Copyright ©2019 Right Angle Publishing Ltd

All rights reserved. No part of this publication may be reproduced in any manner whatsoever without prior permission in writing from Right Angle Publishing.

First published by Right Angle Publishing
161 Rosebery Avenue, London EC1R 4QX

British Library Cataloguing in Publication Data
A catalogue record for this book is available from the British Library

ISBN 978-1-9997931-1-1

ALLIES AND MORRISON

Edited by Ian Latham with essays by Paul Finch and Martin Pearce

Contents

8	**Paul Finch**	Beyond the boundary
10	**Martin Pearce**	On Reading Architecture

17 **Projects 2003–12**

18	Allies and Morrison studios, Southwark, London
34	The Table, Southwark, London
35	Contemporary Applied Arts, Southwark, London
36	BBC Media Village, White City, London
44	Sidgwick Site: University of Cambridge
45	Faculty of English, University of Cambridge
50	Institute of Criminology, University of Cambridge
54	Gatehouse and Auditorium, Fitzwilliam College, Cambridge
64	Finlay Building, Merton College, Oxford
68	Grosvenor Waterside, Chelsea, London
72	City Lit, Covent Garden, London
76	Chelsea College of Art and Design, Pimlico, London
82	Archive and Library, Girton College, Cambridge
88	Royal Festival Hall, Southbank Centre, Lambeth, London
98	Liner Building, Royal Festival Hall, Lambeth, London
100	Canteen, Royal Festival Hall, Lambeth, London
102	Visitor Centre and Footbridge, Welney
106	IQ Business Park, Farnborough
112	Planetarium, Royal Observatory, Greenwich, London
118	Heart of the City, Sheffield
126	Paradise Street, Liverpool
132	One Vine Street, Westminster, London
136	Highbury Square, Islington, London
146	Bankside 123, Southwark, London
154	Bofors Tower, Dunkirk
158	Ericsson Headquarters, Ansty Park, Coventry
162	Mint Hotel, Leeds
166	Great Suffolk Street, Southwark, London
172	River Soar Bridge, Leicester
174	120 Moorgate, City of London
176	St Andrew's Bow, London
182	2012 Olympic Games and Legacy, Stratford, London

201 **Appendices**

202	Chronology
210	Bibliography
211	Credits
212	Exhibitions
212	Awards
213	Team 2003–12

Beyond the boundary
Paul Finch

Any volume in an oeuvre complète produced while the practice still exists is, simultaneously, a stand-alone publication and part of a work in progress. It has had a predecessor and it will have a successor; it marks both moments in time and events in time, drawing on the past and anticipating futures which may already exist. First and last projects discussed in such a publication are far from arbitrary, since the practice could have chosen to include the first in a previous volume, or to have saved the last for the next. However, the choice of Allies and Morrison Studios (2003) and the London Olympic Games and Legacy masterplan (2012) are understandable for a variety of reasons. The former is that most intimate of projects for any architectural practice – its own office, while the latter not only creates a new city quarter, but for the period of the Games, engages the entire world. These significant bookend projects are also interesting because, although entirely different in scale, scope and output, they nevertheless reveal common strands in the work of the practice, which to a greater or lesser extent are evident in the multiplicity of projects that comprise the rest of this volume.

The first and most important of these strands is the ability to 'zoom out' from site and programme at the start of any project, reviewing a series of contexts which then inform design thinking. This attention to context was evident in the first published image of a Bob Allies/Graham Morrison project -the competition-winning entry for the Mound in Edinburgh, which appeared on the front page of Building Design in 1983. That victory, for public space treatment of an area which related to old Edinburgh and the New Town, was the catalyst for the formation of the practice in 1984.

That project, the foundation stone for the practice, dealt with space rather than form, and with public realm rather than private ownership. But most importantly it suggested an attitude to past and present, the historic and the contemporary, and how that relationship could be negotiated, not least by understanding that everything historic was once contemporary itself. The synthesis of past and present in the work of the practice has been fine-tuned in a series of projects illustrated in the pages that follow, not least in Cambridge, that bastion of both tradition and sometimes radical change.

Allies and Morrison have on many occasions found themselves working with iconic works of architecture from history. This volume includes the Royal Festival Hall, the Royal Observatory at Greenwich, and Arsenal's former ground at Highbury, where in each case the architectural task was to respond to the iconic rather than try to create new icons themselves. Graham Morrison voiced the suspicion of the practice towards the growing trend for 'look-at-me' buildings in a talk at the 2004 Royal Academy dinner for winners of the Architects' Journal/Bovis awards. Re-reading his text, it is clear that his criticism centred on designs devoid of cultural meaning or contextual thought; it was not a condemnation of creative imagination or expressiveness (explicit praise was given to work by Will Alsop, Richard Rogers, Marks Barfield and Herzog & de Meuron).

As the works here illustrate, Allies and Morrison are far more interested in exploring contextual responses to each site rather than promoting a stylistic agenda. This is particularly the case at the Royal Festival Hall, where the technical analysis of failings that needed to be addressed were combined with a deep historical understanding not just of what had been built, but of design intention and the ideas that underscored it. However significant the changes brought about to the original fabric of the building, they have never been envisaged as subjugating or negating the inspirations of the original designers, quite the opposite. Even where the opportunity existed to deliver a 'look-at-me' project, for example the Liner Building running parallel to the western flank of the concert hall, the architecture is respectful while determinedly contemporary.

Nor does the practice have qualms about delivering dramatic aesthetic effect – provided it is relevant to programme and location. A striking example is the Charles Street Car Park in Sheffield, part of a city centre masterplan. The description of the thinking behind this marker building and the technical basis for the design (hundreds of single panels are each rotated slightly differently), explain why it is as satisfactory to the mind as it is to the eye.

The practice's most profound urban intervention to date is also outside London: the Paradise Street building, part of the Grosvenor Estate Liverpool One project. Beautifully detailed in pale stone, the building has a dramatic section, and is the most important element in the BDP masterplan which envisaged a new 'shopping centre' as a series of buildings assembled within a street pattern and as a response to dramatic topography. This project involved nearly thirty different architectural practices and proved that Allies and Morrison could take a design lead in a collaborative exercise.

A combination of attention to detail while responding to big challenges has been a hallmark of the practice's work for thirty-five years; inevitably it is the bigger projects that attract most attention, but it is worth noting the many examples of that attention to detail (and detailing) which make an appearance in this volume, and noting the themes that recur: deep windows sometimes with splayed reveals; the subtle use of colour and texture; a material palette which is carefully related to its locale; the balancing of horizontal and vertical elements – each of which would be worth an essay in itself.

But as the commercial and architectural success of the practice increased, particularly in the period under discussion, it became apparent that its real strength was the ability to plan and design at a large scale, without ignoring genius loci. Projects around the practice's Southwark Street offices make the point – in particular the huge office complex for Land Securities across the road (Bankside 123). This saw the replacement of a giant urban obstacle with a considered trio of work buildings, accompanied by a ground plane that is light years away from its nonentity predecessor.

It would be tempting to see masterplanning London's Olympics and legacy as an inevitable conclusion to the work of the practice over the previous decade, but of course there was nothing inevitable about it. For one thing, there was the competition to produce a masterplan which could convince the International Olympic Committee that London should be the location. An incredibly strong international shortlist was assembled, but it was the consortium that included Allies and Morrison which saw off the competition – because they looked, sounded and presented like a real team. At a critical moment in the life of the project, when the masterplan appeared to be stuck; it was their masterly sectional analysis, which found the key to unlock what was to emerge.

The practice's subsequent commission to produce the legacy masterplan is a tribute to the approach described by Bob Allies: provide, first, an inspirational and visionary approach which will be convincing to public authorities; and second, a realisable and robust template which will convince the people paying for the project.

Pragmatism without vision is depressing, but vision without pragmatism is fantasy. The synthesis of the two is what drives and inspires this practice. We should look forward to the next volume.

On Reading Architecture
Martin Pearce

It is a testament to the robustness of Allies and Morrison's approach to architecture that, as the size of the practice and scale of the buildings has grown, the underlying grammar of its work persists. Perhaps that is the greatest test of any design paradigm, that the ideas upon which it is based are durable enough to sustain a variety of projects and circumstances. At the same time we have seen a refinement and maturing of the practice's architectural language.

Speaking of the timeless works of classical literature Henry David Thoreau suggested that 'books must be read as deliberately and reservedly as they were written'. He reminds us that great works of art are intentional, planned and considered, demanding of attention and careful study in order to yield up the jewels of understanding that come to illuminate our own lives. Great works of architecture are no less worthy of careful reading and these characteristics of being both deliberate and reserved distinguish the recent projects of Allies and Morrison.

On Paradigms and Egos
The practice, currently among the UK's largest, retains an ethos of collective endeavour partly because many of the staff who joined in the early years are now partners and continue to refine and develop the architectural language.

In an age of aesthetic permissiveness and technological speed it has become unfashionable to talk of an architectural language or paradigms that identify patterns and iterated design devices, or to speak of precedents and influences from history. Many orthodox avant-garde modernists eschewed ideas of architectural continuity, cutting ties with the past in favour of radical solutions born out of new materials, functions and forms. The continuing legacy of this approach is all too apparent today as the texture and grain of cities are despoiled by so called 'icon' buildings, self referential, hollow gestures that speak more of the individual ego of the architect than a responsibility to use and context. It is paradoxical that out of a movement that viewed architecture as a route to the social betterment and emancipation of the masses, the right of the individual expression by the designer became paramount, their responsibility to the many secondary.

In contrast, the work of Allies and Morrison is concerned with the responsibility of building and adopts a more reserved and thoughtful approach to modernity. This sense of architectural accountability continues the project of post-war English modernism begun by Basil Spence, Leslie Martin and Denys Lasdun. In this they follow the idea that architecture is based on a set of underpinning principles, and which, as in spoken language, has a lexicon of architectural vocabulary structured through syntax to form compositions that have both meaning and relevance.

The search for a simplicity and clarity of expression that resolves the often diverse and conflicting requirements of each project exemplifies this approach. Architecture is difficult and the search for an order that can encompass function, context and form, whilst hard won, is that which makes buildings seem effortless and inevitable. But of course there is nothing inevitable about design; above all it requires testing and good judgement based on sound ideas.

On Composition
Early twentieth-century architecture was in many ways a reaction against the Beaux Arts tradition of composition. Once a subject of study in its own right, even the word 'composition' is today seldom heard in schools of architecture. But to design is to compose – and Allies and Morrison find parallels with orchestral composition, a set of given instruments assembled for the purpose of articulating a work of art. In this, each instrument need not be redesigned, rather its range of musical possibilities and limits understood and acknowledged. The art of composition is the manner in which each element is

combined with, or set against the others to create a beautiful rhythmic whole resulting in a complete work that has the power to move us, to evoke emotions and to touch our hearts.

Fundamental to composition is the idea of order, the structure that provides a framework within which to position and sequence elements. This framework Aristotle called 'taxis', the orderly arrangement of parts that is fundamental to achieving a level of completeness such that all of the parts are integrated with the whole. For Allies and Morrison the structural frame affords this armature and its grid is analogous to the musical stave. The grid is invariably derived from the building's function – the sizes of office spaces, hotel rooms or student bedrooms are in the main typologically determined. Allies and Morrison accept these as givens rather than fighting against commercial and pragmatic realities.

Accepting programmatic determinants provides a framework in which to compose. Of course the tyranny of the grid can result in a stultified architecture too concerned with platonic abstract purity. Mies van der Rohe's adherence to this intellectual clarity could produce an overpowering sense of order, with columns, walls and windows ruthlessly aligned to a universal grid. In contrast Allies and Morrison adopt the possibilities of the grid mediated by the lived world of architecture.

On Symmetry
Symmetry establishes the positioning and relationship of elements within the framework or taxis. The Greek word symmetría means to 'measure together', and is concerned with the balance of elements when considered as one. It goes beyond the beautiful, yet simplistic bilateral of a butterfly or the rotational symmetries of a kaleidoscope.

Allies and Morrison cite the example of the Indonesian proa, an outrigger canoe consisting of two parallel hulls of unequal length, designed so that the force of the wind and ballast of the crew achieve dynamic stability when in motion. Resolving dynamic forces is a characteristic of Allies and Morrison's work and they describe this equilibrium as occurring around a point of 'stasis'. To invoke a feeling of balance and harmony requires good judgement, just as the Indonesian mariner trims his sails and adjusts his course in response to the changing wind and tide. This feeling of being at one with the environment is reflected in the practice's work as through a sense of touch and experience their buildings achieve a feeling of natural fit with the surrounding context.

The stability of an architectural composition by Allies and Morrison is exemplified in the design of their own offices. Here the surrounding warehouse typology is reflected in a concrete structural grid fronting the busy Southwark Street. This robust frame is juxtaposed by a delicate glazed facade of mullions and a filigree of animating shutters. In plan this syncopated order is inflected to accommodate oblique angles of the medieval Farnham Place, the whole composition finding a point of compositional stasis that brings into a delicate balance the asymmetry of the undercroft entrance passage and internal spiral staircase.

Juxtaposing the 'ideal' of linear office space, with the 'circumstantial' particularity of the irregular historic street plan is a recurring theme in much of the practice's work. In this they confront the age-old philosophical problem of an ideal platonic world view set against imperfect empirical realities.

On the City and History
The principle of stasis is nowhere more important than in the relationship of a building to the city. In this Allies and Morrison draw on the work of Aldo Rossi, whose seminal book 'The Architecture of the City' set out to re-assert the status of architecture as an autonomous discipline with a specific body of knowledge.

Giambattista Nolli's 1748 plan of Rome was notable for its accuracy and its use of figure-ground representation

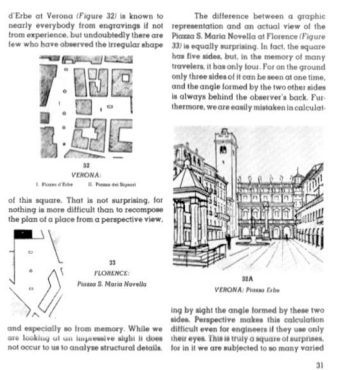

Page from Camillo Sitte's 'City Planning According to Artistic Principles', first published in 1889 but only translated into English in 1945

Rossi had been fascinated by Giambattista Nolli's figure-ground plan of Rome which for him represented an architectural palimpsest of collective memory. Allies and Morrison delight in such drawings as analytical tools to measure their compositions at an urban scale.

Tellingly, this can lead to the point of stasis being positioned outside their building. In thinking about these complex compositions they draw parallels with the Japanese calligrapher who whilst making brush marks is simultaneously thinking about the residual white space. This form of perception was later manifest in Gestalt psychology, which encouraged a holistic understanding of the human mind based on multiple simultaneous readings. In this way the building is never solely an object, but rather a participant in a greater historic and physical whole which recognises that human perception is framed by memory. Allies and Morrison are painstaking in their research to understand the historic layers of a location, the traces of memory that constitute the nature of the place. This reading of context affords a sense of the spirit of a place; what Vitruvius termed the Genius Loci.

To conceive of a location as both past and present or a building as both positive and negative, object and void, both at urban and interior scale is the challenge set out by Robert Venturi in his book 'Complexity and Contradiction in Architecture'. It is the resolution of the difficult whole that derives from a Gestalt approach to building in urban settings and in which Allies and Morrison find territory to liberate architectural potential.

On Scale and Ambiguity

Allies and Morrison embrace these contradictions and play with the ideas of oppositions of function, scale and material. In the practice's earlier work, modest buildings were afforded a sense of grandeur through devices such as delaminating the facade of a small entrance to enhance the scale. In contrast, as the buildings have become bigger, reverse devices are employed to give large structures a feeling of intimacy and reduced scale. The regeneration of Great Suffolk Street in London demonstrates this strategy, as understated linear blocks used to complete an urban corner contrast with a bold crystalline tower behind. A linking undercroft provides an intimate synaptic link of spatial compression between these two worlds.

The Mint Hotel, Leeds, offers further lessons in the juxtaposition of contrasting scales. Here a series of repetitive hotel rooms is faced in a red-brick facade reminiscent of the mill buildings which once stood along this quayside location. The potentially overwhelming grid of rooms is mitigated by the composition of the facade in which discontinuous horizontal string lines subtly merge with vertical elements of deep angular reveals brought to slender edges. This basic arrangement of two rooms above and two below creates a giant order that tempers the visual scale.

On Public Space

The complex understanding of scale shifts, and the relationship of buildings to the external spaces they create have become ever more significant as the practice has undertaken strategic urban projects. The contrast between big buildings and small multifaceted spaces follows notions of the City Beautiful movement that drew on the work of the Austrian architect Camillo Sitte and were later developed by Gordon Cullen and the English Townscape movement. Sitte identified aspects of European urban squares that made them feel warm and inviting. His 1889 treatise, 'City Planning According to Artistic Principles' emphasises the creation of an irregular urban structure with small plazas enhanced by monuments and other aesthetic elements. Opposed to overly formal planning he suggested that 'a square should be seen as a room: it should form an enclosed space'. In contrast to the grand Beaux Arts axial and bilateral symmetry, he advocated the consideration of spaces from a psychological viewpoint. The perception of a space, he said, should be considered from the pedestrian's viewpoint, moving through as a series of discrete and intimate conditions, each linked to the next by a sense of intrigue.

Allies and Morrison are equally concerned with the need for spaces to have a sense of enclosure. Recent work often employs the device of a subtle axial shift in each block to give a sense of altering the perspective and drawing each facade into each other's neighbourhood. This serves to evoke a dialogue between the buildings, emphasising the oblique rather than flat-on view. In this Allies and Morrison have revived the instruments of the English picturesque tradition, employing the device of a layering of foreground, middle and background that recalls the allegorical canvases of Nicolas Poussin and Claude Lorrain, but here used to create new urban narratives.

On Facades

Some have suggested that the composition of a typical Allies and Morrison facade owes much to the paintings of Piet Mondrian, of frames within frames, a two-dimensional exercise in abstract composition. But this is to ignore their concerns for the third dimension in a facade. Never seen in pure elevation, the facade of a building is an object in its own right, more attuned to the low reliefs of Ben Nicholson, its character only revealed when seen through the movement of shadows on materials in changing light and invariably viewed from the oblique angle of the street looking upwards. This modelling of the facade becomes paramount in Allies and Morrison's work as the reveals, cills and heads of openings, the choice of materials and depth of relief form an architectural palette. For this reason Allies and Morrison's office is filled with facade study models and exquisite perspective drawings, the optimal means to understand and test these nuances.

This concern for oblique views is particularly effective in Bankside 2 and 3, where reveals set to the same angle wrap the buildings. The effect is to create an architecture of two strikingly different appearances when approached from alternate directions, the same facade appearing as a rich mass of solid terracotta or as a crisp steel and glass grid. The adjoining Bankside 1 'Blue Fin' building employs externally-fixed shading fins each of the same colour, but through slight changes in angle and spacing these are perceived as a myriad of hues evoking the shimmering reflections of the nearby river Thames.

In considering the external envelope Allies and Morrison often refer to the shell or carapace of an animal such as a turtle or crab, a delicate internal organism shielded by a hard exoskeleton. The nature of this mediating interface between the internal life of a building and the external environment is a preoccupation for the practice. The challenge of expressing the interior logic of the building whilst simultaneously responding to the surrounding context, often within the outer 200mm of the building depth, has provided fertile ground for the development of a sophisticated architectural vocabulary.

At times Allies and Morrison have used an alternative approach to the layering of the facade, instead finding a very different external reading, which sees the building as a solid ingot of fine material. The Greenwich Royal Observatory and Welney Visitor Centre have the volumetric character of being cast from a single substance and follow a language developed at the earlier Abbey Mills Pumping Station. The singularity of material gives these buildings solidity and conveys the feeling of a precious jewel delicately placed into the landscape. At the City Lit building, the mass of brickwork forming the urban block is 'excavated' to provide deep battered reveals that speak of the weight and density of a clay block from which the building has been 'sculpted'.

On Technology

There is a tendency among some architects to employ ever advanced technological means with little concern for

Bankside 123, London (2012)

Mint Hotel, Leeds (2011)

Abbey Mills Pumping Station (1997)

Welney Visitor Centre (2006)

Royal Observatory, Greenwich (2007)

their ultimate goals. Much so-called high-tech and 'green' architecture is reductive in that architectural ambition is subverted by the pursuit or expression of a singular idea. Reinforced concrete, glass and steel were initially employed by the masters of the Modern Movement not for their own sake but rather at the service of greater architectural ideals. In some respects their early use exceeded the technological possibilities with regards to environmental performance and durability. We too easily forget Madame Savoye's dissatisfaction as Le Corbusier's villa at Poissy haemorrhaged heat, leaked and crumbled. Yet the building remains a prescient anticipation of the separation of structure from cladding, a disjunction in which Allies and Morrison have found the potential for much experimentation. This exploration of the expressive possibilities of two seemingly opposing ideas - the free facade and traditional materials - has delivered a play of textural and visual material qualities contrasted and juxtaposed to develop a novel language of abstraction. This sense of abstraction however is met with an equally strong sense of appropriateness. The choice of materials is often drawn from the surrounding context, as for example the deep tones of brown brick set against white concrete at Fitzwilliam College acknowledges Denys Lasdun's existing buildings. This sense of appropriateness is nowhere better seen than at the Royal Observatory Greenwich in the choice of a sumptuous patinated bronze cladding for the blind oculus. It evokes Mies van der Rohe's use of bronze at the Seagram building not for its structural honesty but rather for the way that the patina produced a play of shadows within shadows and gave the building a timeless quality. At the Royal Observatory Greenwich the innovative technological processes that were employed to manufacture each huge bronze shell of the conical form are secondary to the poetic manner in which this material captures the spatial and temporal expanse of the celestial realm, as the conic section's surface becomes the heavens' terrestrial distiller.

On Drawing

As Allies and Morrison buildings embody poetic ideas so too the manner in which those ideas are represented in drawing says much of their lyric quality. Drawing is the principle communicative tool of the architect and the threshold across which imagination passes. To inscribe ideas on paper and the way those marks are executed is the depiction of intention, and can tell the story of a beautiful idea that underpins a building. In the act of drawing all the rules of composition, hierarchy and articulation of elements are captured, and the plans of Allies and Morrison are memorable for the precision and clarity with which they convey these relationships. There is a generation of architects whose obsession with representational means above realisable ends has led to a plethora of virtual buildings which, without the limits of gravity, materials, climate or users, result in seductive yet ultimately irrelevant fantasies. Paradoxically, in valuing the tool above that which it creates, many have become so deskilled by specialised software as to render them unable to draw or make physical artefacts. In contrast, Allies and Morrison's insistence on the primacy of the hand drawing and physical model makes for an immediate and inseparable linkage of representation and reality. As with their buildings, Allies and Morrison's drawings are beautifully crafted. The weight of line, subtleties of balance and composition are exquisitely refined to capture the essence of an idea, and become works of art in their own right.

On Use and Identity

To employ an architectural language and elevate a building to a work of architecture has but one end, that of facilitating and enhancing the experience of those who use it. Louis Sullivan's famous dictum that 'form should ever follow function' was to become a founding tenet of modern architecture. Today rapidly evolving needs and new technology have called this into question as buildings are faced with potentially undetermined changes of use through their lifetime. The tyranny of the open-plan office has led to many flexible, yet anonymous and banal buildings, devoid of character and unloved by their inhabitants. Similarly, the rational economic organisation of apartment types has resulted in much efficient yet alienating housing. In this they ignore the fundamental requirement of architecture to establish identity and character, to create places as opposed to spaces that serve the most primordial human needs, those of orientation and belonging. Forty years ago Herman Hertzberger recognised these requirements, identifying the importance of entrances, staircases and incidental areas as the places of human interaction with the thresholds of public, semi-public and private spaces the vital elements in our psychological security and wellbeing. Allies and Morrison are equally aware of these needs and the paradoxical collision of universal function with our psychological requirements for a building to be particular, embodying character and creating a unique identity.

At the BBC White City site the rapidly changing world of broadcast technology made for a brief that necessitated an organisational structure that accommodated the 'churn' of reconfiguration. The scale of this organisation could have resulted in an anonymous behemoth, yet there is an extraordinary understanding of the need for individual identity. Devices such as a hierarchy of entrances subdivide the buildings and afford a sense of ownership at a human rather than corporate scale. Atrium spaces have a strong sense of orientation as the structure syncopates with the floor slabs and generous staircases provide important incidental meeting places. Further care in the organisation of service cores creates layers of privacy that make these large buildings legible and clear at the macro scale whilst maintaining a sense of intimacy and ownership at a human scale.

The sense of identity is also seen in the English Faculty and Institute of Criminology at the University of Cambridge. Here two similar building typologies are afforded distinct identities. Again the importance of entrance and staircase gives each a unique internal ambiance whilst the external appearance inflects to the surrounding context. The English Faculty, faced in terracotta, is composed to express a strong vertical mass around a courtyard while the Institute of Criminology's delicate horizontal lines reflect the linear site. The two buildings transcend the mere expression of internal function. Rather they are representations of more complex ideas as they address the tension between internal requirements and external obligations and speak of the necessity for a building to establish a sense of distinctiveness, not by overt means but through quiet appropriateness and identity. Above all they fulfil the sense of place-making that gives their users a feeling of belonging and ownership.

On Reading this Book

The great pioneer of British modern architecture, Berthold Lubetkin, wryly observed in his speech on receiving the Royal Gold Medal for Architecture in 1982 that much of architectural culture today seems 'to beget artists who scream to be noticed and remembered for a quarter of an hour'. We do well to recall his words as the cacophony of individual expression continues to turn the city into an architectural zoo. The recent work of Allies and Morrison marks a more considered, humane and responsible approach to architecture. Rather than shouting, the works chronicle a rich yet reserved and deliberate architecture. There is wit, intelligence and clarity such that each building presents itself to be read as carefully as it was written.

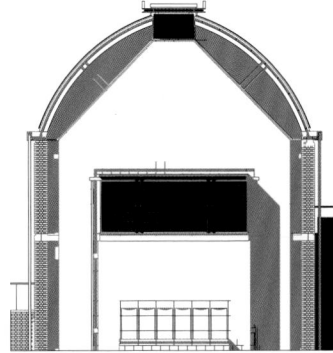
Horniman Museum, London (2002)

The Faculty of English, Sidgwick Site, University of Cambridge (2004)

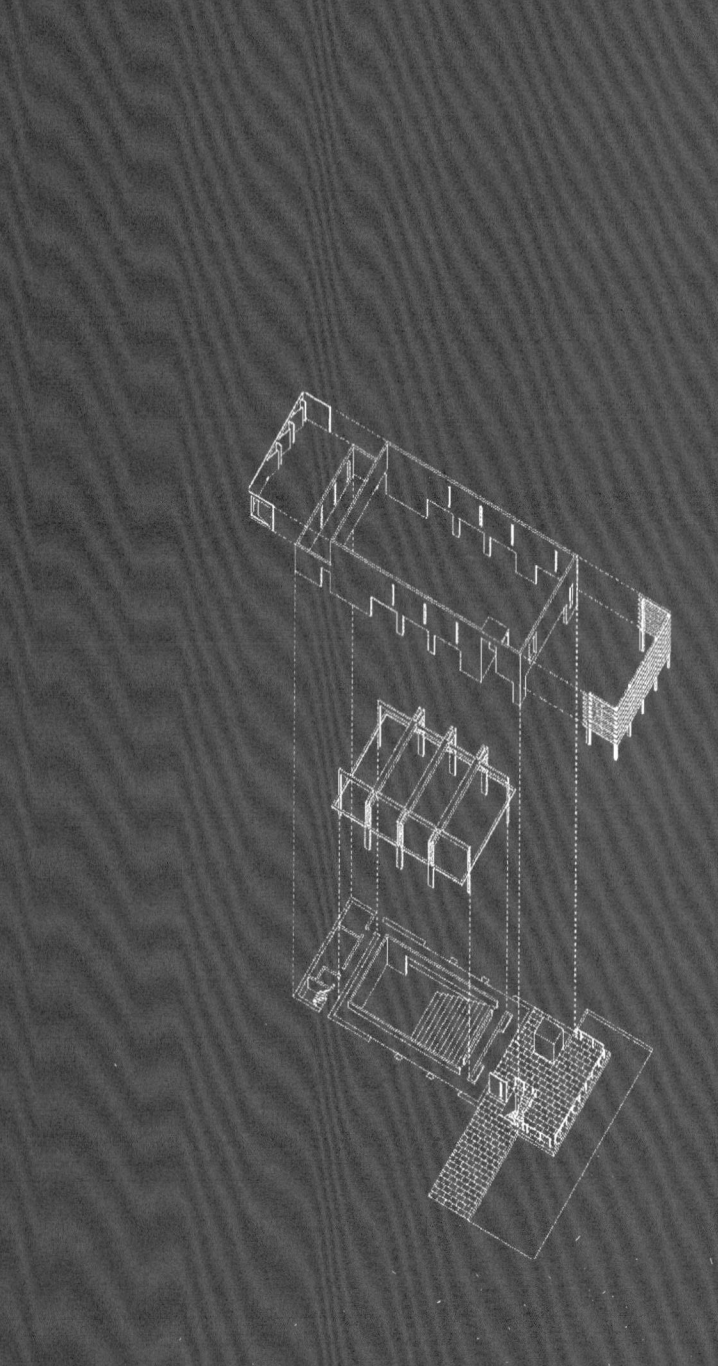

Projects 2003–2012

ALLIES AND MORRISON STUDIOS

85 Southwark Street, London
1999–2003

Built on a site that had remained underdeveloped since it was bombed during the Second World War, 85 Southwark Street accommodates the studios of Allies and Morrison. The building includes basement workshops, a ground-floor reception and exhibition space, three studio floors and a rooftop terrace.

The unusual shape of the site derives from the line of Southwark Street, a Victorian thoroughfare that was cut across the existing medieval street pattern, leaving a remnant of Farnham Place to the south. The long urban block, bounded

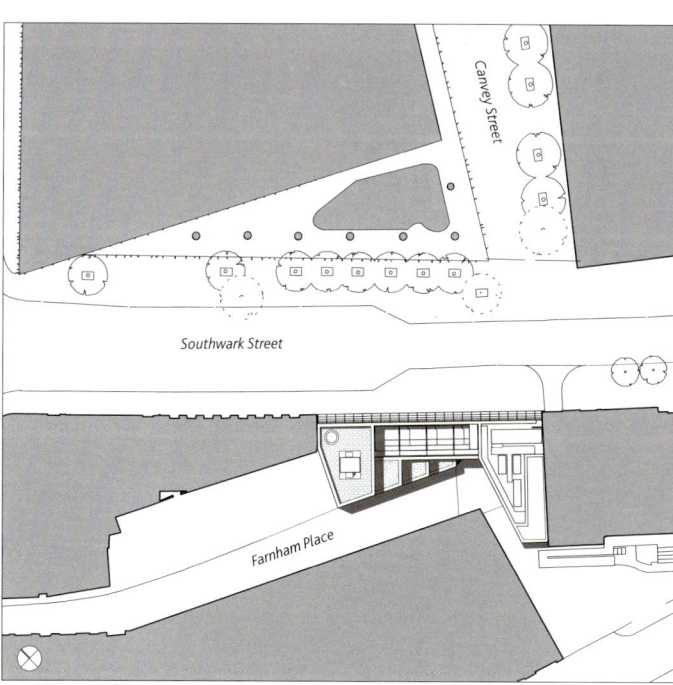

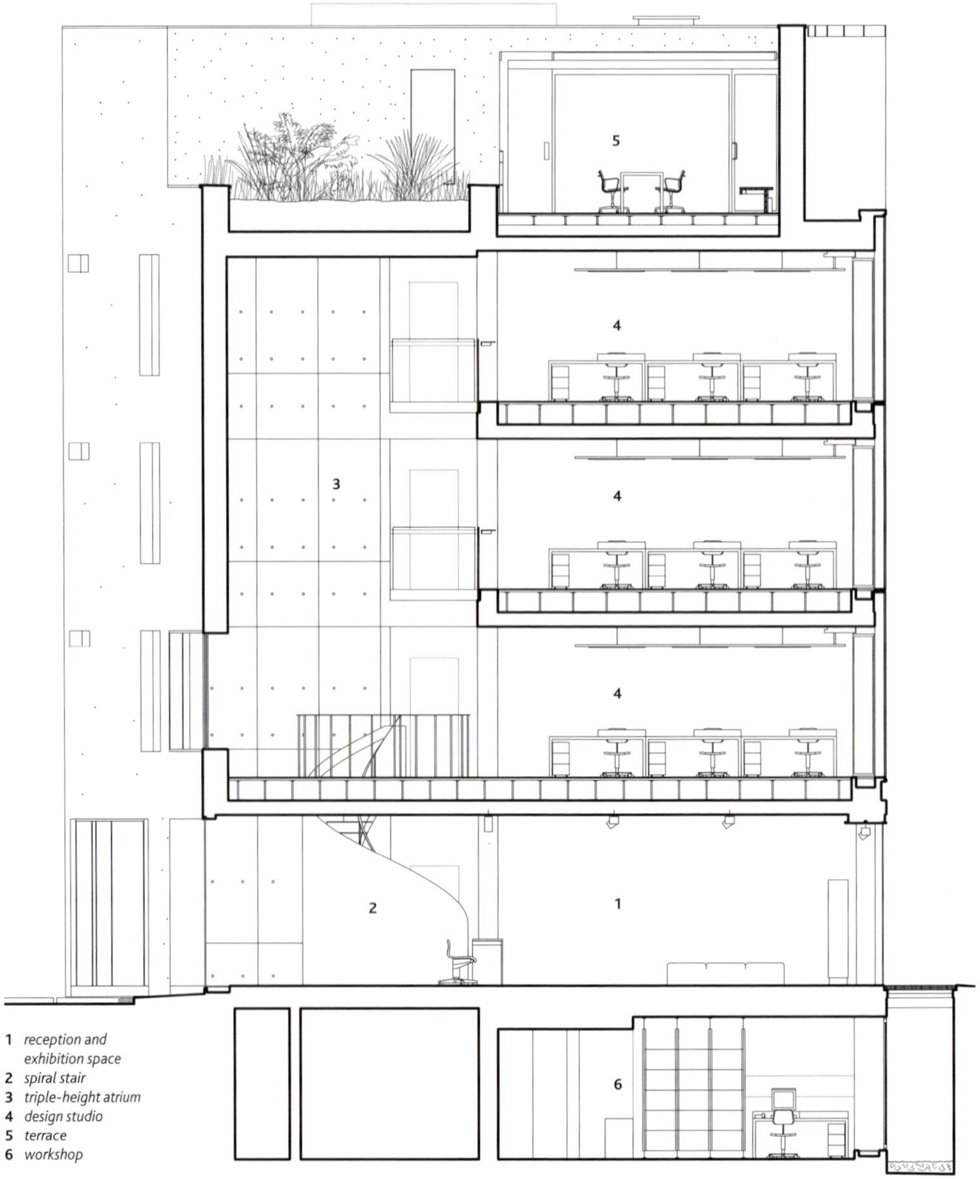

1 reception and exhibition space
2 spiral stair
3 triple-height atrium
4 design studio
5 terrace
6 workshop

Section through atrium

by Great Suffolk Street and Great Guildford Street, is now relieved by a passageway that provides a shortcut between Farnham Place and Southwark Street. Passing between The Table cafe/bar and the studio reception space, the passageway links a series of lanes that connect Union Street to Tate Modern and ultimately across the river Thames to St Paul's Cathedral. It can be closed off by two sliding metal screens when required.

The role the studio building plays within the urban context, and the contrast between its front and back, are reflected in the elevational composition and cross-sectional organisation. Whereas the north facade on Southwark Street comprises sealed, full-height glazing, the southerly aspect facing the quieter Farnham Place is rendered, with openable windows. This facade is indented and angled in plan in

◀ *Roof gardens*
◀ *Spiral stair connecting the ground floor with the atrium and studio spaces*
▶ *Three-storey atrium aligning the studio floors*

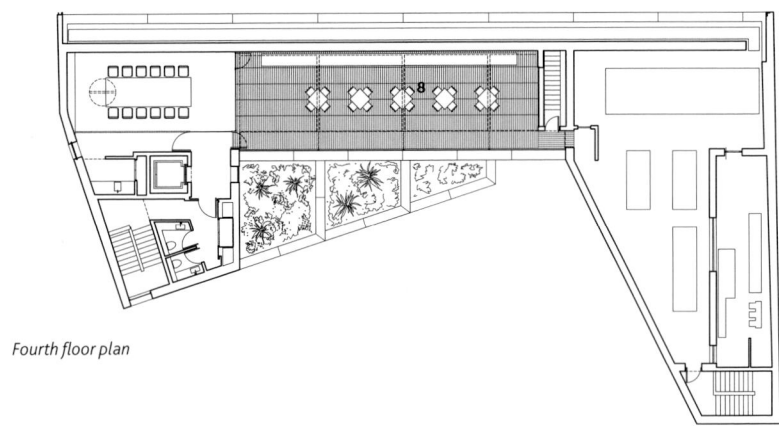

Fourth floor plan

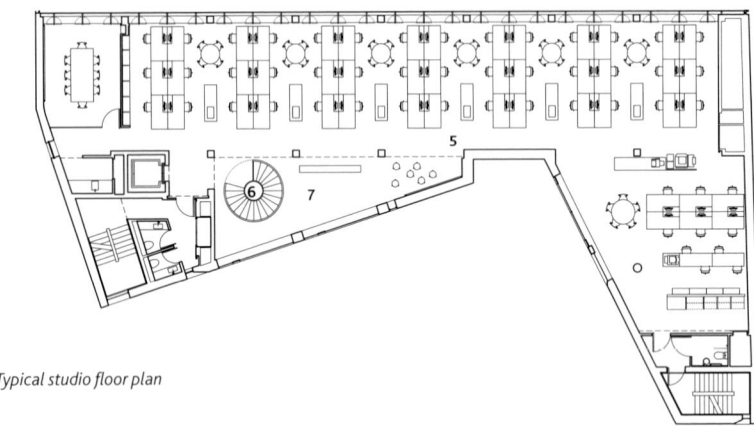

Typical studio floor plan

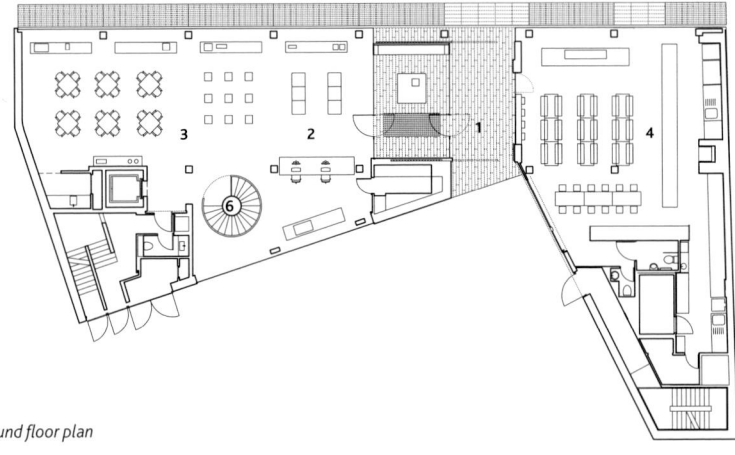

Ground floor plan

1 entrance
2 reception
3 exhibition space
4 The Table cafe
5 open-plan studio space
6 spiral stair
7 three-storey atrium
8 roof terrace

response to the street, and steps back to accommodate three planted upper-level terraces.

Inside, to the south, a triple-height atrium connects the design studio floors that are aligned along the long north Southwark Street elevation.

Direct sunlight thus lights the atrium rather than falling on desks and computer screens. Here, pairs of internal perforated metal fins modify the light and reduce any potential glare. Hinged like butterfly wings, they are spaced at 1.5 metre intervals to correspond with the facade window mullions. Silver when closed, they reveal a yellow colour when opened.

The open ground floor, divided by the glazed entrance passage, accommodates a cafe on the east side and the main reception with space for meetings and exhibitions on the west. A steel spiral stair leads up through the triple-height studio atrium and down to the basement that contains a modelmaking studio, print room, library and IT workshop.

The building is constructed in exposed in-situ concrete that acts as a heat sink to moderate temperature fluctuations, while the underfloor displacement air system is supplemented in the spring and autumn by the openable windows.

▲ *Entrance and reception with informal meeting areas on the ground floor atrium*
▶ *Third floor studio*

◄ Fourth floor terrace and meeting room
▶ Pairs of perforated fins open like butterfly wings

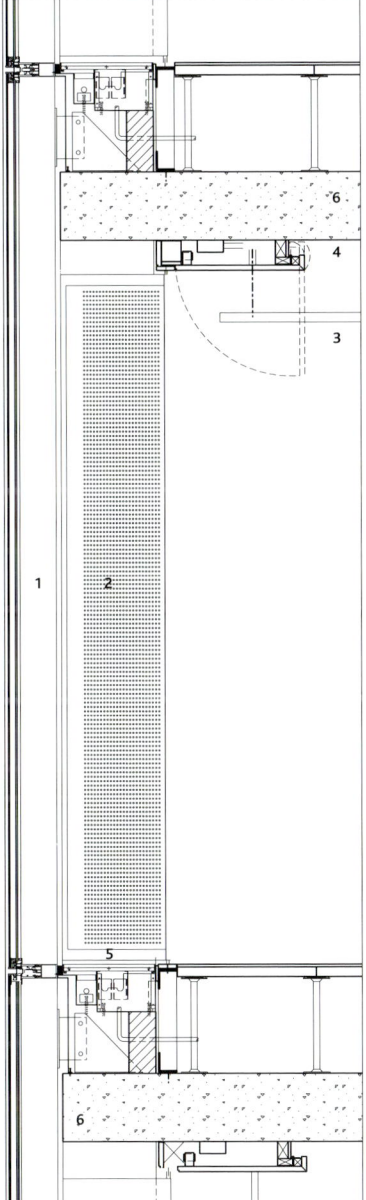

Facade section detail

1 glazed curtain walling
2 fin in open position
3 light fitting suspended from ceiling
4 exposed concrete soffit
5 trench heater grille
6 concrete slab

ALLIES AND MORRISON STUDIOS
89 Southwark Street and Farnham Place, London
2009–12

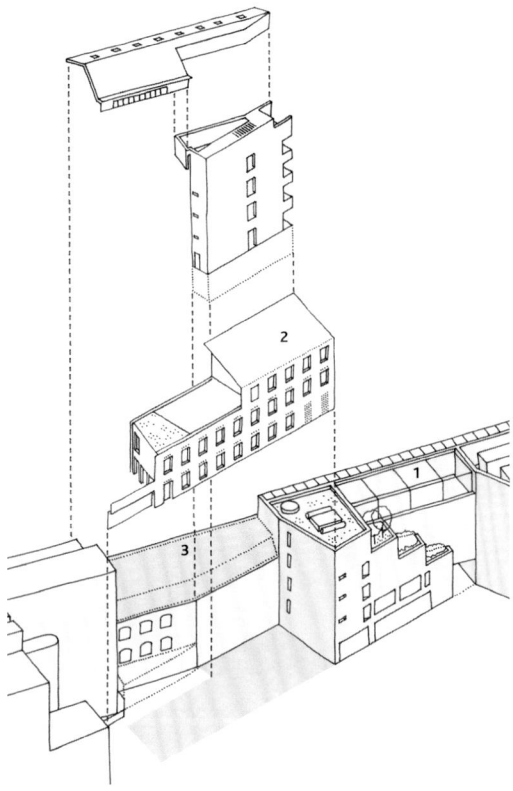

The need for additional studio space led the practice to extend its original building at 85 Southwark Street with the acquisition of the neighbouring grade-II listed Victorian warehouse at 89 Southwark Street and the construction of a new extension building on Farnham Place to the rear.

Together these two additional buildings almost match the floor area of the original building, forming a cluster that provides the practice with an enlarged, integrated 'campus'.

The refurbished warehouse and the rear extension face each other across a new courtyard that reconciles the different angles of Southwark Street and Farnham Place. At the narrow eastern end of the courtyard the two buildings converge to share their vertical circulation in a core that also links to the original studios. This organisational strategy allows the three buildings to operate as a single office while also allowing for the door openings in the party wall between them to be closed so they can operate separately or be sublet floor-by-floor if required.

The three studio buildings have been conceived with similar features, including dual-aspect fenestration, and with a variety of visual and physical connections between them they can accommodate a range of open-plan office spaces. Linked by generous, naturally-lit stairs, they also have access to a cascading sequence of external spaces.

1 *85 Southwark Street studio*
2 *Farnham Place studio – new building*
3 *89 Southwark Street studio – conversion*
4 *Courtyard*

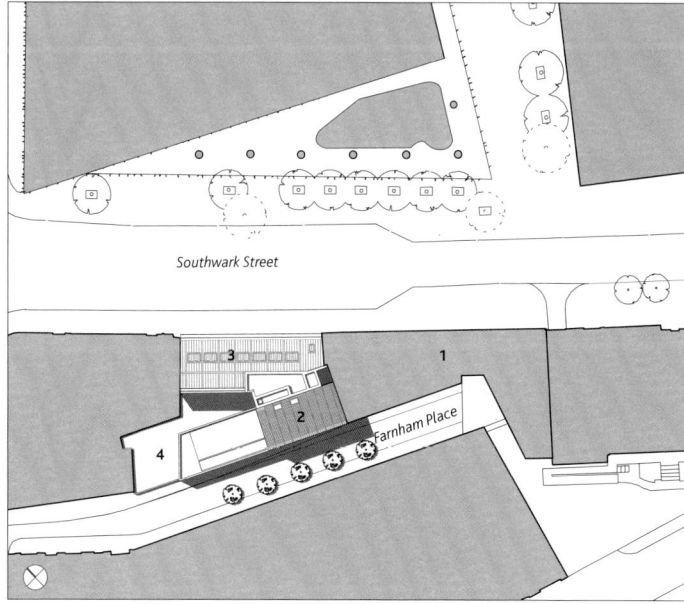

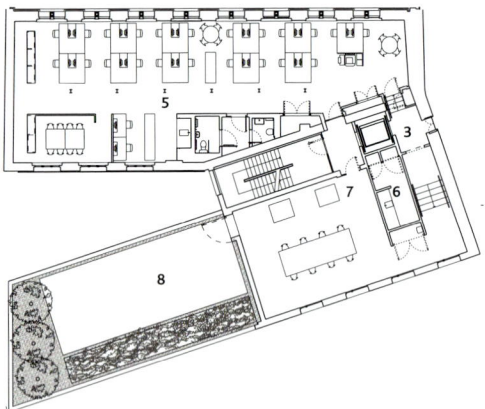

Second floor plan

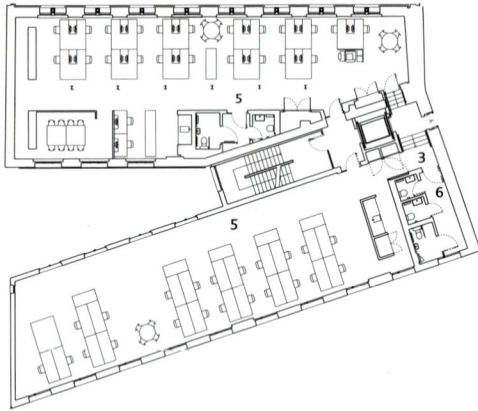

First floor plan

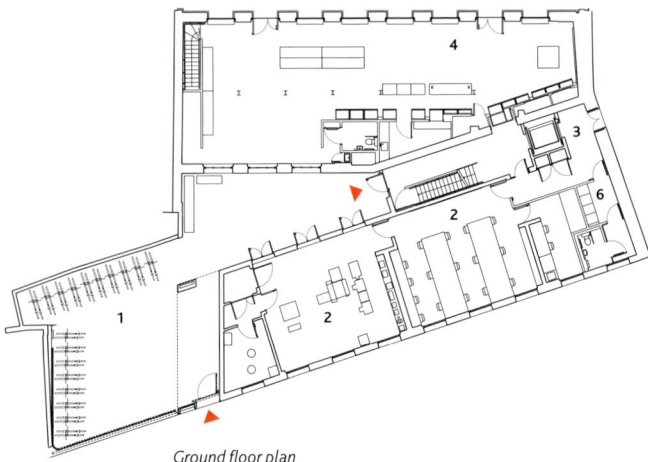

Ground floor plan

1 courtyard
2 workshop
3 new core connecting the three buildings
4 Contemporary Applied Arts, Southwark
5 studio space
6 kitchen and wcs
7 meeting room
8 roof terrace

However, each of the buildings retains an individual character. Internally, the most obvious distinction is in their structure. The original studios were built using a concrete frame that is exposed internally and apparent through the glazed Southwark Street elevation. The refurbished warehouse retains its industrial character, with its brick walls and riveted steel frame revealed throughout. The identity of the new rear extension, smaller in scale, is more akin to a workshop, with its cross-laminated timber frame exposed in the ceiling. The fit-out, furniture and fittings, however, are common to all three buildings, lending coherence to the overall workplace.

The Victorian warehouse was originally used for type manufacturing. It was built in the early 1870s, occupying the plot of one of the many buildings to accommodate Bazalgette's plans for Southwark Street, completed in 1856. The building's grade-II listing recognises the qualities of the elaborate polychromatic brickwork and carved stone of its facade to Southwark Street. Behind, the rest of the building that was badly damaged by wartime bombing had been rebuilt in an unsympathetic idiom.

Allies and Morrison's intervention sought to reinstate the original massing of the building. The post-war mansard roof was replaced with a simpler pitched roof, an awkward rear extension was removed, and the top of the facade was extended to align with the original parapet.

Third floor office space

The rest of the facade was repaired and its sash windows replaced with double-glazed replicas.

Internally, the building has been completely rearranged. Insensitive additions were removed, revealing the riveted steel frame and brick walls, and the steel frame painted in a muted green to match its original colour. Set against the windowless part of the rear wall is a new timber-boarded enclosure containing toilets, kitchens and service risers. The rest of the space is fitted out as open-plan office space, ordered by the positions of windows and the exposed steel frame. The rhythm of the layout is reinforced at high level by service routes, concealed within rafters, that alternate with the downstand beams. On the top floor, services are contained above the boarded enclosure, exposing the flitch beams that support the new roof.

The ground floor level was lowered to allow the art gallery occupier to open its frontage to Southwark Street and its rear openings to the new courtyard.

Across the courtyard, occupying the entire ground floor of the new building, is the practice's workshop. It is possible for passers-by to glimpse right through the two buildings, establishing a visual connection from Southwark Street to Farnham Place.

The upper floors of the extension building are occupied by studio space. The first floor is designed for open-plan office accommodation

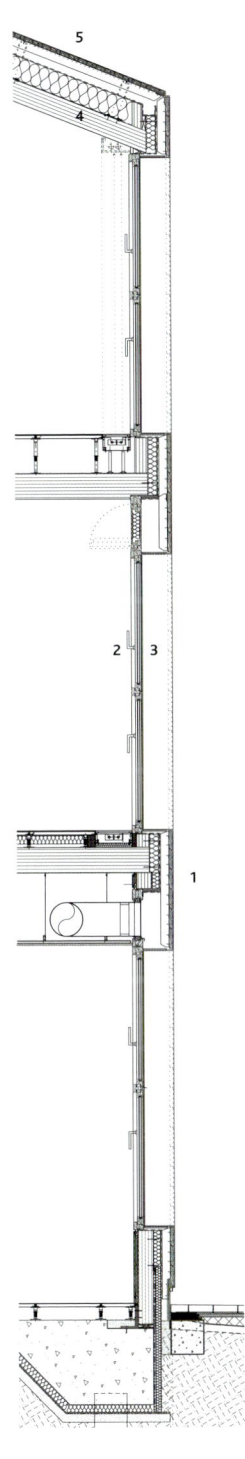

1 Siberian larch horizontal cladding
2 oak window
3 anodised aluminium lining
4 cross-laminated timber panel
5 pitched warm roof with Siberian larch horizontal rainscreen cladding

◀ Workshop
▶ Timber facade detail

and the second floor provides a large meeting room that opens onto a terrace. The cross-laminated timber frame, finished in a light stain, is left exposed in the ceilings of all three floor levels. The setting out of the timber panels follows the space planning grid, with open joints between each panel providing a channel for the electrical services.

Externally the street facade is clad in a stained timber rainscreen, a reference to the timber buildings that were commonplace in eighteenth-century Southwark. In contrast, the elevation facing the courtyard is finished in white render, brightening the space between the two buildings and enhancing daylight levels in the studios.

The extension also further develops the public realm improvements of the original building. Beyond the entrance, passage and terrace created by the original studio building, Farnham Place had remained effectively a service road. Restricting vehicle access and servicing to the west end of the street has allowed the road to be pedestrianised. Dutch bricks are laid to the level of the terrace and run along Farnham Place before ramping down to meet the road. Offset to one side are five planters, each containing a tree and incorporating an oak bench and lighting.

◀ *View of Farnham Place with The Table cafe*
▶ *Rendered wall to courtyard and view of courtyard with doors to Contemporary Applied Arts gallery*

1 studio
2 workshop
3 Gallery
4 roof terrace
5 courtyard

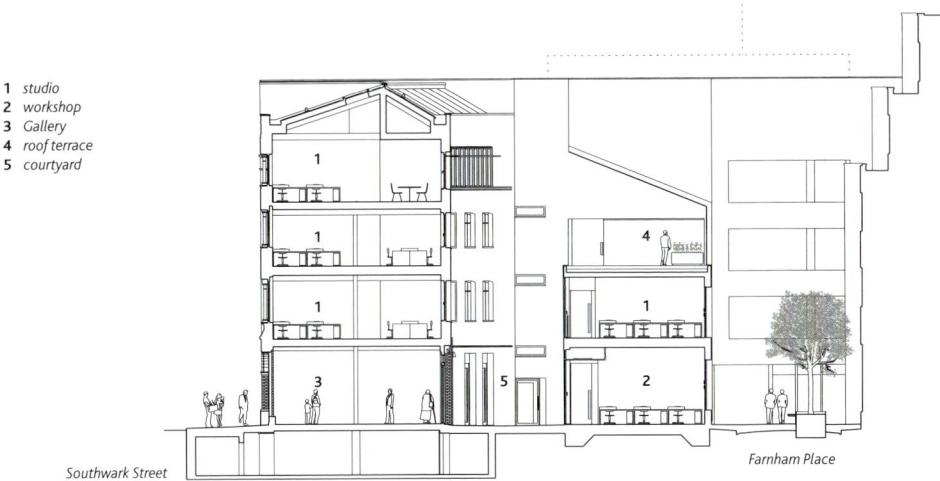

Southwark Street

Farnham Place

THE TABLE
83 Southwark Street, London
2005

Established by the partners of the practice, The Table cafe/restaurant occupies the easternmost part of the ground floor of Allies and Morrison's original studio building at 85 Southwark Street. When it was first opened The Table was the only restaurant in the immediate vicinity, and its launch was symptomatic of the practice's faith in the potential regeneration of this part of Southwark. It was also envisaged as a demonstration of how new developments can help foster activity at street-level – even on a street as apparently unpromising as Southwark Street – and it provided a staff canteen.

In time, the significance of The Table's location would become clear: the venue faces a new street that leads from Southwark Street to Tate Modern where the second-phase Switch House extension establishes a new south entrance; and it also addresses a new route through to Farnham Place. This emerging network of streets and passages has forged an important new pedestrian route between Southwark and St Paul's Cathedral, via the Millennium Bridge.

Set at the end of the formerly run-down Farnham Place, The Table anticipated its gradual improvement in its large window and paved terrace which, particularly in summer, bring some of the activity of Southwark Street back into the quieter passage.

The Table's interior is designed to convey a domestic atmosphere, with an open kitchen providing simple food, served at wooden tables. Its evident success has made it a hub of activity throughout the day, with tables spilling out onto Farnham Place in fine weather.

◀ *Interior of the cafe and Southwark Street elevation*
▶ *Interior of the gallery with exposed steel structure*

CONTEMPORARY APPLIED ARTS
89 Southwark Street, London
2012

Founded in 1948 to promote British craft, Contemporary Applied Arts was based, between 1996 and 2010, in Percy Street, in London's West End, in a gallery designed by Allies and Morrison. It subsequently moved to the basement and ground floor of Allies and Morrison's own studios, a listed Victorian building at 89 Southwark Street.

The ground floor shop and gallery showcase the work of CAA's members in a single volume, either side of a central desk. A full-height display wall extends from the shop, occupying the narrower, east end of the space, into the gallery where it encloses a small office and kitchenette. The deeper exhibition space opens onto a brick-paved courtyard, which it shares with Allies and Morrison's model workshop. The courtyard can be used to display large sculptures and provides a spill-out space for private views. At the end of the gallery space is a freestanding exhibition wall, which conceals a new staircase to the basement storage area and meeting room.

In the main space the original brickwork and riveted steel structure have been exposed, while the ground floor level has been lowered, the arched street-front openings extending to the ground to provide level access and full-height shop windows. Low-iron glass is set deep within each arch, fully exposing their polychromatic brick reveals while wide internal sills facilitate basement ventilation and act as gallery plinths.

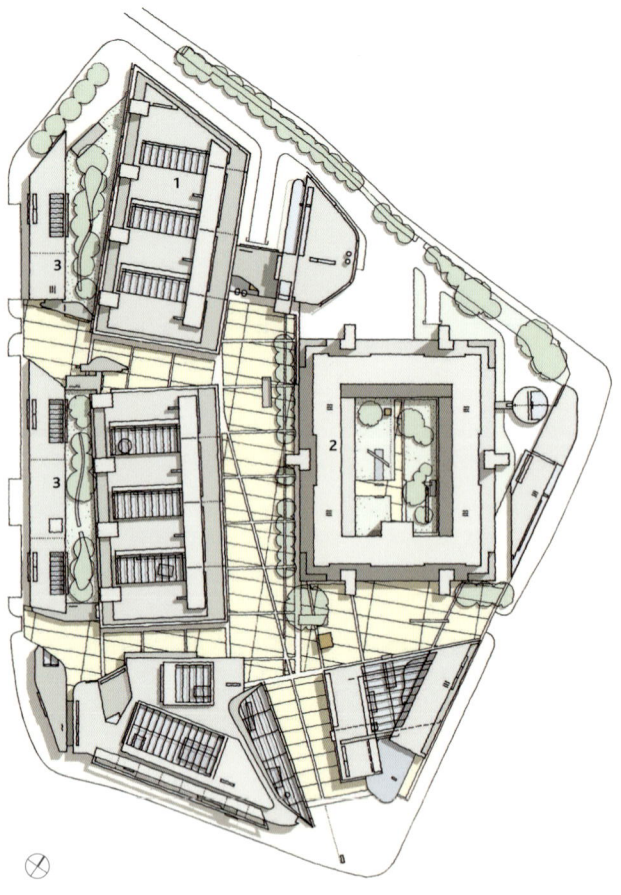

1 *Broadcast Centre*
2 *White City One*
3 *perimeter buildings*

▶ *The site in 1999 and new public space*
▶ *Facade detail*

BBC MEDIA VILLAGE

White City, London
2000–04

Occupying the site of the former White City Stadium, built for the 1908 Summer Olympics, the BBC Media Village comprises a group of buildings, most of which were designed by Allies and Morrison, that house many of the corporation's broadcast operations.

Allies and Morrison's eight new buildings form a series of urban blocks that frame a sequence of new public spaces. While the plans of the buildings are relatively straightforward, the character of the spaces is fluid and complex. At ground level the new buildings contain shops, cafes and restaurants which can open out onto the external realm, animating and introducing new facilities to the area. As well as transforming the environment for those who work at the BBC, the new streets provide a network of pedestrian routes that are fully accessible to the general public and connect directly with the surrounding residential area. The landscape of the new public spaces was designed with Christopher Bradley-Hole, who also contributed gardens related to the new buildings.

The first stage of development involved the construction of a new energy centre, two major buildings and two subsidiary buildings containing office and production space. The two main buildings share a similar plan configuration, with four 18-metre-deep arms of floor space arranged around three rooflit atria. The office areas open to the atria, which contain staircases that provide direct circulation between floors, an arrangement intended to encourage informal communication between departments. One side of each atrium is relatively open, with glazed balustrades and a continuous walkway; the other is more enclosed, with timber panels providing privacy to working areas.

These large, robust buildings are intended to be functional and flexible. They are clad in aluminium and glass, with brises-soleil on the south and west elevations and opening shutters wherever natural ventilation is viable. The shutters, located behind metal louvres, are painted different colours, lending variety to the otherwise repetitive facades. The colour selection and sequence, chosen by artist Yuko Shiraishi, formed one of the project's public art projects. Elsewhere, Tim Head was commissioned to create a light installation for the Energy Centre.

◄ *Staircases form a feature within the atrium*
▶ *View across atrium to open-plan office floors*
▶ *Escape stair handrail detail*

1 atrium
2 office
3 core

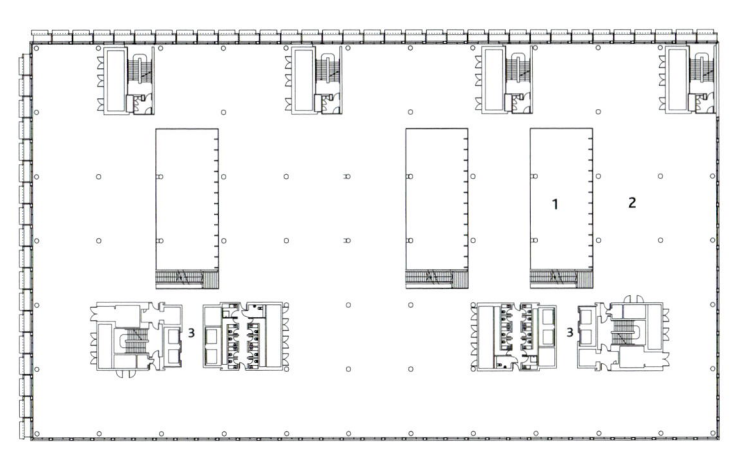

Typical upper floor plan

39

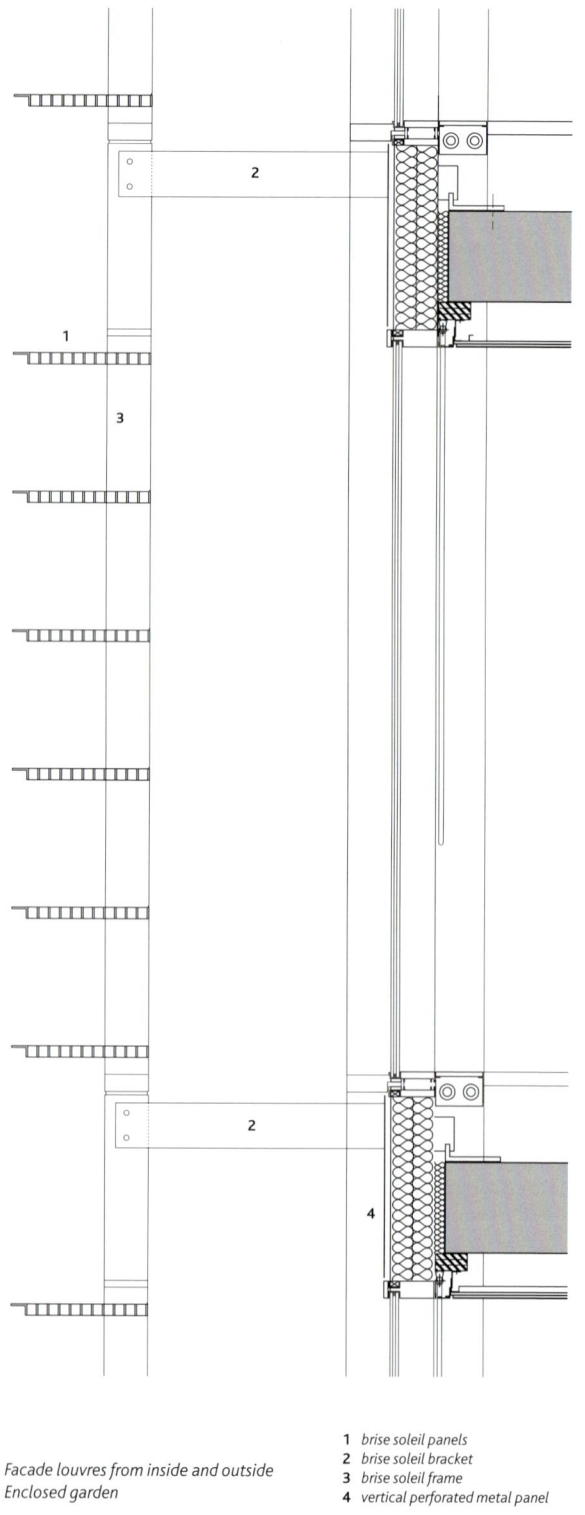

◄ Facade louvres from inside and outside
► Enclosed garden

1 brise soleil panels
2 brise soleil bracket
3 brise soleil frame
4 vertical perforated metal panel

40

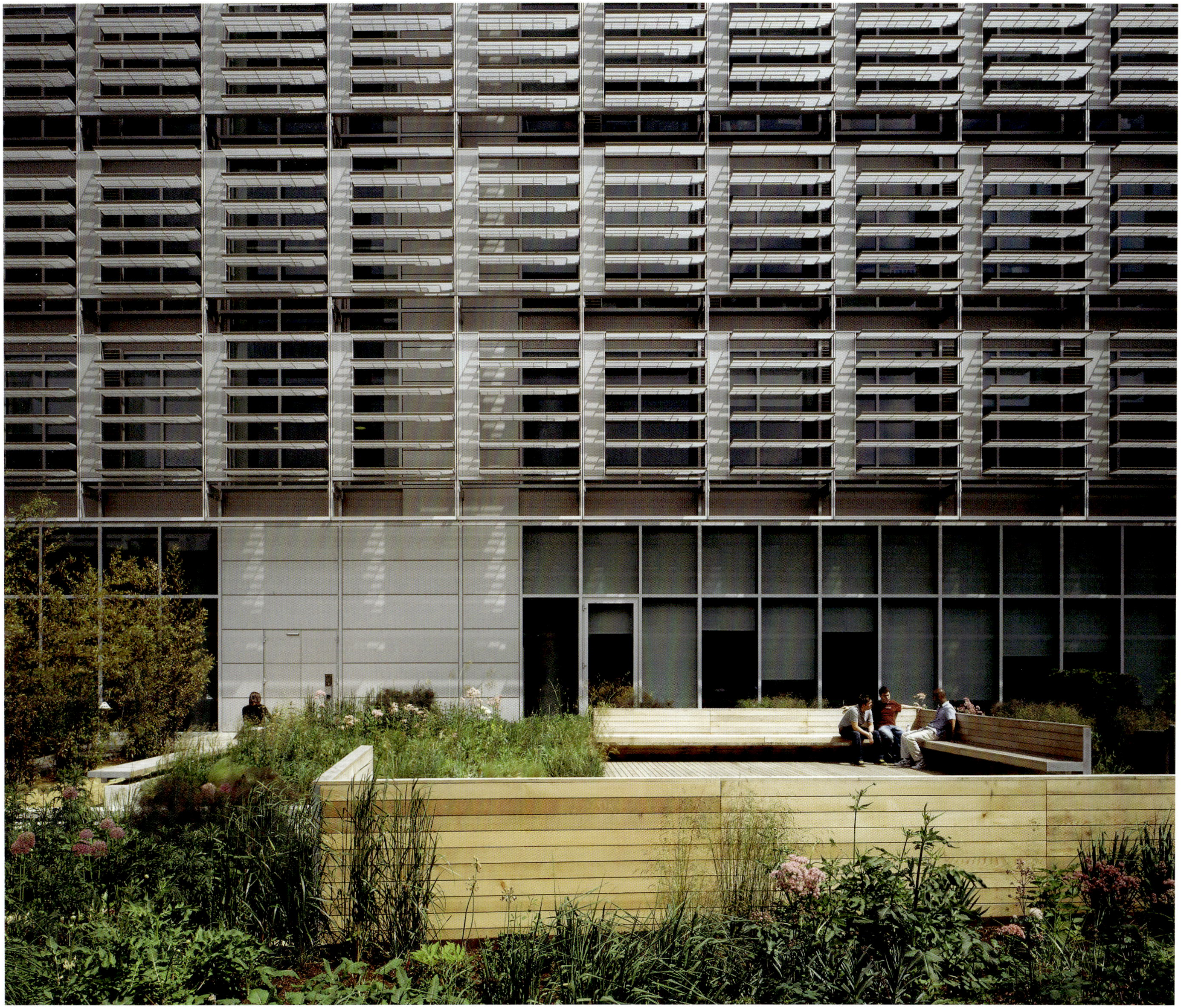

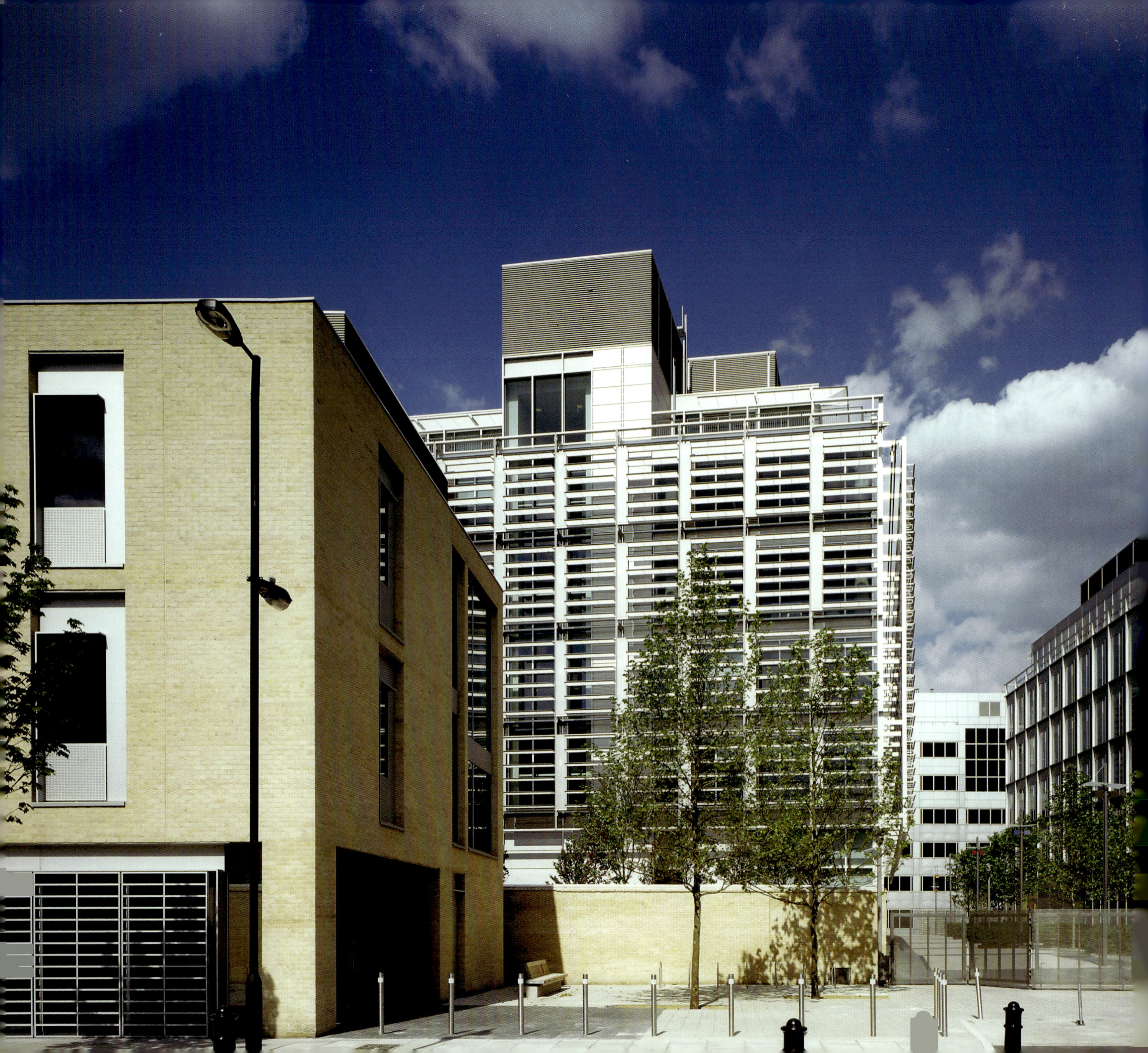

The buildings required for the BBC's own use logically faced towards the centre of the site. Because of this, two additional buildings were introduced at the perimeter of the site to ensure that the surrounding streets were addressed by fronts rather than by backs of buildings. Also designed for office use, these buildings form a continuous street frontage of brickwork with a simple pattern of aluminium-framed windows.

◀ *Cross street leading into the site*
▶ *Street frontage at the perimeter of the site*

SIDGWICK SITE
ARTS AND HUMANITIES CAMPUS
University of Cambridge
2003

The original plan for the Sidgwick Avenue site – the arts and humanities campus of the University of Cambridge – was drawn up by Casson Conder in 1952. Envisaging a series of linked buildings arranged around a sequence of informal courts, the plan represented a contemporary interpretation of the characteristic medieval college plan. Hugh Casson's vision was never fully realised, although significant interventions were made by James Stirling in 1968, Norman Foster and Partners in 1995 and Edward Cullinan Architects in 2000.

Allies and Morrison were asked to set out a plan for the completion of the site with the intention of not only defining possible locations for additional buildings but also clarifying movement routes across the site and reviewing the potential of its public spaces.

Locations for four new buildings were identified: the Faculty of English, the Institute of Criminology, the Department of Land Economy and a building for East Asian Studies (only the latter remained unbuilt).

Each new building, by means of its siting and its plan configuration, contributes towards a new understanding of the site. A main north-south circulation spine through the centre of the site links the University Library to the north with the Raised Faculty Building in the centre of the site, and on to the Sidgwick Avenue frontage to the south. All the principal building entrances are oriented towards this main route, improving legibility of the campus for visitors and students alike.

The limestone-clad Raised Faculty Building was regarded as the finest of Casson's original buildings on the site, but its central courtyard was largely unused. With new trees and seating providing a relaxed setting for informal exchange and discussion, it now it forms a significant public square at the heart of the campus.

1 *Raised Faculty Building (Casson Conder)*
2 *Department of Land Economy (Nicholas Hare Architects)*
3 *Faculty of English (Allies and Morrison)*
4 *Institute of Criminology (Allies and Morrison)*
5 *East Asian Studies*
6 *Museum of Classical Archaeology (Casson Conder)*
7 *Faculty of History (James Stirling)*
8 *Faculty of Law (Norman Foster and Partners)*
9 *West Road Concert Hall (Leslie Martin)*

FACULTY OF ENGLISH
University of Cambridge
2001–04

The Faculty of English faces north towards West Road and the University Library and south towards James Stirling's History Library. It also looks inward, its accommodation forming three sides of a west-facing courtyard. The U-shaped building form is set back at its south-east corner to accommodate a protected holm oak tree. Here, at the narrowest point of the plan, the main entrance and staircase are located. Glazing on both sides allows views from the staircase through to the interior courtyard while also appearing to dissolve the mass of the building at this key point.

The composition of the elevations is generated by the three-metre module of the academic offices. Adaptations are introduced in response to orientation, such as the brises-soleil on the south and courtyard facades. Offices overlooking the garden have full-height French windows, while terraces allow meeting rooms at various levels to enjoy external space.

▲ Courtyard elevation
▶ Detail of west facade

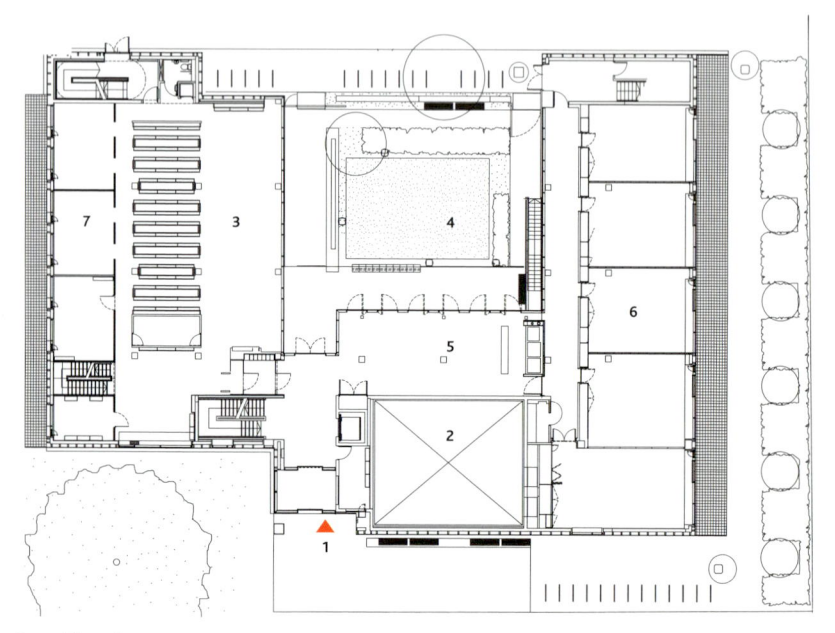

1 entrance
2 void over drama studio
3 library
4 courtyard
5 social space
6 seminar room
7 study rooms
8 conference room
9 academic offices
10 Head of Department

Ground floor plan

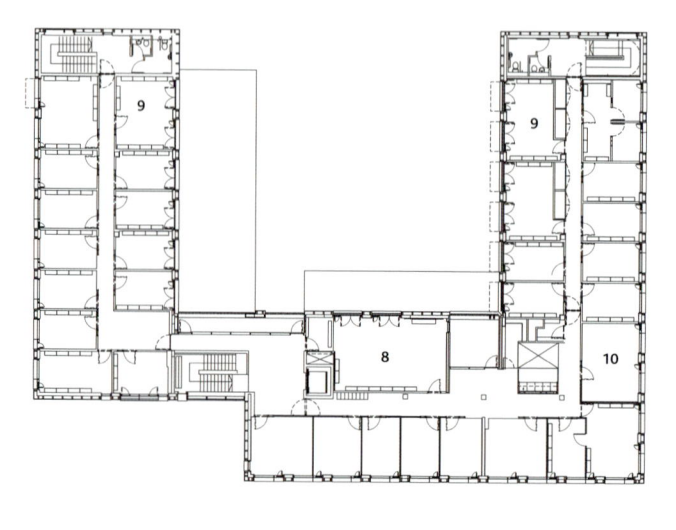

Third floor plan

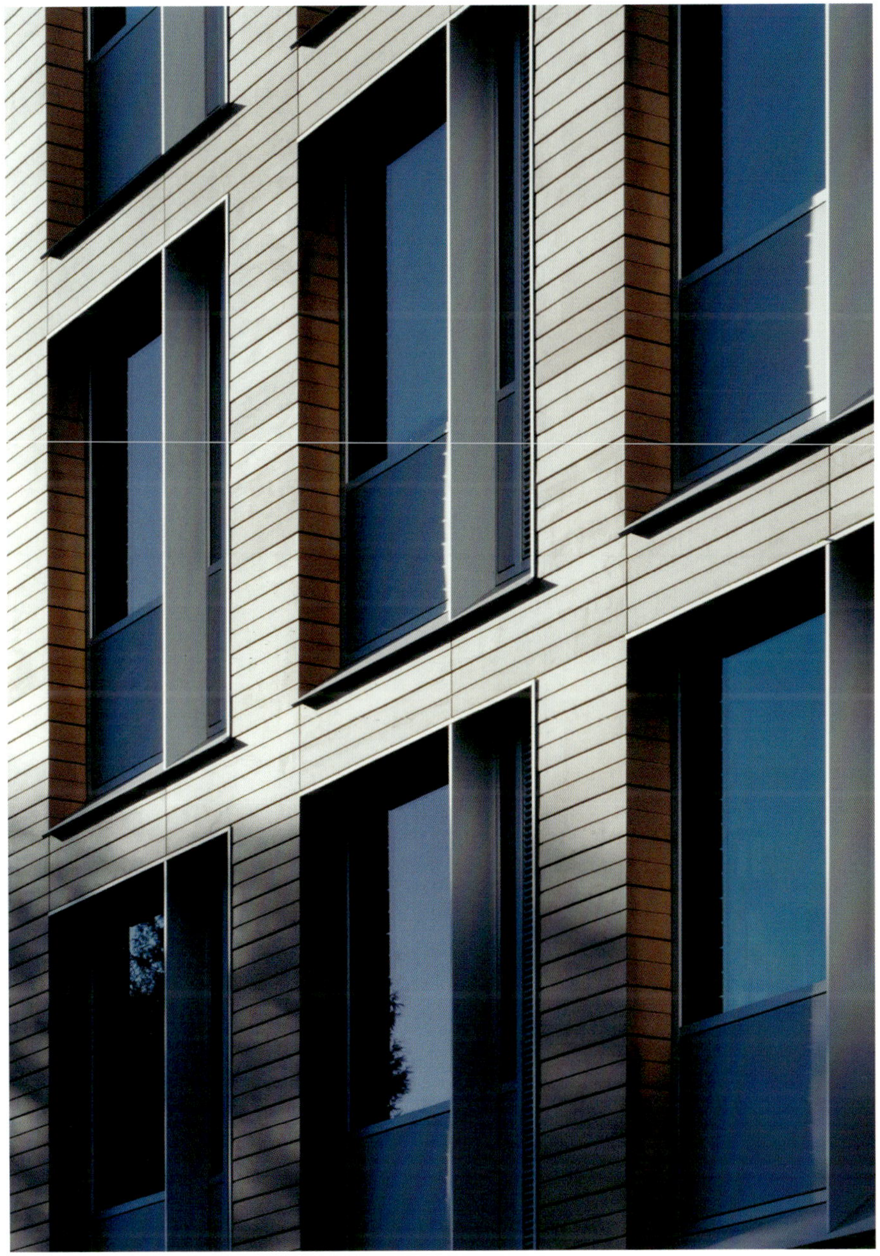

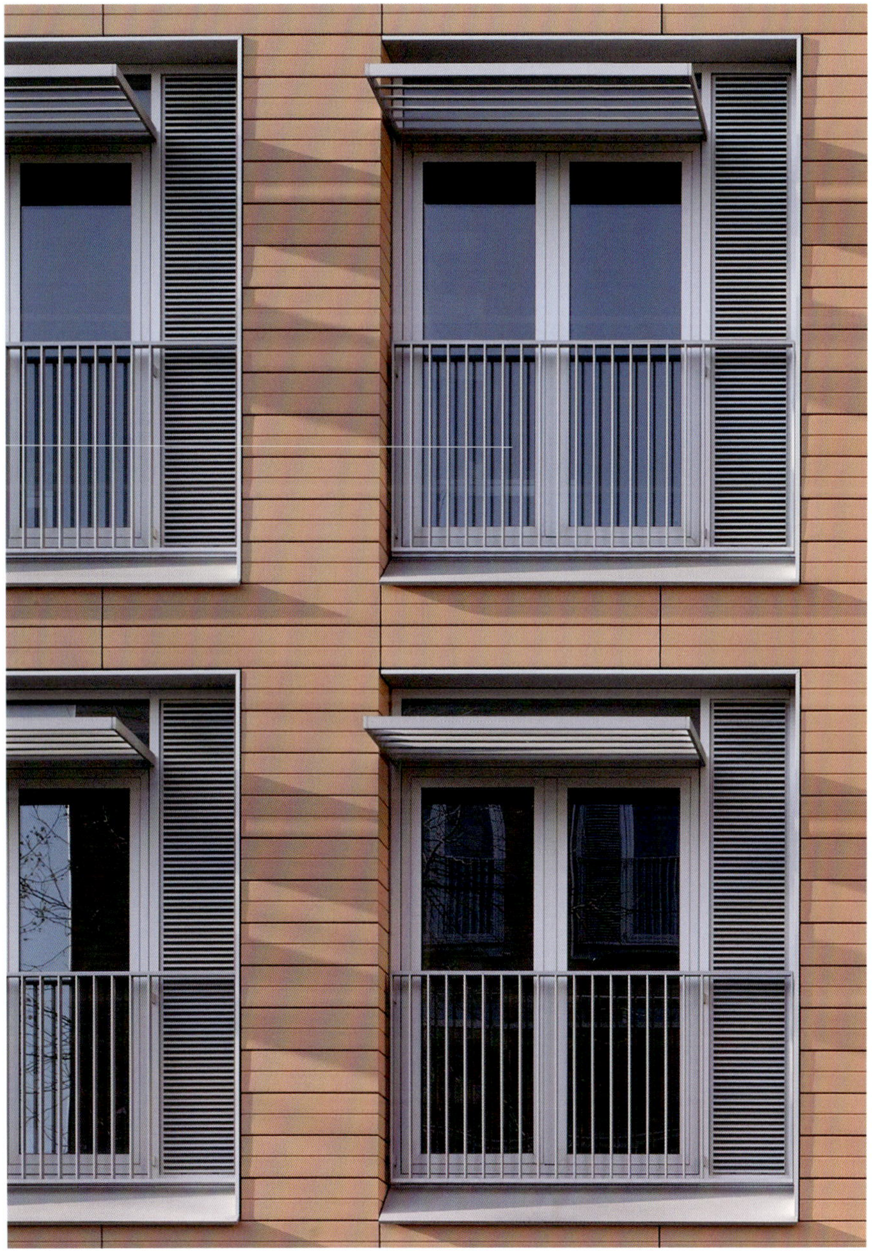

◀ The library overlooks the central garden
▶ The library, social spaces and staircase

1 library
2 courtyard
3 seminar room
4 academic offices
5 plant room

North-south section through courtyard

49

CRIMINOLOGY

INSTITUTE OF CRIMINOLOGY
University of Cambridge
2001–04

The Institute of Criminology establishes a new built edge to the eastern boundary of the Sidgwick Avenue site and creates a new courtyard adjacent to the Raised Faculty Building. Its simple rectangular plan is disrupted at the north-east corner by a projecting entrance 'pavilion'. Above the glazed entrance are the institute's main meeting room and staff room.

The pavilion shares the material vocabulary of the remainder of the building – precast concrete and dark grey anodised aluminium.

However it breaks from the otherwise regular rhythm of the main elevations to make a distinct response to its location.

Internally the four floors of accommodation house a variety of research, administrative and library spaces. Open staircases provide informal connections between the different floor levels. The basement, which accommodates the main teaching and social spaces, extends underneath the courtyard. Daylight enters via three circular rooflights that punctuate the landscaped

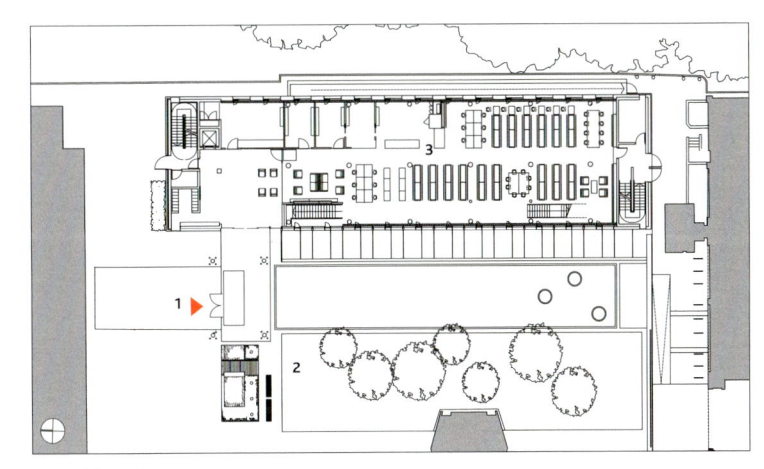

Ground floor plan

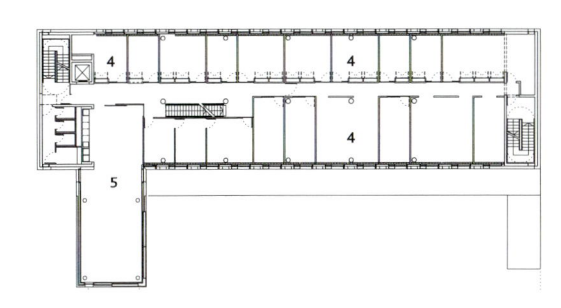

Third floor plan

1 entrance
2 garden court
3 library
4 offices
5 meeting room

garden above, as well as from a strip of roof glazing that runs parallel to the facade above the main circulation route.

The facade is composed of fixed full-height windows alternating with vertical panels of cladding and louvres. Behind the louvres are openable shutters that provide natural ventilation to individual office spaces. The regular rhythm of the facade is differentiated in response to the presence of the library, where more glass and shading are introduced.

The building's white precast concrete panels and dark grey aluminium cladding recognise a relationship respectively with Hugh Casson's Raised Faculty Building and Foster & Partner's Law Library. The reveals of the concrete cladding panels are lined with metal plates on the north but not to the south, provoking a different reading of the building according to the direction from which it is approached.

◄ *Courtyard facade*
► *Library and circulation space*

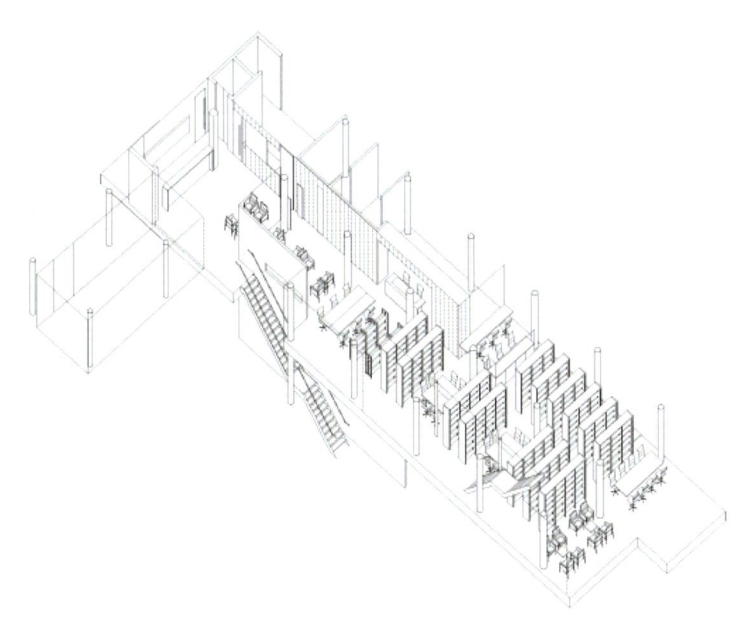

1 garden court
2 library
3 research
4 meeting room
5 phd workspace
6 office
7 seminar room
8 storage

Axonometric of library interior

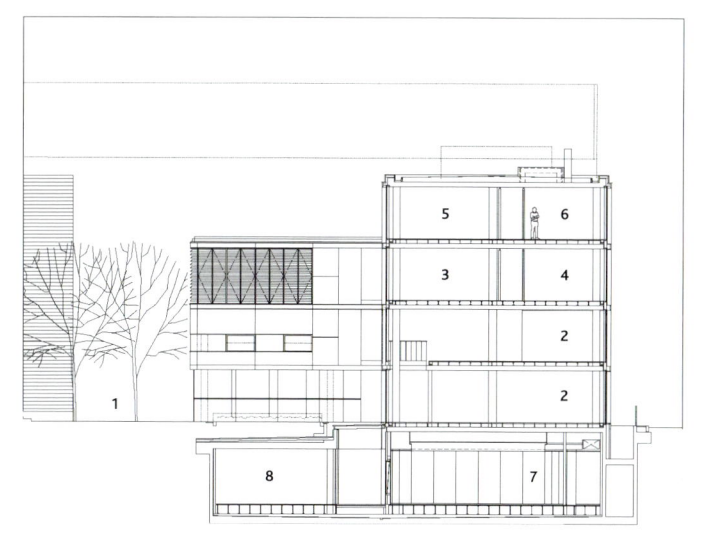

Cross section through library

53

GATEHOUSE COURT AND AUDITORIUM
FITZWILLIAM COLLEGE
University of Cambridge
1999–2004

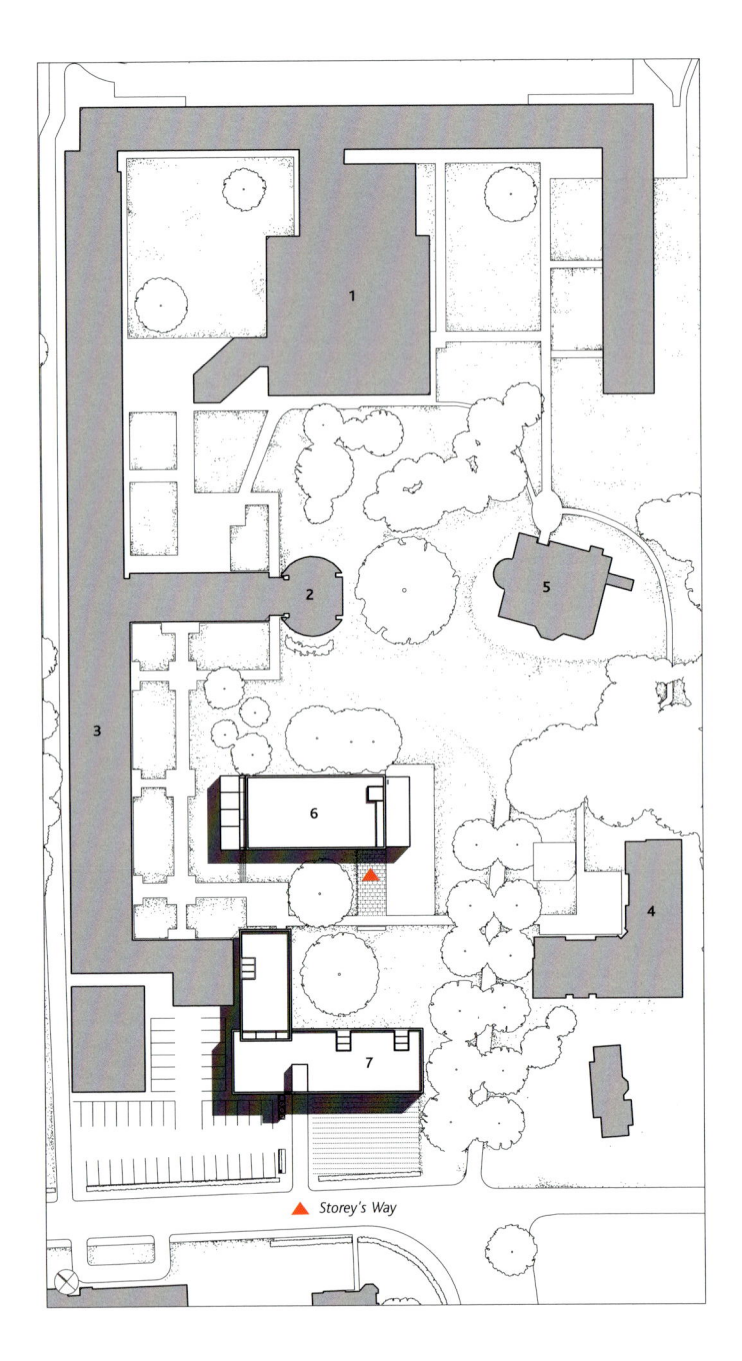

The central precinct of Fitzwilliam College was planned and built by Denys Lasdun between 1959 and 1963, although the overall masterplan remained uncompleted. MacCormac Jamieson & Prichard and subsequently van Heyningen & Haward extended Lasdun's perimeter buildings, establishing the west and south corners of the college site.

Allies and Morrison's Gatehouse Court, which provides administrative accommodation at ground level and 42 student rooms above, effectively completes the Lasdun masterplan by forming a new college entrance on Storey's Way in accordance with the original aspiration.

The two wings of Gatehouse Court define the edge of a new courtyard containing two large copper beech

1 *Hall and Central Building – Denys Lasdun & Partners*
2 *Chapel – MacCormac Jamieson & Prichard*
3 *New Court – MacCormac Jamieson &Prichard*
4 *Wilson Court – van Heyningen & Haward*
5 *The Grove*
6 *Auditorium – Allies and Morrison*
7 *Gatehouse – Allies and Morrison*

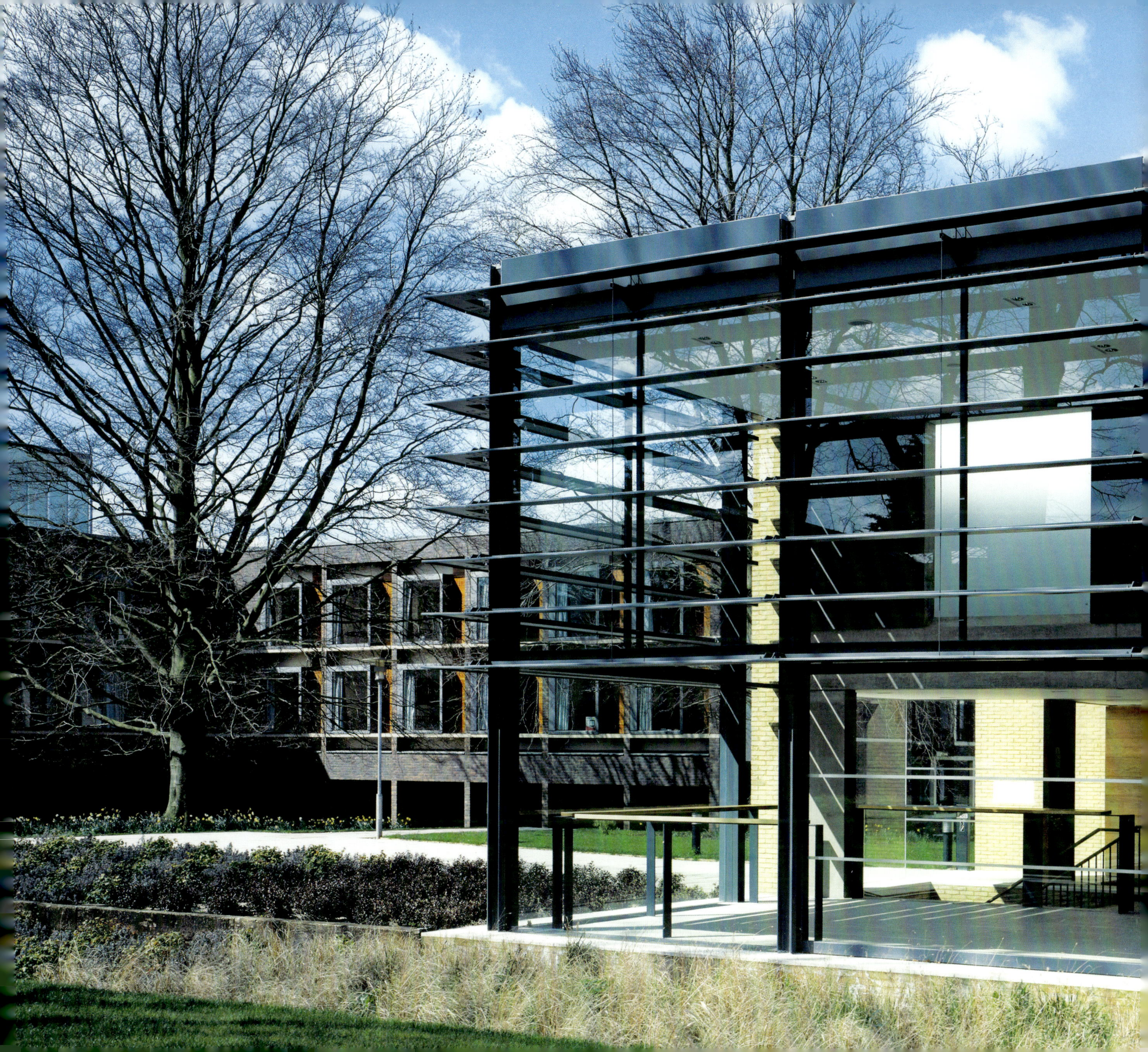

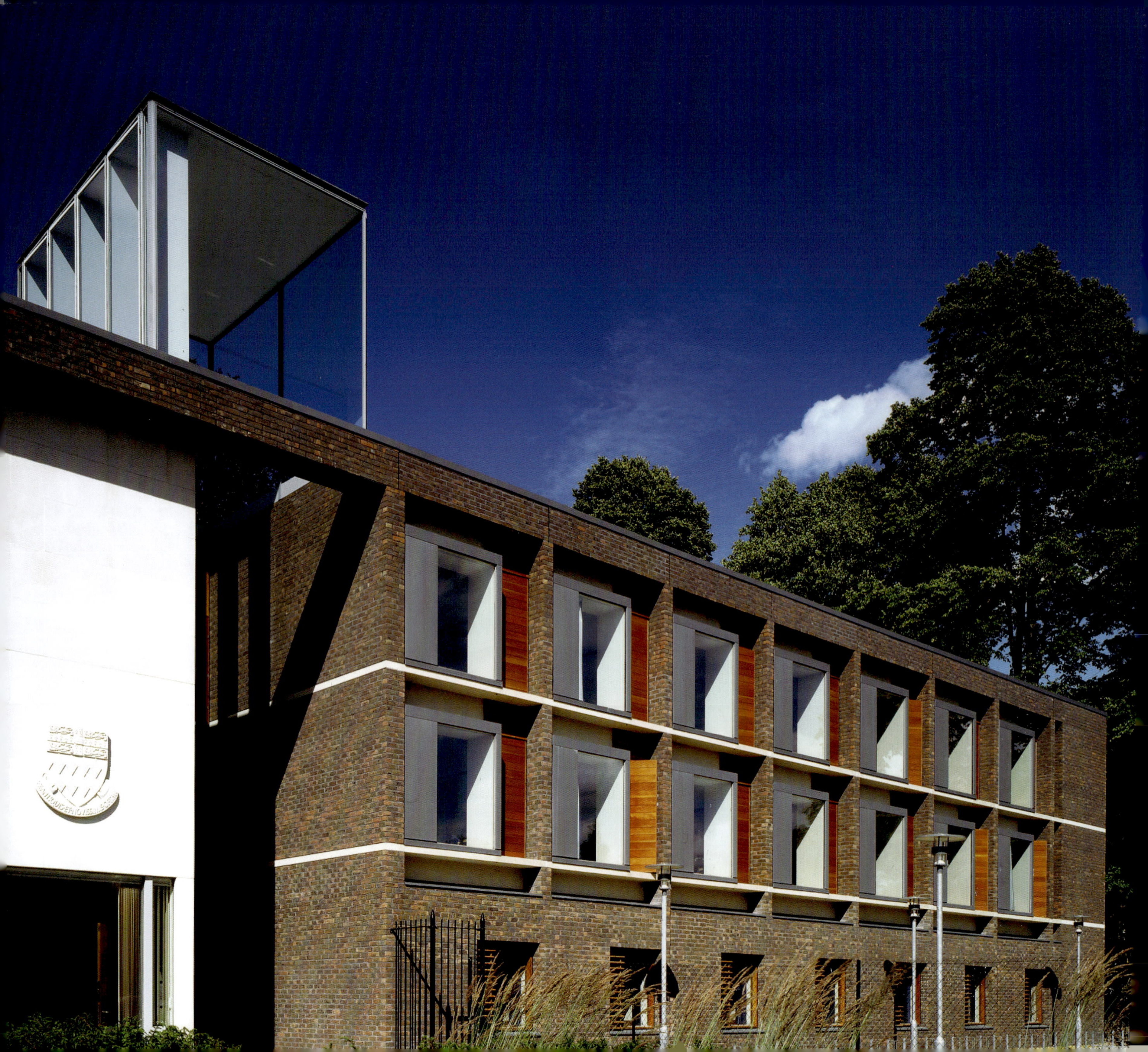

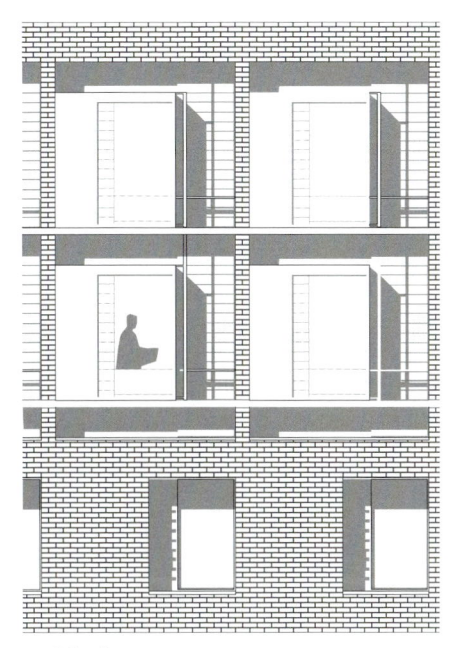

South facade 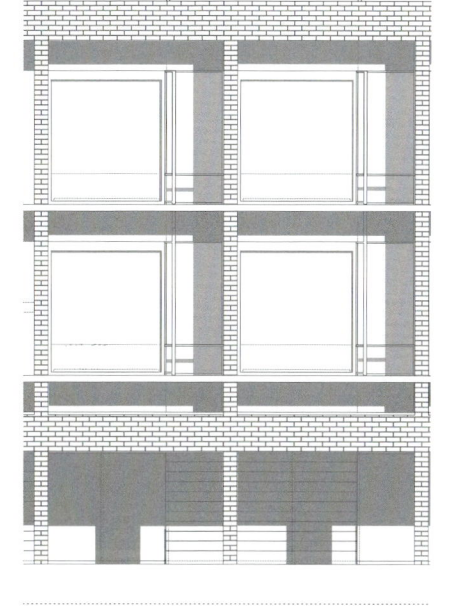 *North facade* 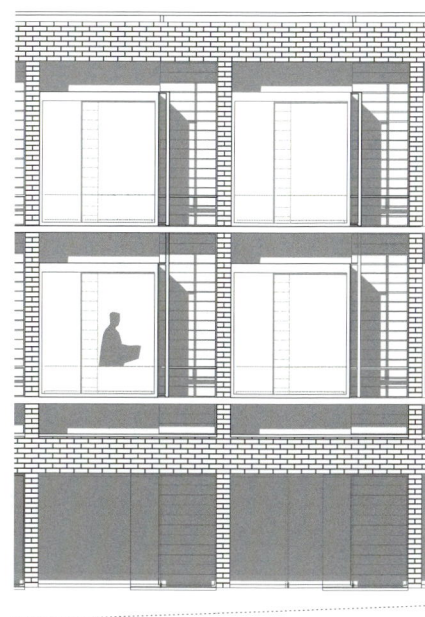 *East facade*

trees. A third side of the courtyard is aligned with a new auditorium which includes a multipurpose performance space, foyer and music practice rooms.

The new courtyard forms one of the series of garden spaces anticipated by Lasdun's masterplan, an interplay between a residential perimeter and an informal central landscape.

Gatehouse Court extends the language of dark brick and pale banding instigated by Lasdun and reinterpreted by MacCormac Jamieson & Prichard. This rhythm provides a framework for a series of standardised student rooms, each with a bay window and prefabricated bathroom pod. The zinc-clad window bays of the student rooms are adjusted according to the orientation so that each room has optimum levels of daylight and natural ventilation. The repeated pattern of bays is broken by the college entrance, a three-storey void rising to a glass lantern, and the adjoining stone-clad seminar rooms and porter's lodge.

◄ *Entrance with windows to student rooms*
▲ *Elevations differ according to orientation*
▶ *View from cloister*

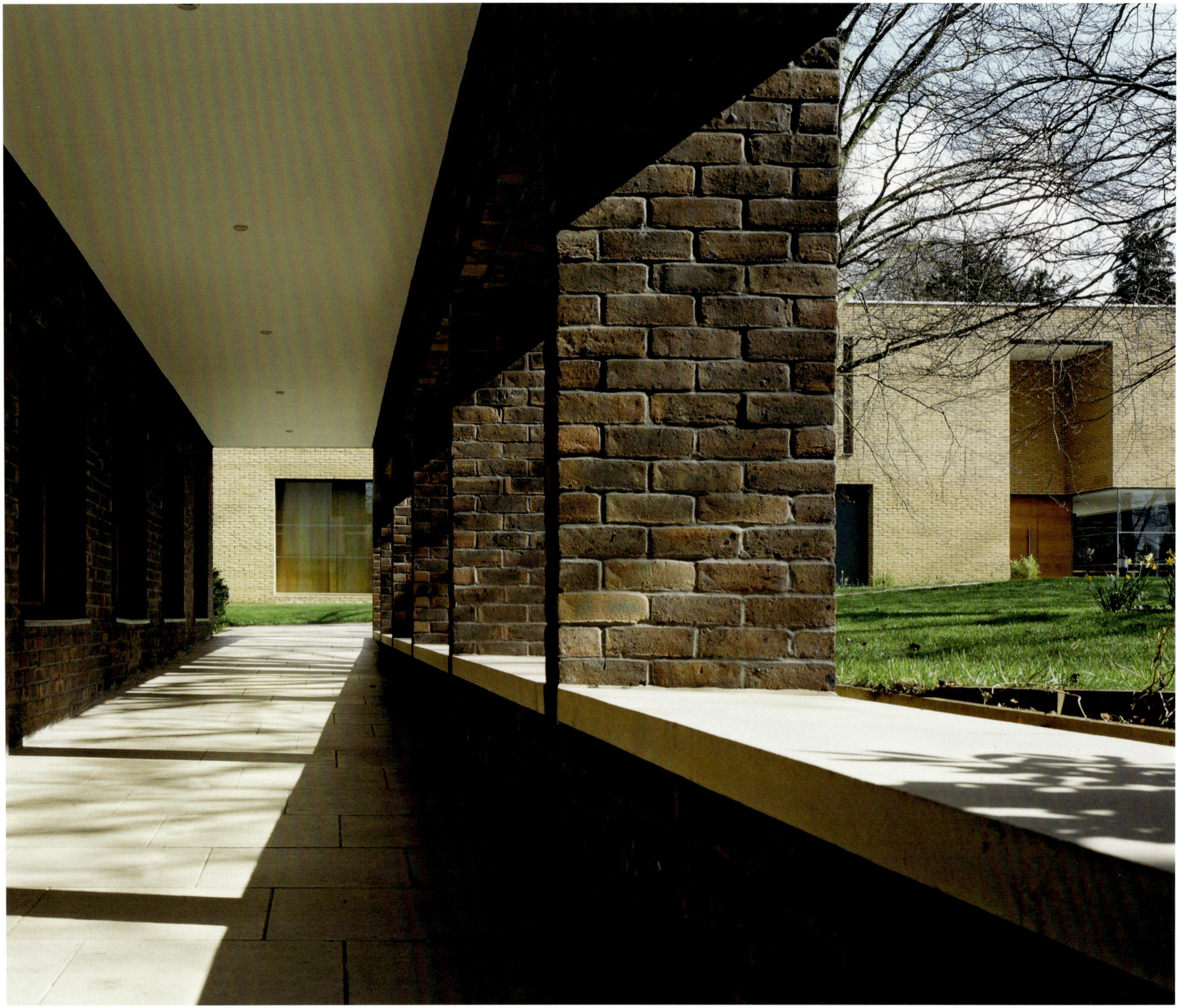

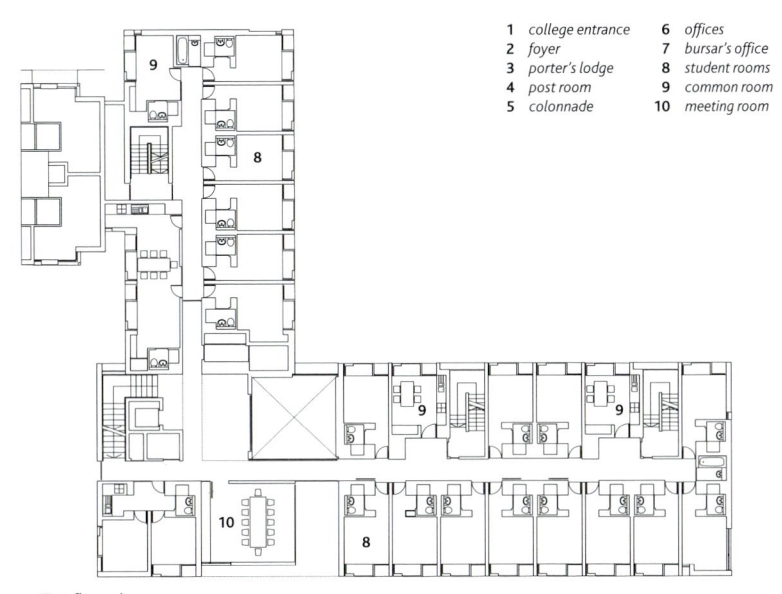

1	college entrance	6	offices
2	foyer	7	bursar's office
3	porter's lodge	8	student rooms
4	post room	9	common room
5	colonnade	10	meeting room

First floor plan

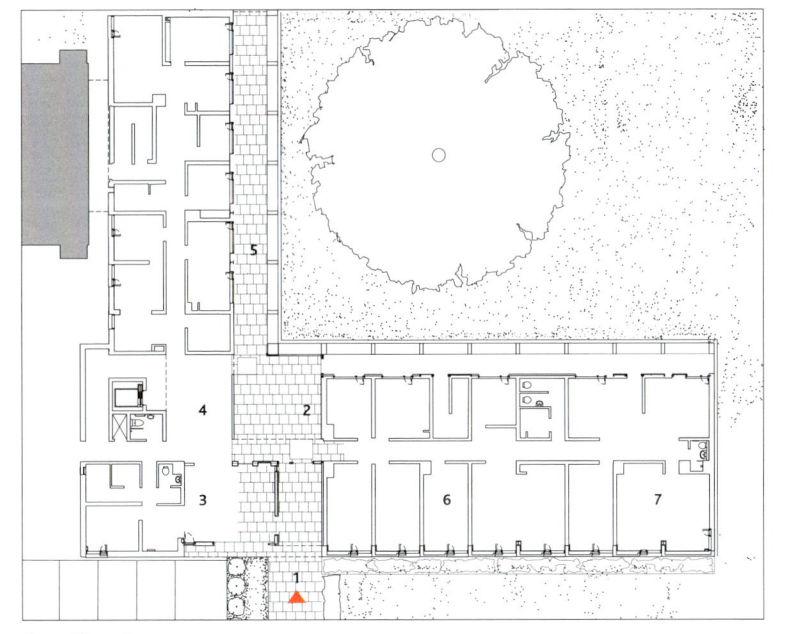

Ground floor plan

◄ *Gatehouse cloister and auditorium*
► *Student room with views into the courtyard*
► *Post room with view towards the cloister*

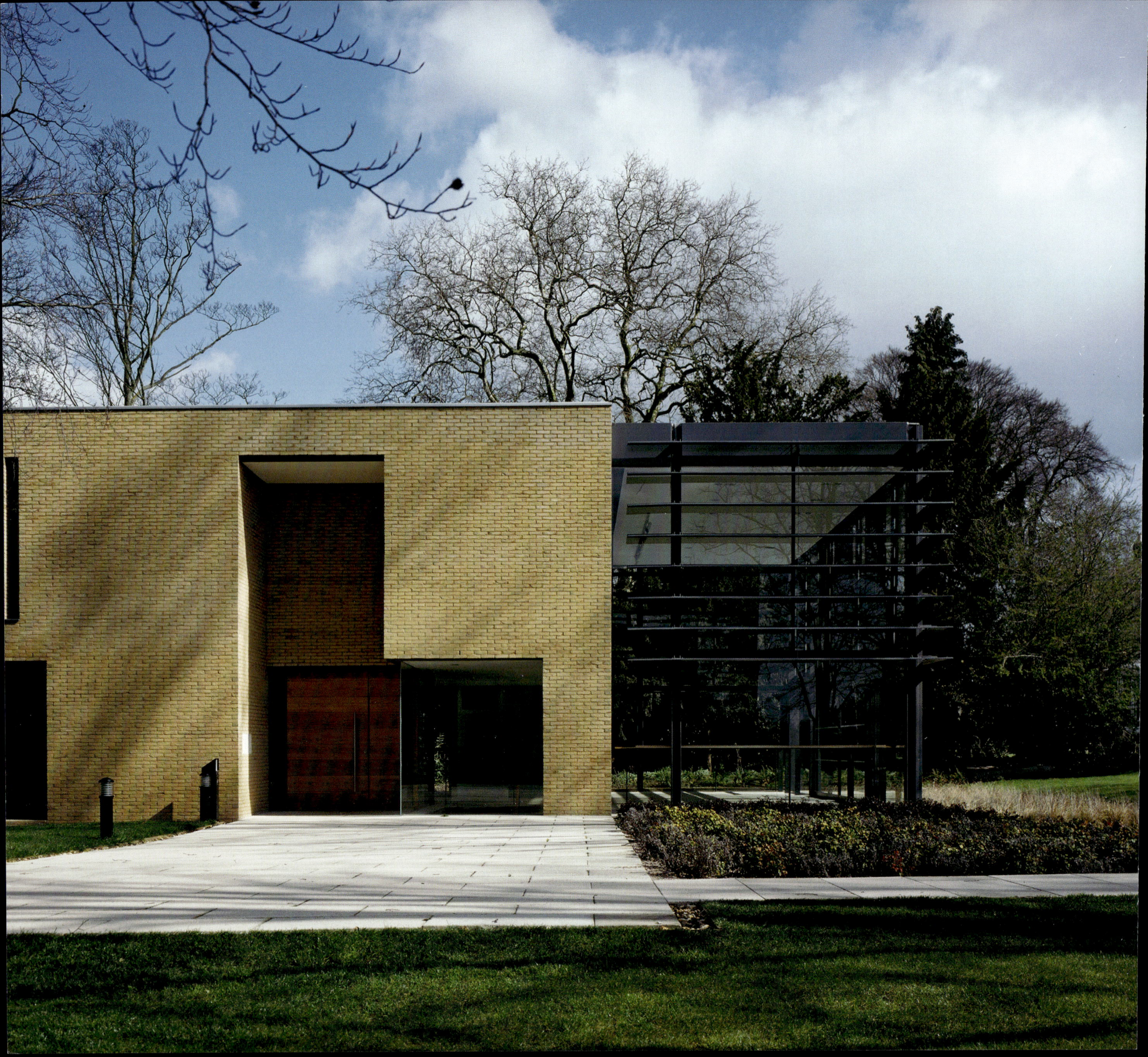

The Auditorium takes its place among the freestanding structures within the rectangular perimeter building of Lasdun's masterplan – Lasdun's own refectory, MacCormac Jamieson and Prichard's chapel, van Heyningen and Haward's lecture hall and The Grove, the early nineteenth-century house that originally occupied the site.

The overall height and impact of the auditorium is tempered by placing the stage at basement level, with the audience arriving at a ground-floor gallery. This 'upper' level is naturally lit by large windows that also offer views out. Sliding glass doors to the foyer can be fully opened, if wished, for summer concerts.

Manually-operated sliding oak shutters provide blackout to the auditorium, if required, just as openable panels at high level in the auditorium allow the acoustic performance of the auditorium to be adjusted.

The exterior is clad in pale Cambridge cream bricks to match those of The Grove, and acknowledge its continuing significance within the gardens since plans for its demolition were abandoned.

▲ *View from auditorium foyer to Gatehouse Court*
◄ *Auditorium entrance and foyer with sunken garden*

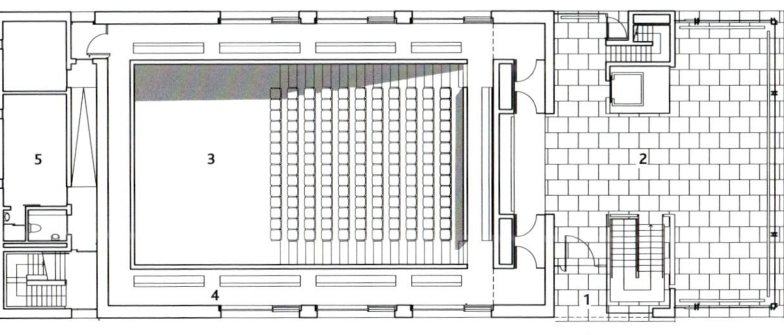

Ground floor plan

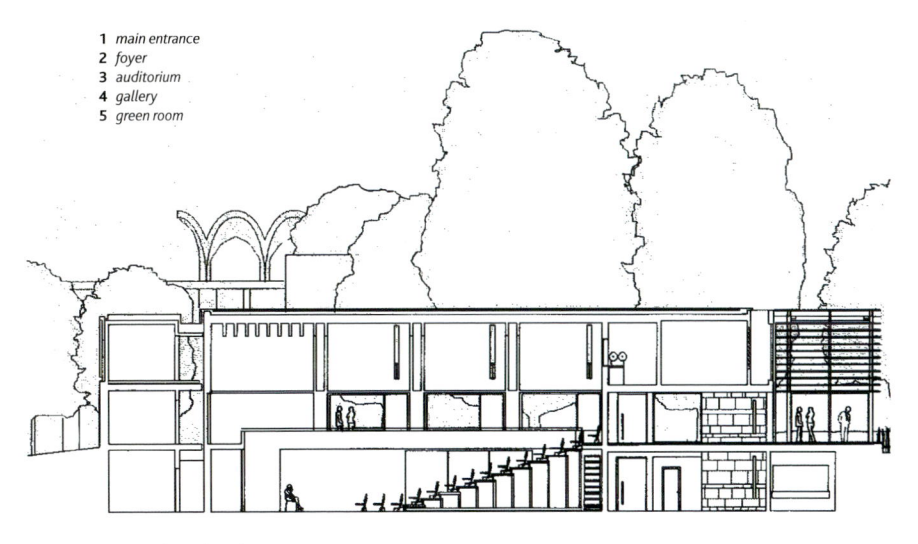

1 *main entrance*
2 *foyer*
3 *auditorium*
4 *gallery*
5 *green room*

Section through auditorium

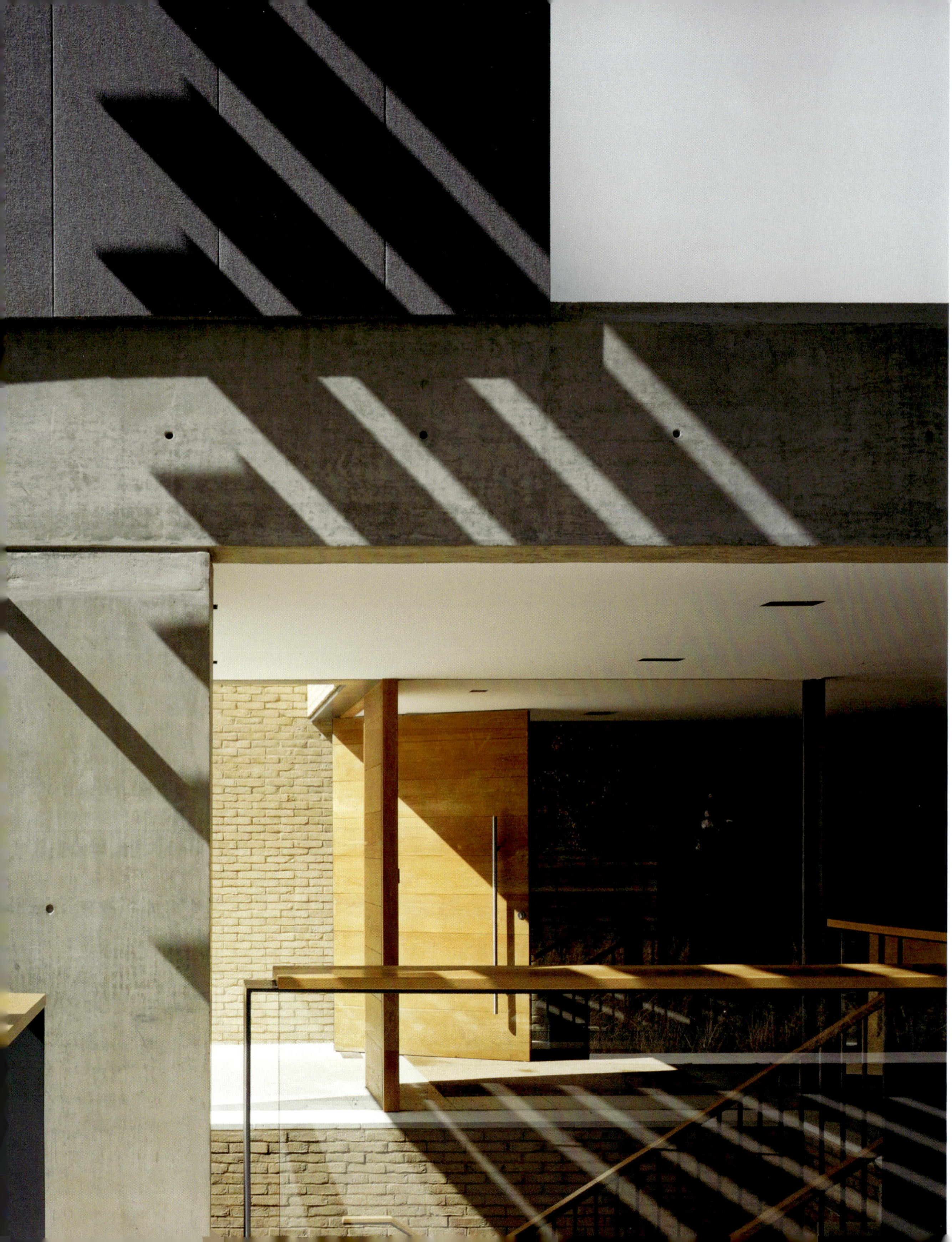

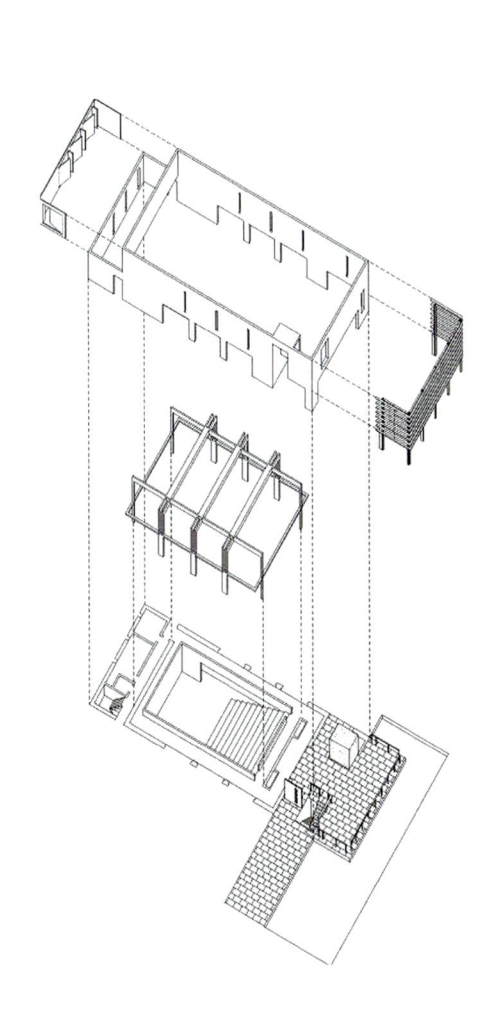

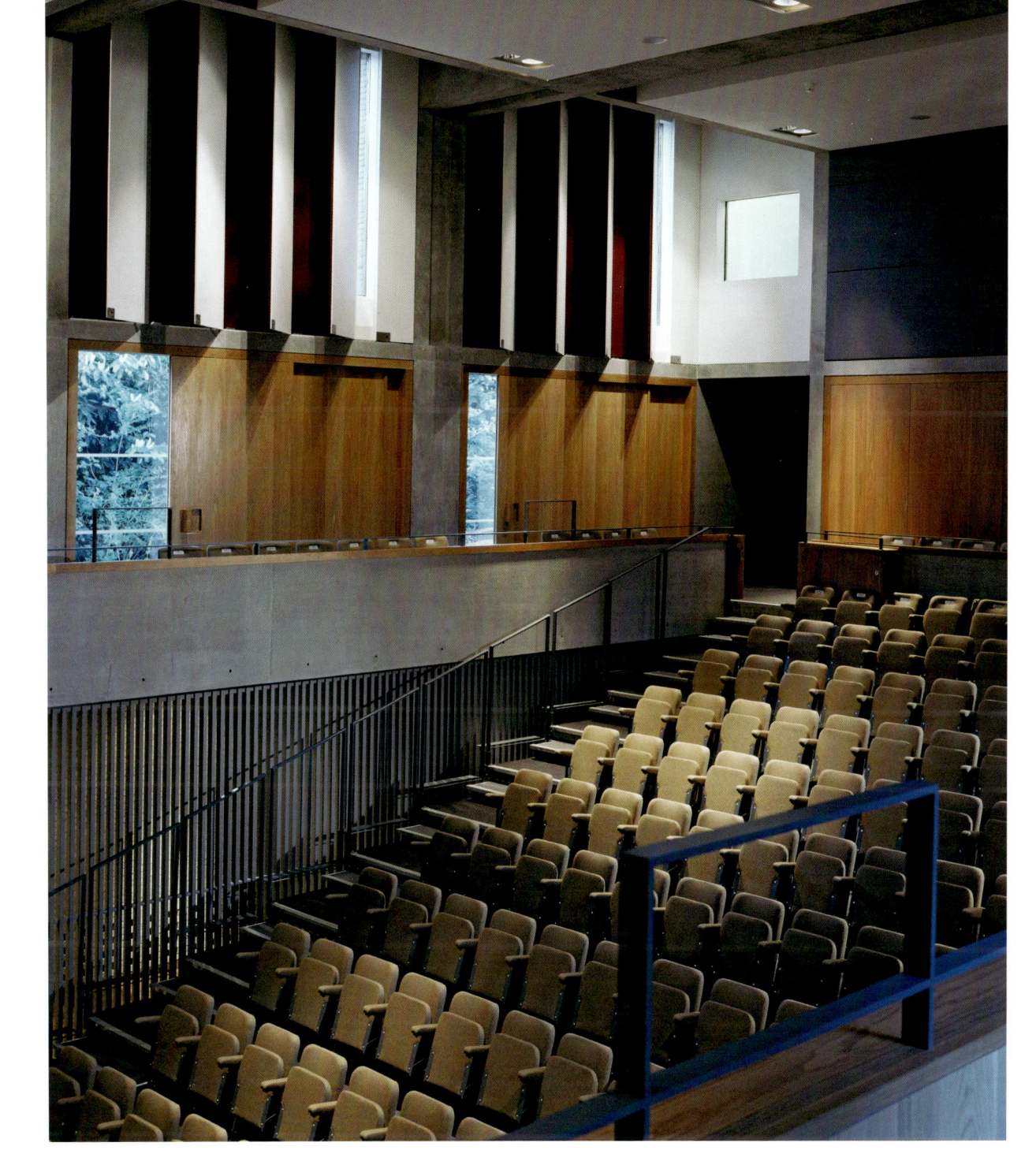

◀ *Foyer looking towards the auditorium entrance*
▶ *Auditorium interior*

FINLAY BUILDING
MERTON COLLEGE

University of Oxford
2002–04

The Finlay Building accommodates the administrative offices of Merton College on three floors, while a basement level houses storage and archives. Located off Merton Street and opposite the main college precinct, the new building occupies a constricted site, ringed by medieval buildings and containing fragments of the medieval city wall. It is configured so as to establish a sequence of small courtyards, linking existing spaces together and adjusting them to the geometry of the earlier buildings.

The body of the new building follows the western perimeter of the site, rising above a medieval stone wall that forms the boundary with Corpus Christi College. The elevations are faced in a combination of ashlar and freestone, with stainless steel reveals and cills providing definition to the window openings. Ashlar also features in the lower plinth to the building and in the two-storey link building that abuts the stone wall of the Real Tennis court to the east, and contains the new building entrance. Here, at first-floor level, the main meeting room faces south across the courtyard, its windows set back within a balcony to protect it from the sun. The second floor is contained within the roof space, with projecting mansards allowing light into the interior.

◀ *Courtyard by night*
▶ *Entrance facade*

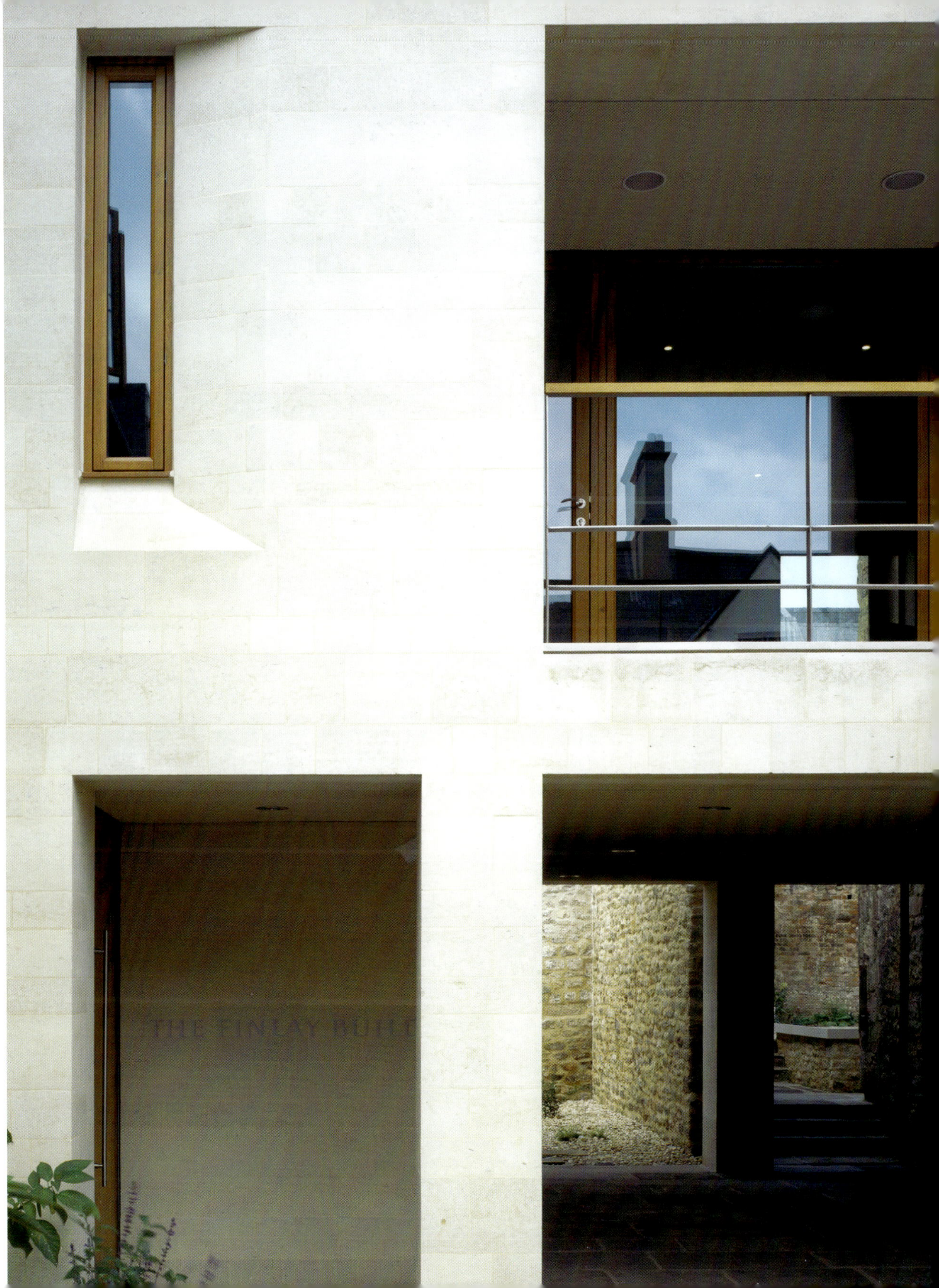
THE FINLAY BUIL

▼ *View from meeting room into courtyard*
▼ *Balustrade detail*
▶ *Cantilevered precast concrete stair*

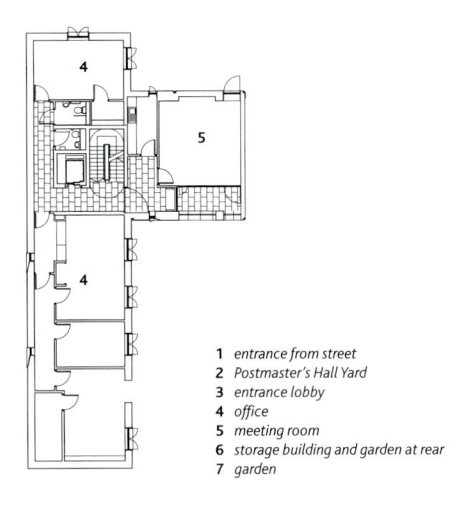

1 entrance from street
2 Postmaster's Hall Yard
3 entrance lobby
4 office
5 meeting room
6 storage building and garden at rear
7 garden

First floor plan

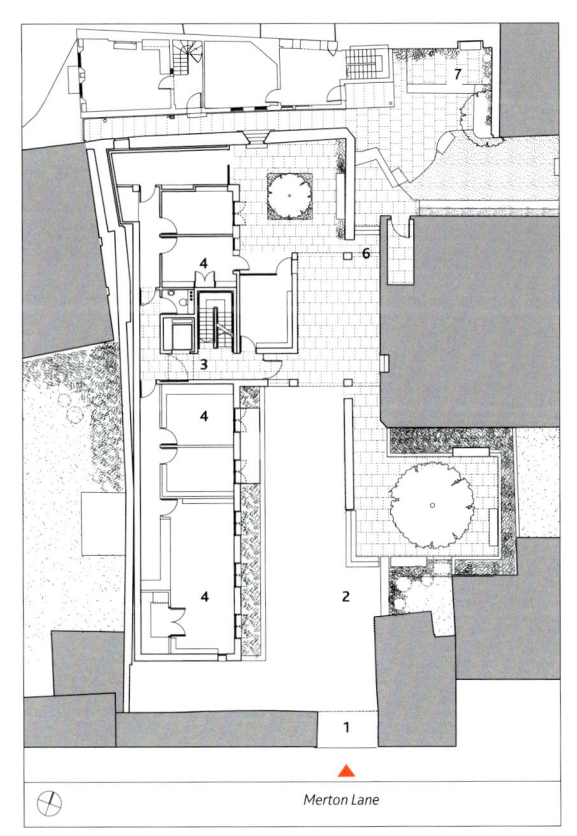

Ground floor plan

Merton Lane

67

GROSVENOR WATERSIDE

Chelsea, London
2001–05

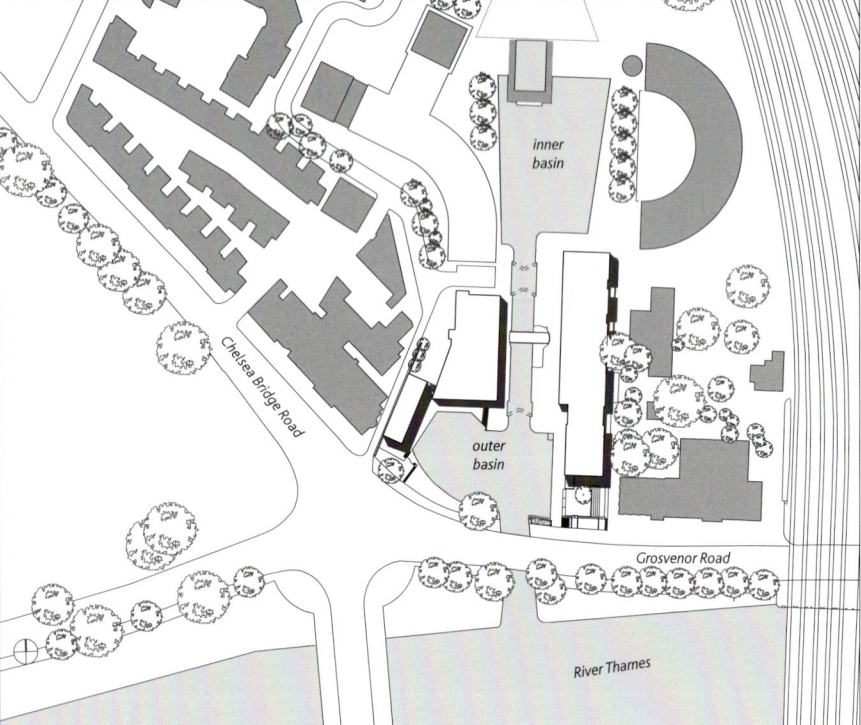

Grosvenor Waterside is a residential development prominently located on the north bank of the Thames immediately adjacent to Chelsea Bridge. At its heart is Grosvenor Dock, which in the nineteenth century served as Thomas Cubitt's building yard, facilitating the development of Belgravia and Pimlico.

The practice was appointed in 2001 by developer St James to design two key buildings within the context of a new masterplan, as well as a third, smaller building that initially housed the marketing suite for the development before being adapted.

The two main buildings face one another across a lock that links the inner and outer dock basins before opening out to the Thames. Their siting and massing provide enclosure to the outer basin and lock area while establishing an appropriate scale and relationship with the adjacent historic structures of the pumping station to the east and the Lister Hospital to the west. As such the two buildings are conceived as complementary structures, with a similar architectural language and employing the same materials.

▲ *South-facing Thames frontage*
▶ *Elevation of facade from the outer basin*

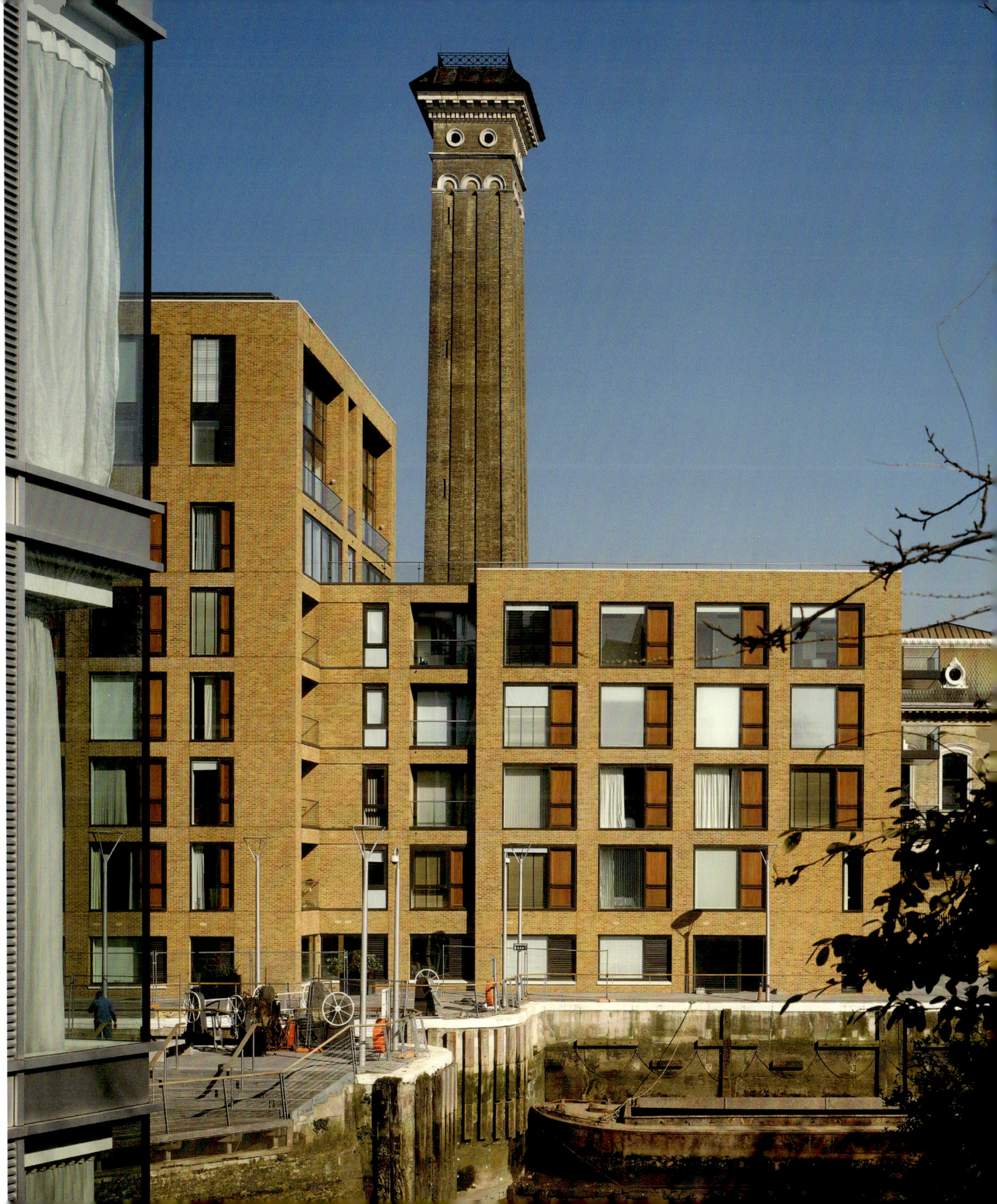

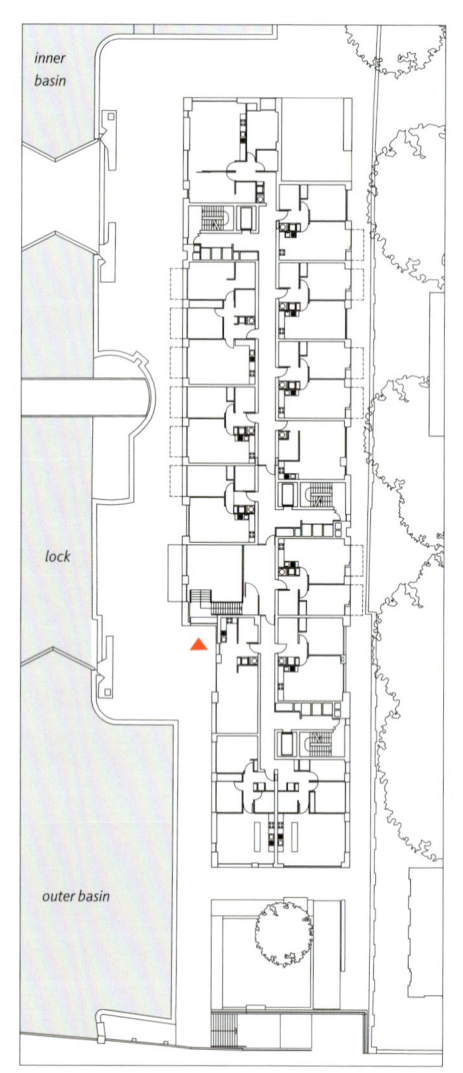

Ground floor plan

The larger, eastern building has a simple linear plan that is oriented north-south to run parallel with the lock. It is composed of two conjoined blocks of differing scale: an eight-storey block at the northern end that relates to the massing of the smaller building facing it across the lock; and a five-storey block at the southern end, near the outer dock, which establishes a relationship with the Western Pumping Station to its east.

The plan of the shorter rectangular building on the east side of the lock has been modified by a splay to its western flank that widens the southern elevation to the outer basin, creating a more horizontal facade which in turn provides a stronger contextual relationship with the Lister Hospital buildings on the western boundary. The east elevation of this building mirrors the matching western facade of the larger, linear building across the dock, both comprising four rows of balconies and regular punctuated openings which recall the historic industrial setting of the lock.

◀ *Facades to basin*
▶ *Balconies face across the dock*

CITY LIT
Covent Garden, London
1998–2005

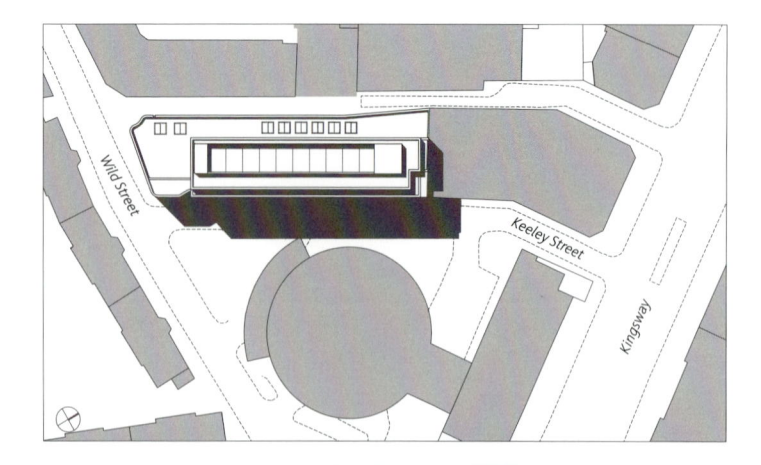

Founded by the London County Council in 1919, the City Lit is an adult education college situated in Holborn, central London. In 2005 the institute relocated to new premises, built on a narrow, east-west orientated site between two existing streets with a party wall on its eastern boundary.

The building is arranged over eight floors and contains 25 teaching rooms as well as special needs and specialist spaces, including a multi-use theatre, a recital room, a centre for the hearing impaired and a music department. One floor is dedicated to the arts, with bookbinding, painting, drawing and pottery studios, printmaking, graphics, digital arts, jewellery and silversmith and general workshops. The plan is arranged with a public core at one end and a smaller service core at the other, linked by a central corridor.

From the main Keeley Street entrance a double-height internal 'street' gives access to the principal performance spaces and a cafe at the eastern end. Periodically the space is charged with activity, such as during times of enrolment, exhibitions of student work or public performances in the theatre or recital room.

The building is clad almost entirely in brick, with the entrance faced in aluminium and marked by a pair of

◀ *Keeley Street facade*
▶ *Main entrance on Keeley Street*

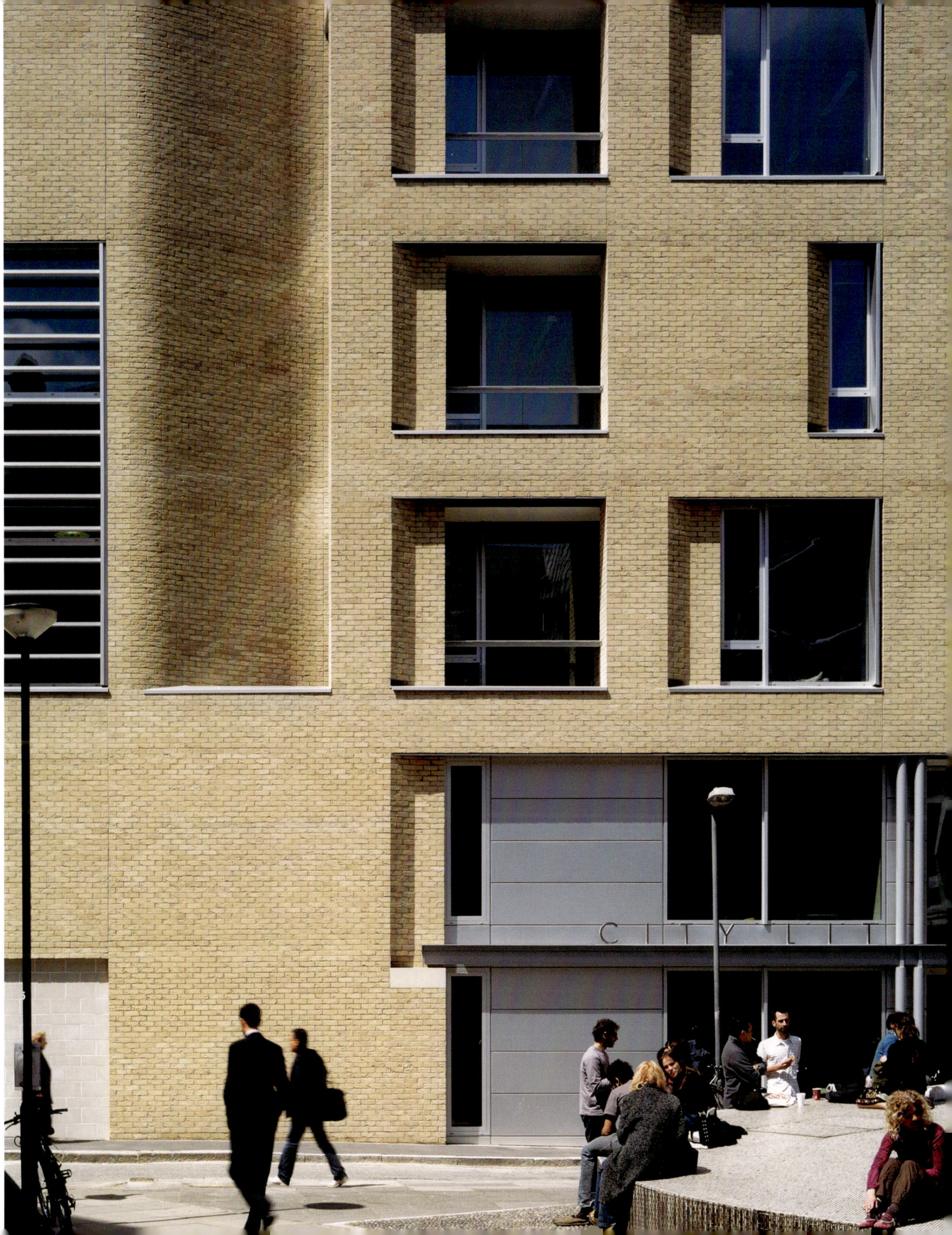
CITY LIT

◄ Ground floor entrance and cafe
▶ Painting and drama studios

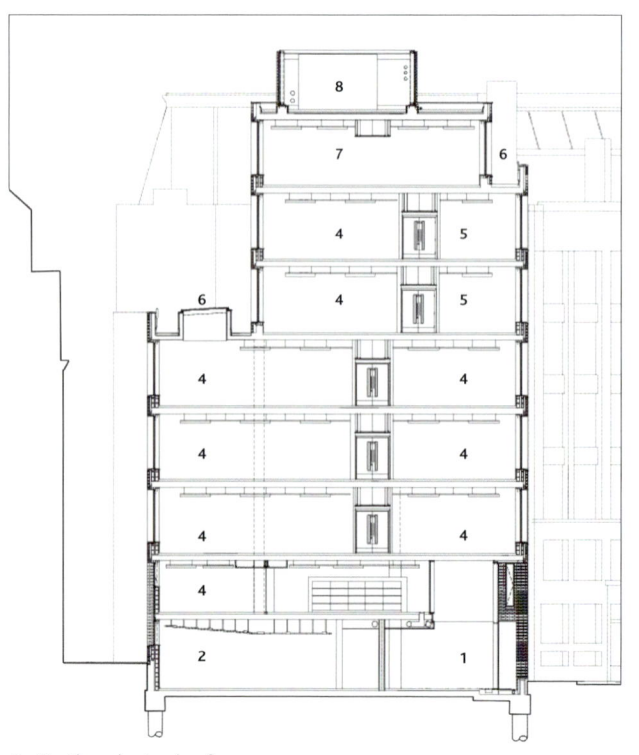

Section through art and performance spaces

Ground floor plan

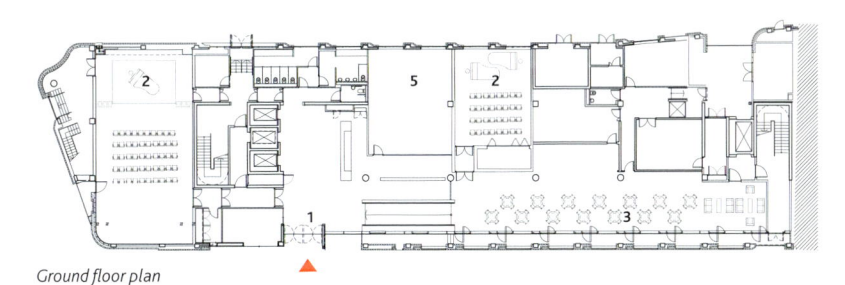

1 entrance
2 auditorium
3 cafe
4 class room
5 office
6 terrace
7 student lounge
8 sculpture terrace

round columns and a canopy. The introduction of a mezzanine floor, largely set back from the elevation, has enabled the representation of this scale in a tall brick colonnade, behind which sits a more lightweight screen. Double-height timber doors open to extend the width of the internal street.

On the upper floors the brickwork is conceived as a continuous plane that wraps around the building, with cuts and folds that reveal a depth to the facade and form the window openings. Aluminium plates emphasise these reveals, producing a different appearance when viewed obliquely from Wild Street to the west or Kingsway to the east.

At its western end, the building reduces in height in response to the scale of the adjacent residential buildings, assuming a more sinuous form as it turns the corner. Within this corner component are the large double-height spaces of the performance theatre and dance studios, health and fitness rooms and a television and radio studio.

75

CHELSEA COLLEGE OF ART AND DESIGN
Pimlico, London
2001–05

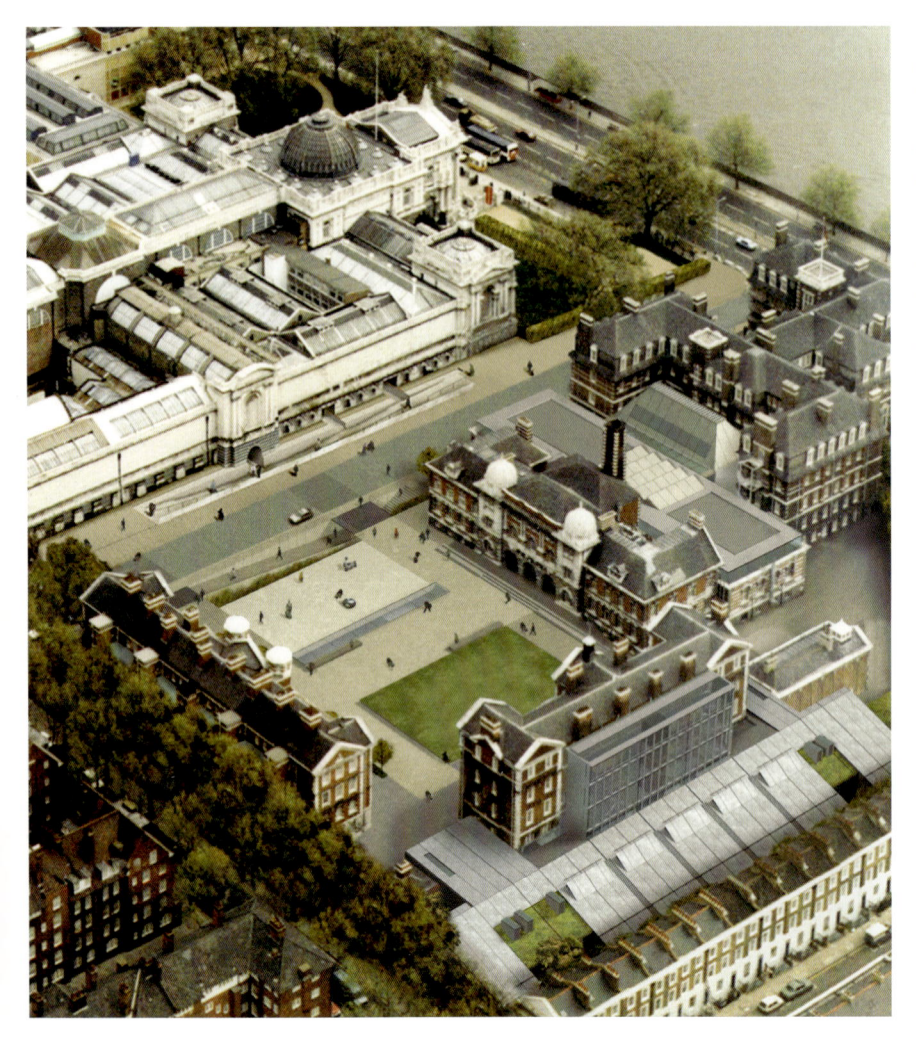

This project brings together the previously dispersed schools of Chelsea College of Art & Design onto a single site in the former home of the Royal Army Medical College at Millbank. The existing Edwardian buildings, clustered around a generous but hidden parade ground, offered great potential for a twenty-first-century art college. However, a century of pragmatic adaptations and uncertain maintenance had stripped them of their original gravitas.

The arrival of Chelsea College of Art allowed the removal of nearly all of the ad-hoc and inferior additions from within and behind the principal buildings, leaving large, adaptable rooms facing the parade ground and a series of cleared sites to the rear. This facilitated the construction of new, purpose-built structures whose highly serviced and specialised spaces, such as workshops and large sculpture and painting studios, could not be easily accommodated within the existing buildings.

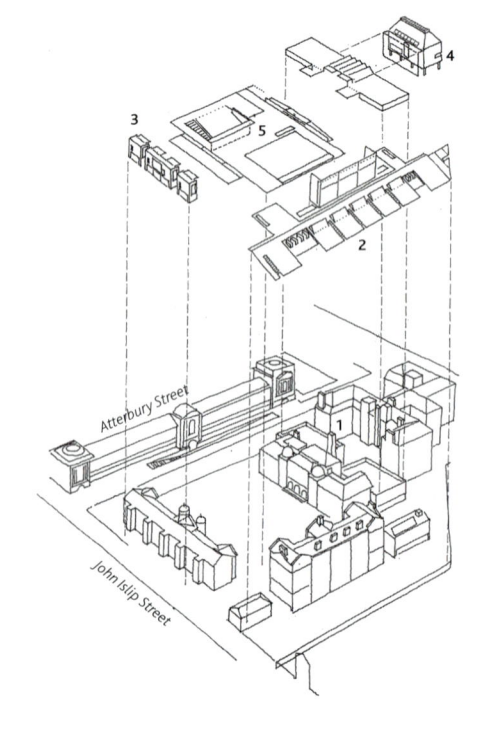

1 *College and Mess Building*
2 *workshops*
3 *seminar rooms*
4 *painting pavilion*
5 *central square*

▲ *Visualisation showing new interventions and Tate Britain beyond*
▶ *New gallery building from John Islip Street*

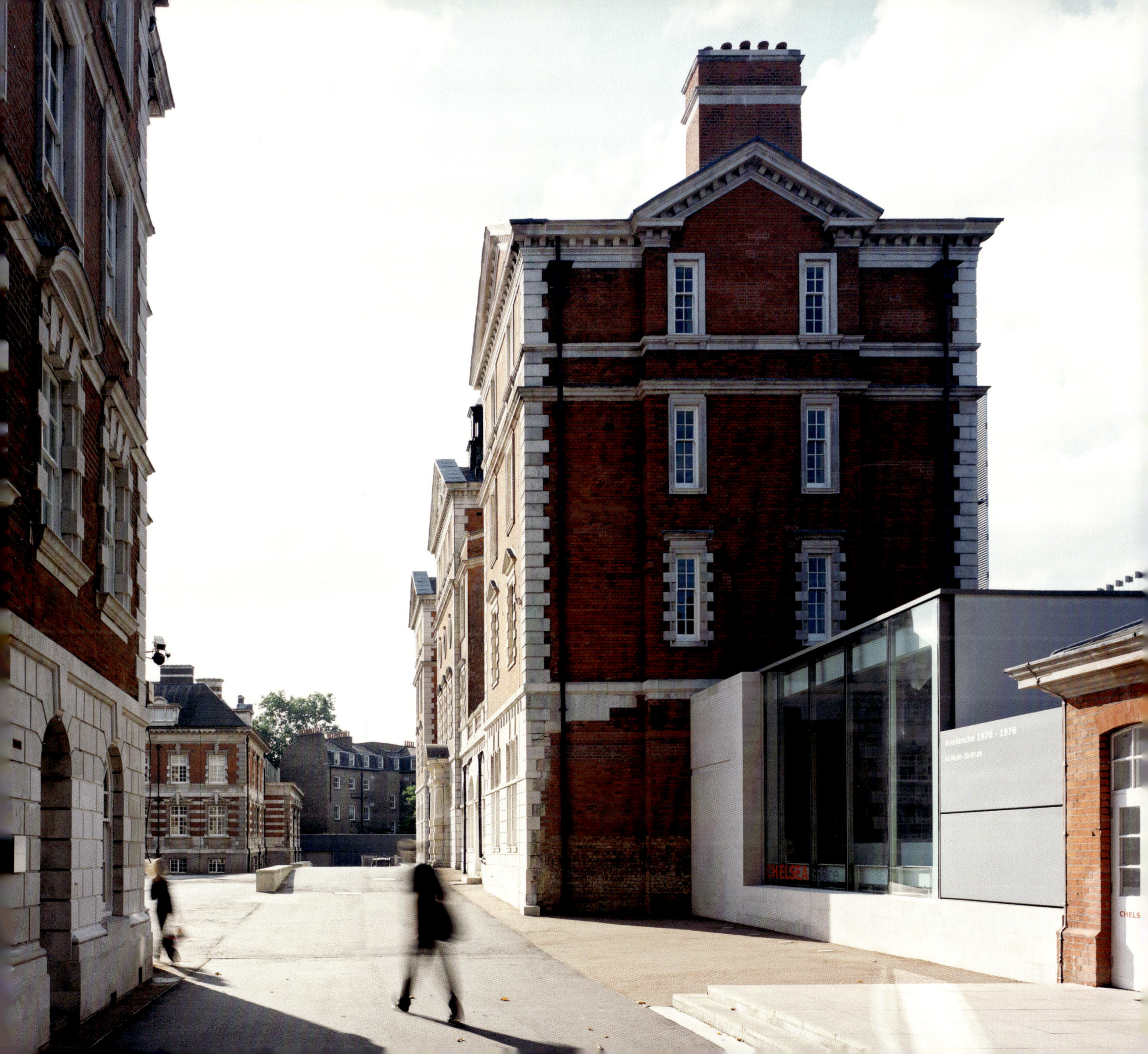
Avalanche 1970 - 1976
CHELSEA space
CHELS

The circulation, including lifts and open accommodation stairs, occupies generous, top-lit space between the new and existing buildings. Not only does this set up a simple, legible pattern of circulation, but it also provides a series of meeting places and informal exhibition spaces that have become a focus for the life of the college.

Behind the former barracks building a naturally ventilated and unheated three-storey space creates an environmental buffer zone which provides access to the original spaces, stripped now of awkward corridors and escape staircases. An external screen of aluminium rods filters natural light and controls views to and from the neighbouring residential backs. Behind this, a suite of large, open-plan workshops stands one metre back from the site boundary, exposing the perimeter wall of the nineteenth-century Millbank Prison and allowing daylight to reach the workshops.

Likewise, a new pavilion building, its translucent walls screening daylit painting studios, occupies a previously underused courtyard behind the former main Medical College building. An extension to the third parade ground building, the former married quarters, provides a series of seminar spaces, replacing unsightly lavatories with a more generous frontage to John Islip Street.

◀ *New workshop building behind the old barracks*
▶ *Exhibition, sculpture and painting studios and circulation space*

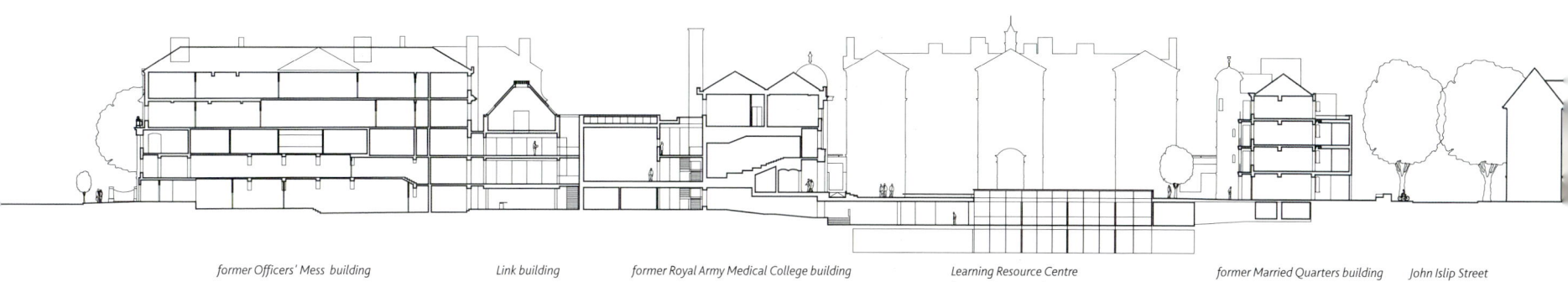

former Officers' Mess building   *Link building*   *former Royal Army Medical College building*   *Learning Resource Centre (not implemented)*   *former Married Quarters building*   *John Islip Street*

79

The new interventions reconfigure the organisational arrangement of the former medical college but reinforce its formal relationship with the parade ground, now a sculpture court at the heart of a new arts quarter. The removal of a high security fence that separated the old parade ground from Atterbury Street establishes a direct relationship with Tate Britain opposite, which effectively acts as a fourth side to this new public square.

At the same time, the new buildings evoke a memory of the large octagonal footprint of Millbank Prison, whose former wall defines the western boundary of the college.

Built at a time when a number of other arts institutions were abandoning their valuable urban sites, this project deliberately set out to explore the relationship between the art school and the city, prioritising a robust adaptability that was provoked by the existing context over generic, idealised buildings. It has been rewarding to see that, in the years since its completion, this architectural approach has found a resonance in the work of some of the students.

◀ *Triple-height circulation space*
▶ *Existing fabric and new intervention*

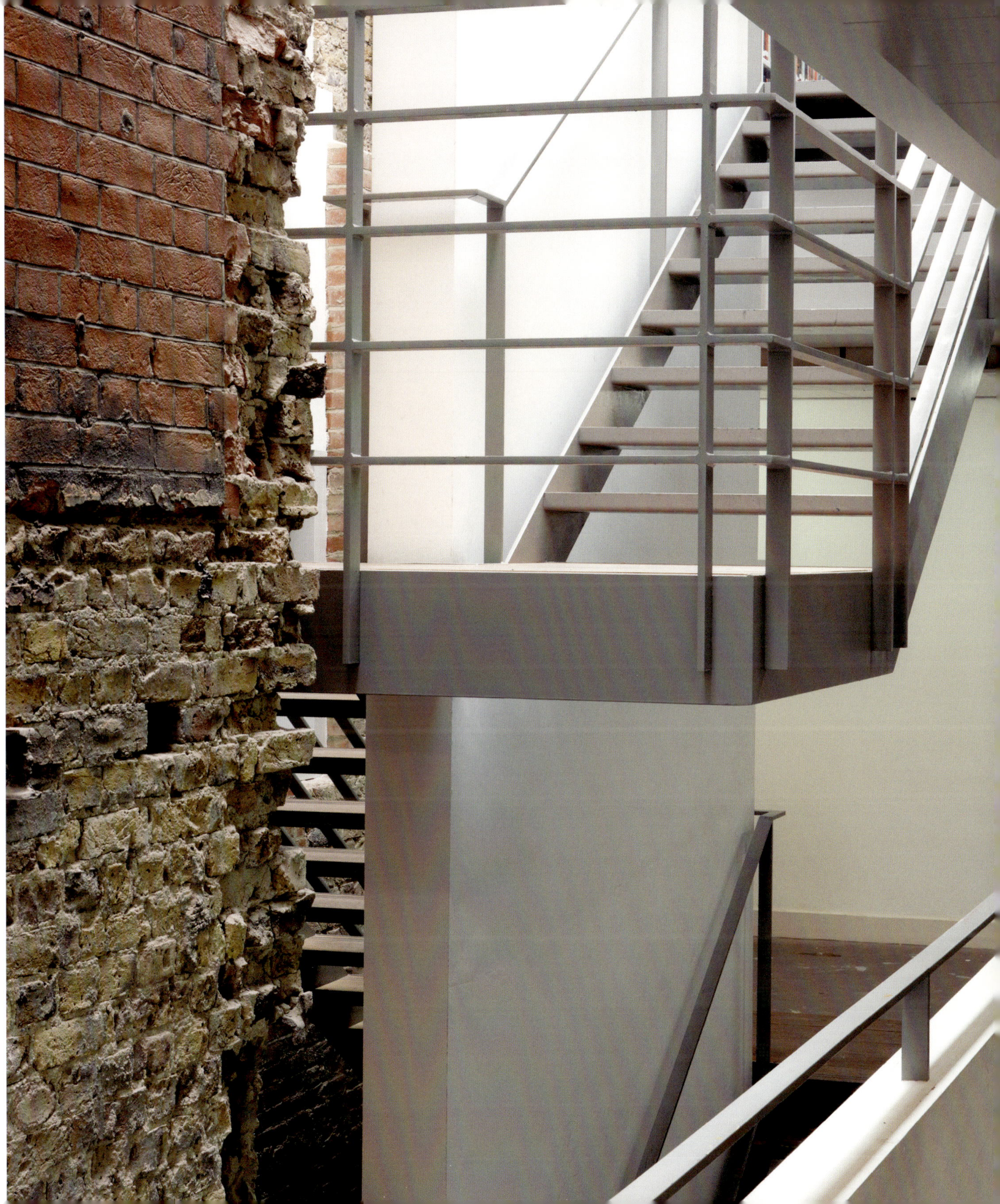

**LIBRARY AND ARCHIVE
GIRTON COLLEGE**
University of Cambridge
1998–2005

The original buildings of Girton College were built in six phases between 1872 and 1932, and designed by three generations of the Waterhouse family of architects – Alfred, Paul and Michael – the latter in collaboration with Giles Gilbert Scott. The nature of the successive phases was determined by the college's requirements at the time rather than conforming to a guiding masterplan. Over the course of this development the character of the college evolved from an initial, almost domestic appearance to a more collegiate structure of residential buildings arranged around a sequence of linked courts.

The principal public rooms within the college, including the main McMorran

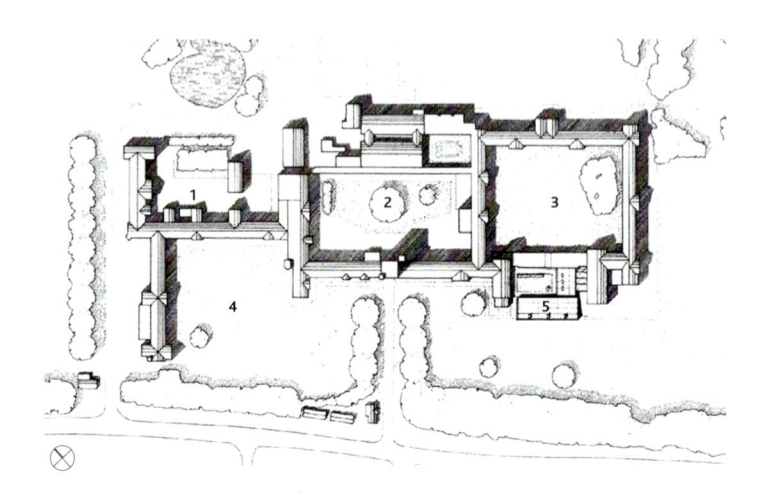

1 *Ash Court*
2 *Cloister Court*
3 *Woodlands Court*
4 *Emily Davies Court*
5 *new library and archive*

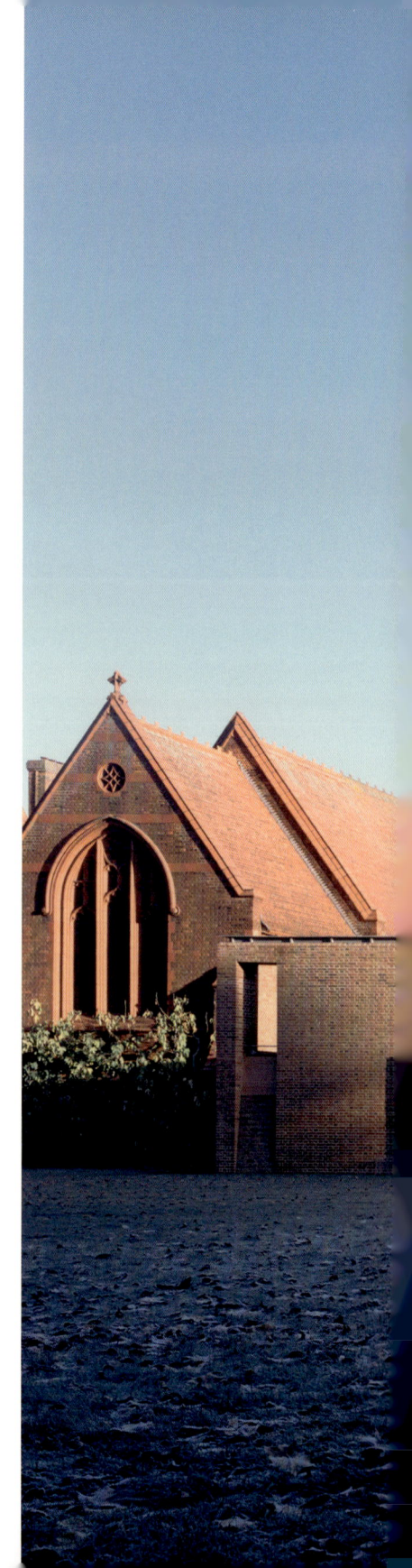

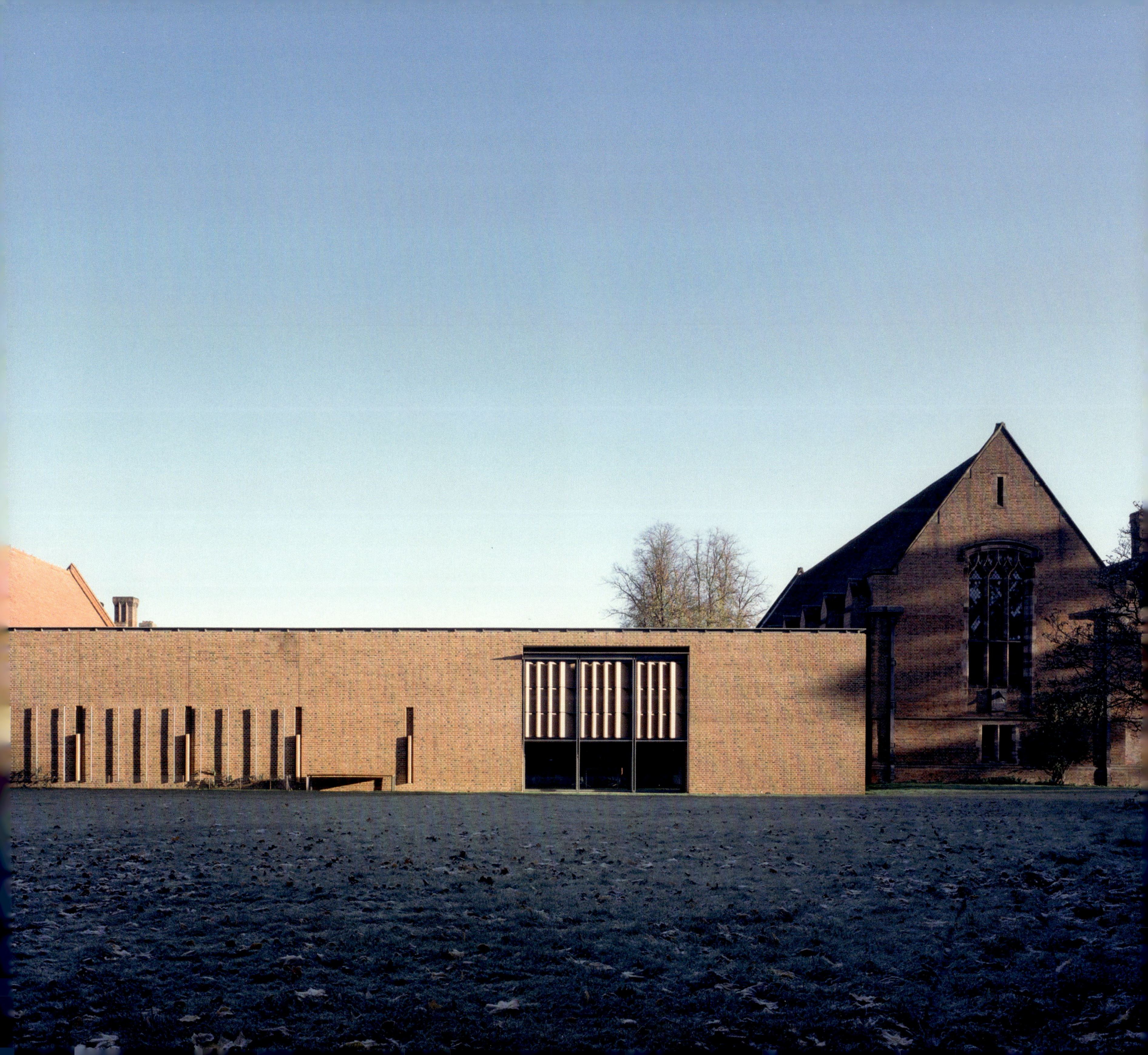

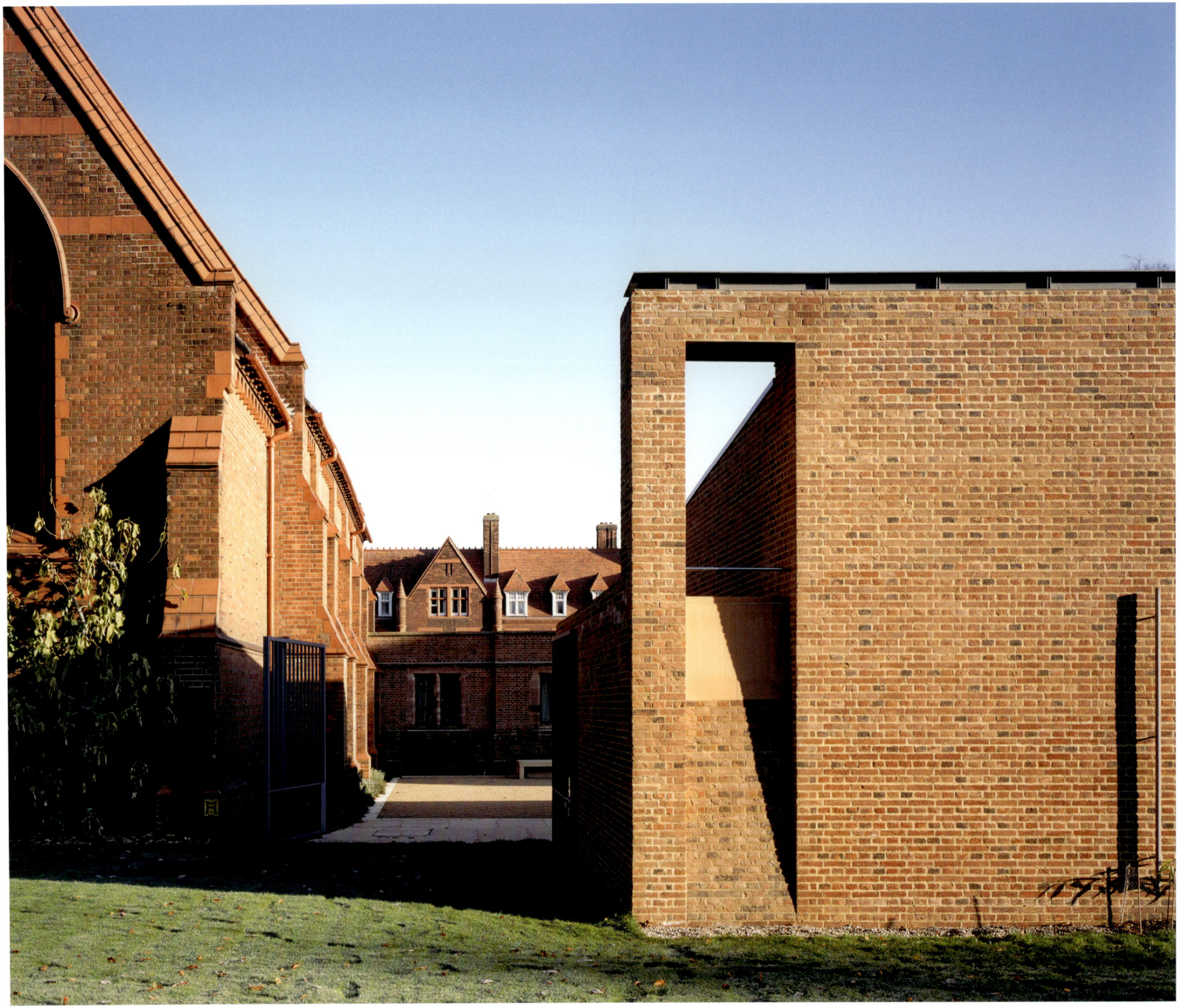

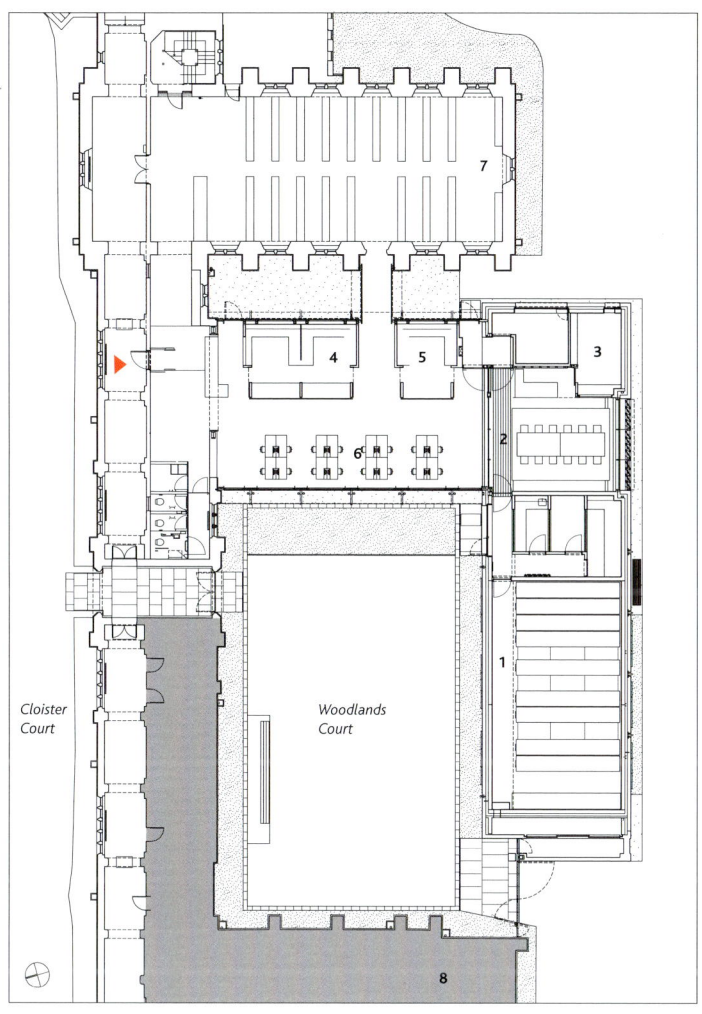

Ground floor plan

1 archive and special collections store
2 reading room
3 archivist's office
4 library office
5 librarian's office
6 IT suite
7 existing lower library
8 existing chapel

◀ Entrance from garden into courtyard
▶ Courtyard at dusk
▶ Library with reading room beyond

Library, tended to project out into the landscape, away from the rectangular enclosures of the courts. This approach was also adopted with the new library building, which sits between the existing library and chapel.

The project comprises three distinct parts. The first, a highly-insulated single-storey brick enclosure with a lead-faced monopitch roof, houses the college archive and rare books collection together with a reading room, archivist's office and conservation laboratory. The second, a steel-framed glazed structure with a sedum-covered flat roof, contains the library offices and IT support areas and links the new archive to the existing library and to the main circulation within the college. The third element is a new courtyard formed between the new buildings and the original library and chapel.

A relocated entrance brings visitors to the issue desk within the new building and sets up a direct view into

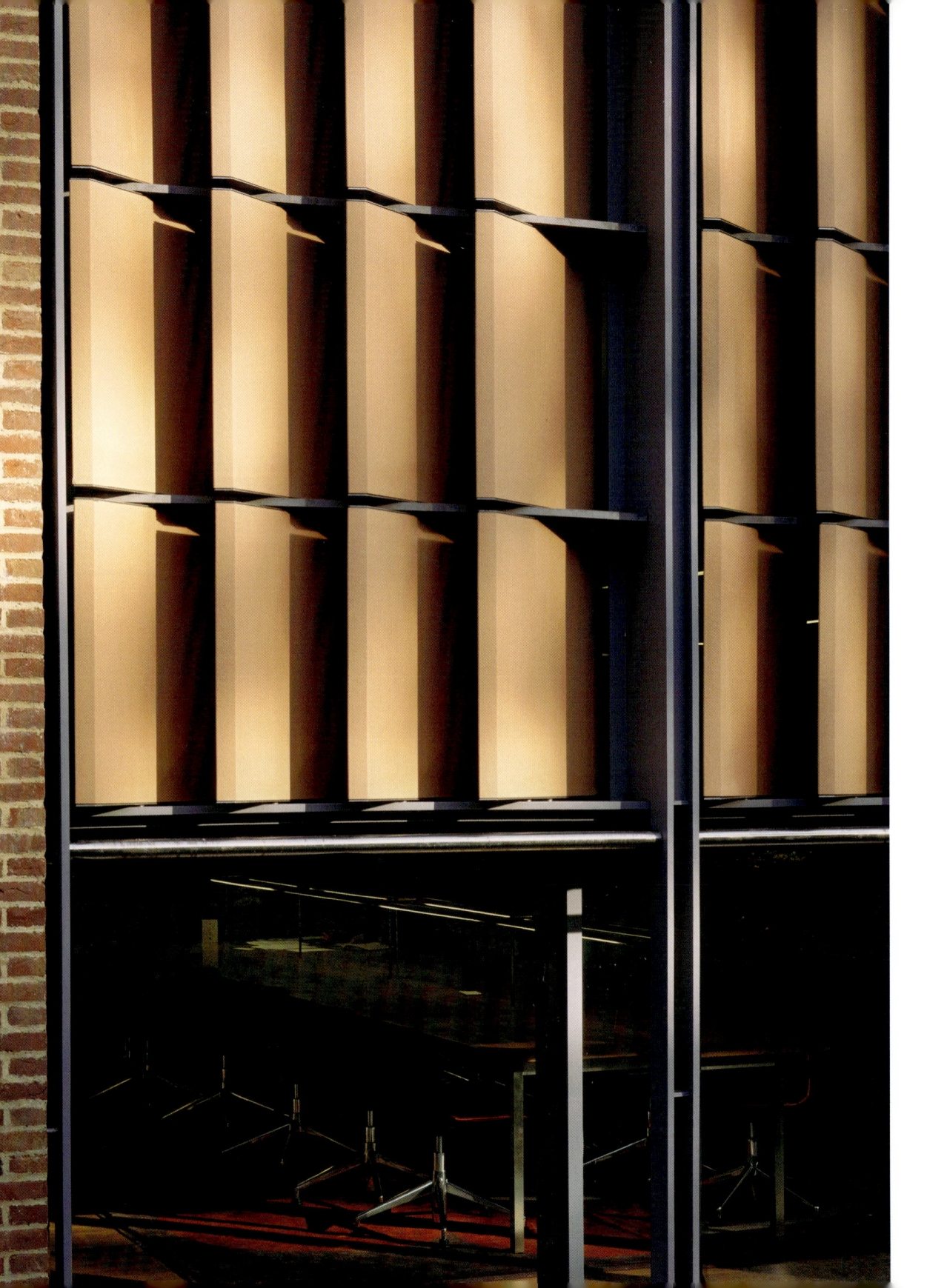

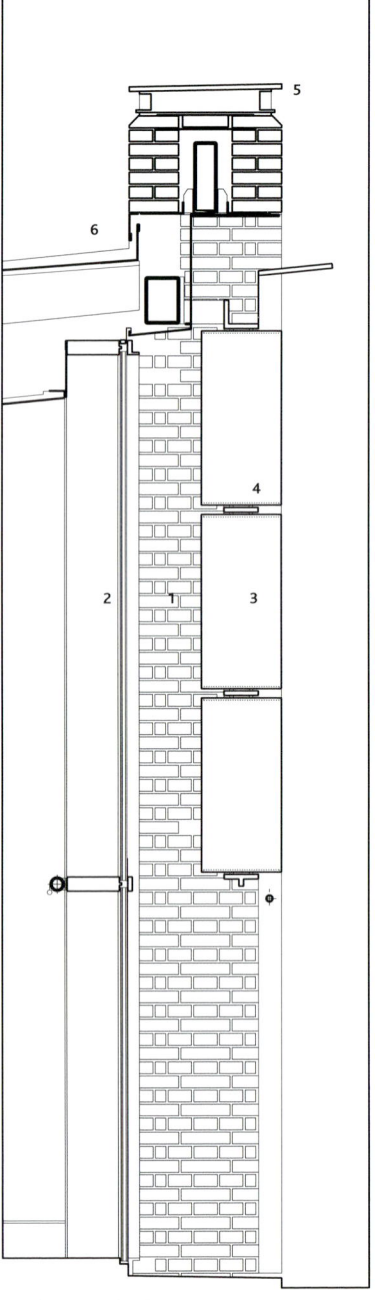

Facade section detail

1 50mm English bond brickwork
2 double-glazed window unit
3 terracotta louvre assembly
4 painted metal frame assembly
5 metal coping
6 lead roof

the reading room and through to the landscape of the gardens beyond. The library offices, which form one edge of the link building, are punctuated in the middle by a new route linking to the lower floor of the existing library where the main book stack is located.

In order to maximise the potential environmental stability of the archive building, openings in the masonry walls are limited. The one large opening that provides light to the reading room is protected from solar gain by a screen of terracotta panels held within a metal frame.

◀ External facade to meeting room
◀ The meeting room looks out to the garden

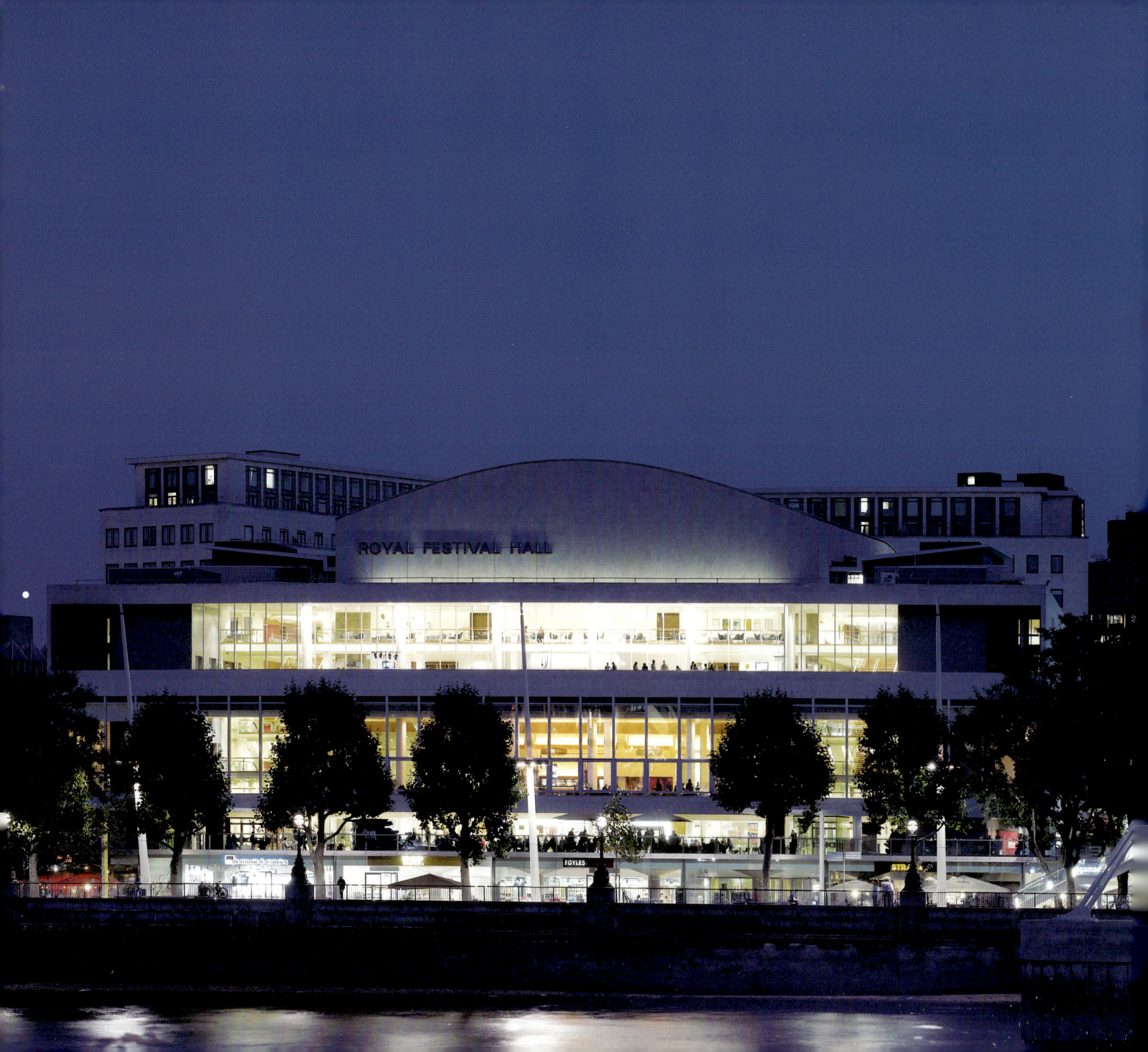
ROYAL FESTIVAL HALL
FOYLES

**ROYAL FESTIVAL HALL
SOUTHBANK CENTRE**

Lambeth, London
1999–2007

By the early 1990s the Royal Festival Hall, the grade-one-listed concert hall designed by Leslie Martin and Peter Moro for the 1951 Festival of Britain, was in need of comprehensive renewal. The clarity of its generous public spaces had been undermined by a problematic 1960s reconfiguration and the gradual incursion of service accommodation into the foyers. In addition, the Festival Hall's relationship with the surrounding context had been compromised by a crude yoke of concrete raised walkways, and the auditorium itself, though much

◀ *Riverside terrace in 2007*
▼ *Royal Festival Hall and Hayward Gallery in 1980*

1 auditorium
2 Liner Building
3 stairs towards the river
4 raised street

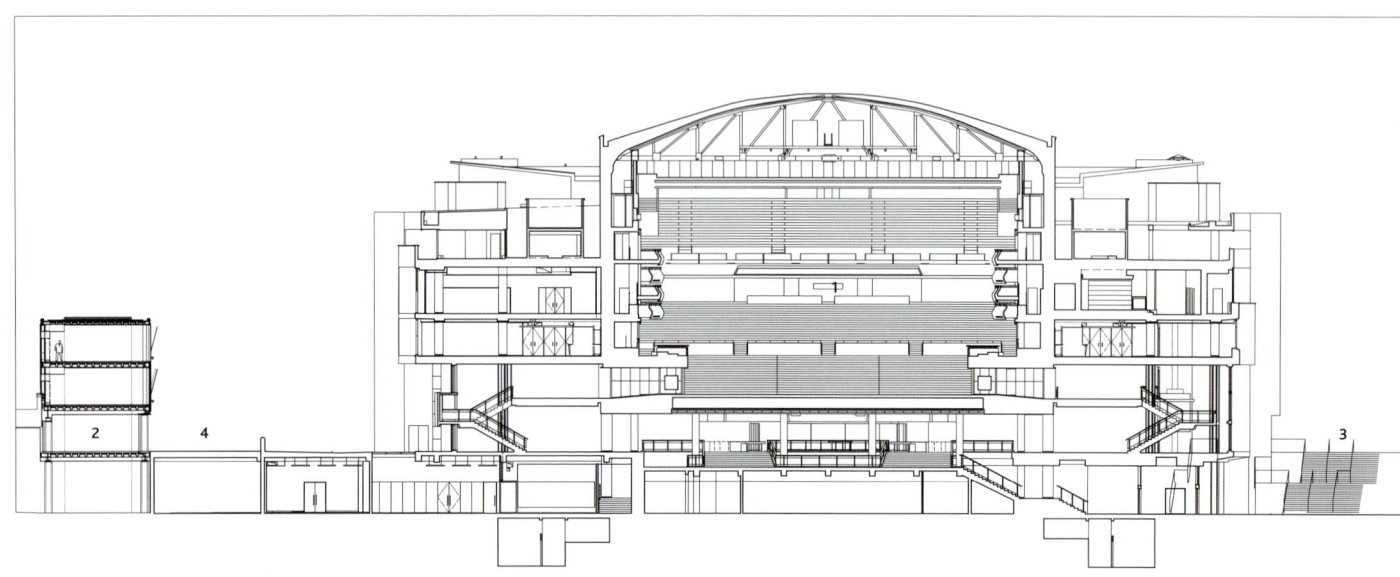

Cross section through the main auditorium

loved, was regarded as acoustically dry and unresponsive. Allies and Morrison's appointment in 1992 as house architects to the Festival Hall culminated in a major programme of restoration between 2005 and 2007.

It was in the repair of the auditorium that a unifying approach to the care and conservation of this exemplary modernist building was most keenly sought. The space had been substantially unchanged since 1951, a testimony to Moro's compositional deftness within Martin's conceptual framework: the 'egg', as it was described, within the 'box' of the foyers. Yet it was becoming dilapidated — a function of operational inadequacies — and its acoustic qualities had never matched its authors' aspirations and, increasingly, modern expectations. It became clear that looking after this modern icon was in essence about the management of change.

The tools for this 'management of change' ranged from the repair and pure restoration of the original fabric to extrapolation from and extension of this fabric to solve some problems not originally anticipated, and finally to quite discrete new additions.

◀ *Auditorium during and after the restoration*
▶ *Detail of restored balconies*

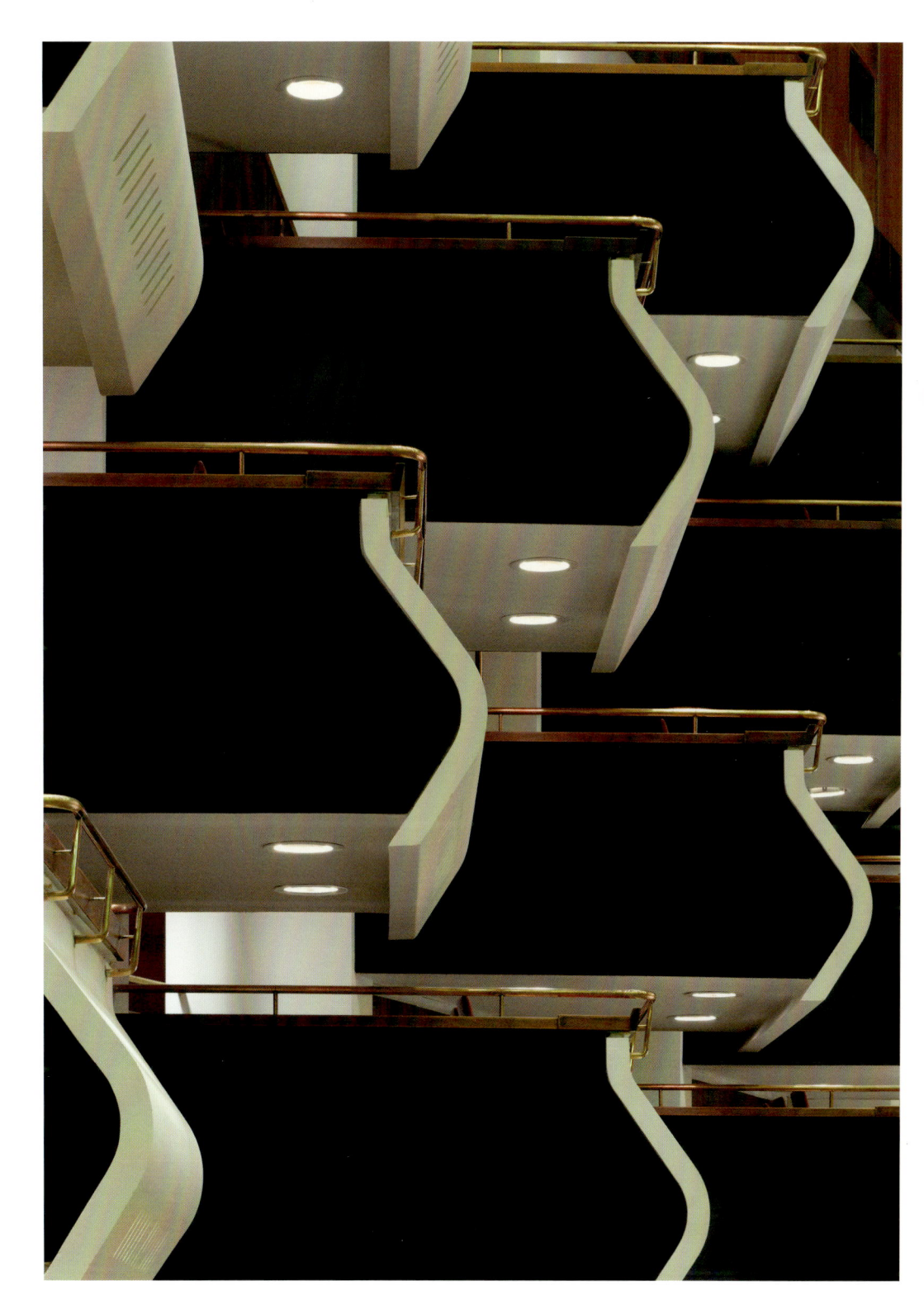

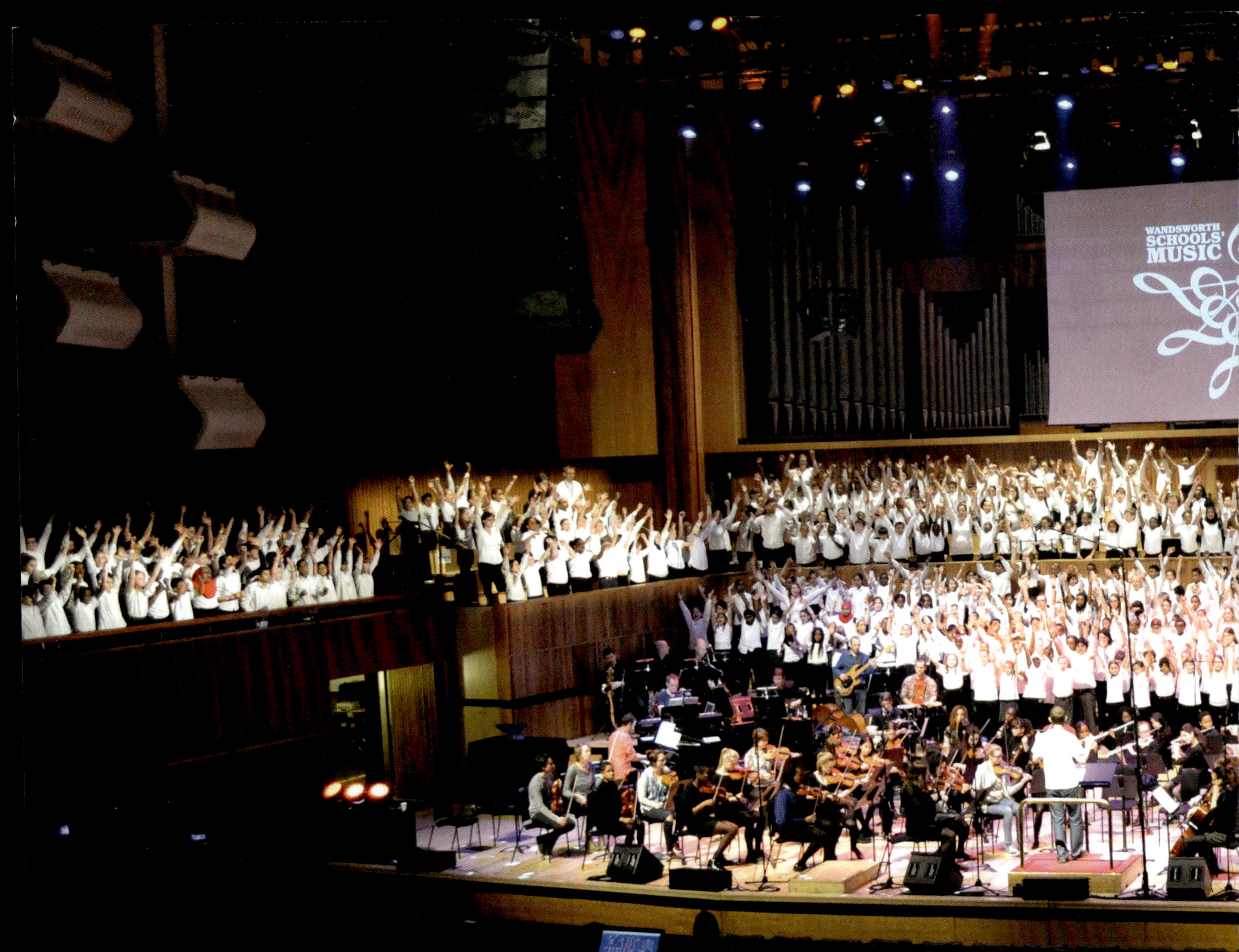
WANDSWORTH
SCHOOLS'
MUSIC

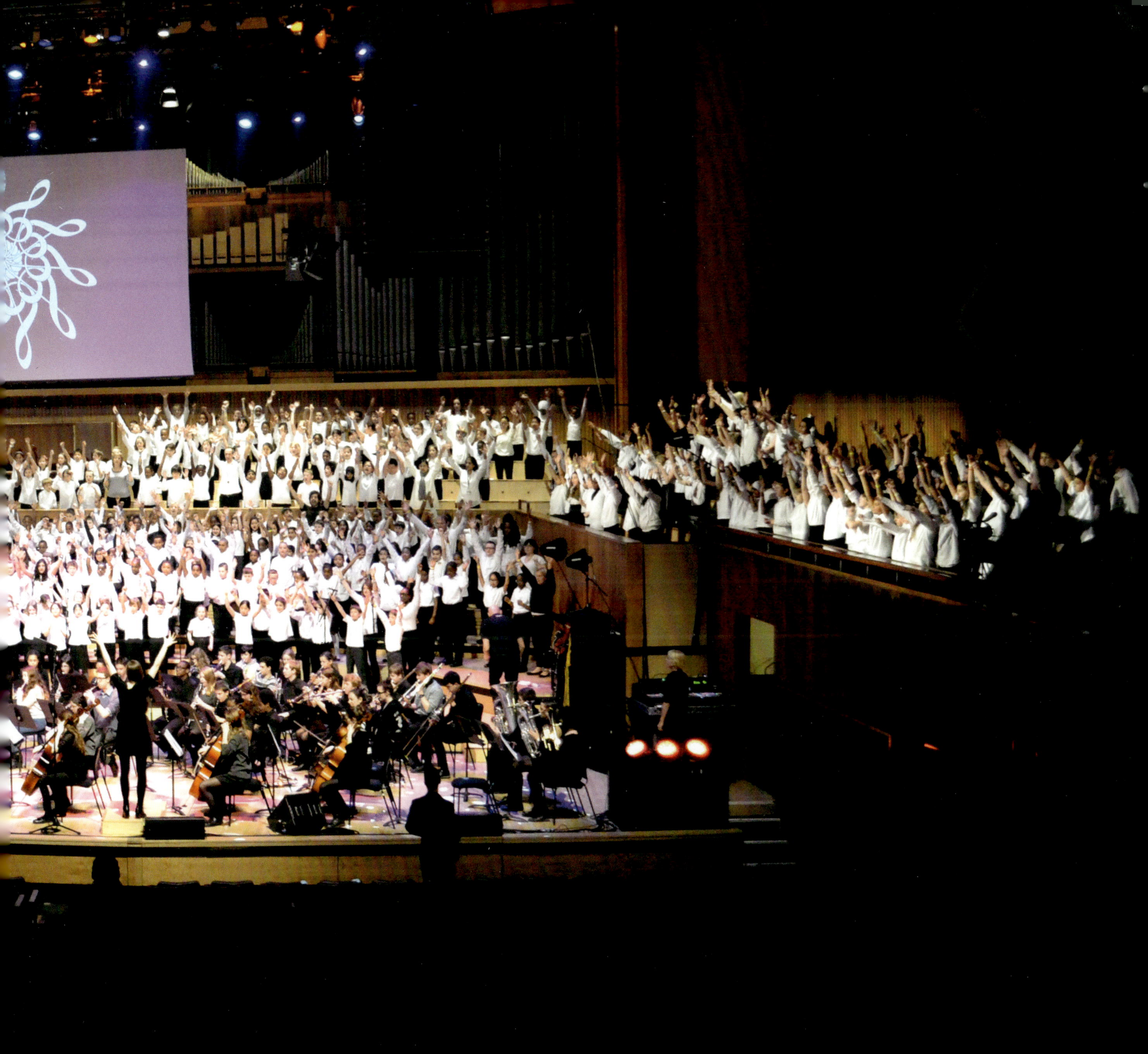

Underpinning each decision was a discipline set out in a conservation plan, which identified not only the physical significance of the parts of the building but also the intellectual significance of their relationship to the whole. So, for example, while the entire rake of the auditorium was rebuilt to allow wider seat spacing and under-floor delivery of heating and cooling, the original concept of a terraced 'hillside' falling down to a Westmorland slate 'lake', was emphasised rather than diminished.

The key challenge with the auditorium was to preserve the unique physical character of the space while transforming its acoustic and environmental performance and the experience of all its users. To accomplish this almost every visible surface was painstakingly removed, upgraded and replaced. This process allowed the significant amendments to be made to the seating rake, the geometry of the stage surround, the adjustable components connected with performance, and the over-stage acoustic reflectors, adding further legibility and adjustability to the warmth and character achieved by the newly reverberant surfaces elsewhere in the hall.

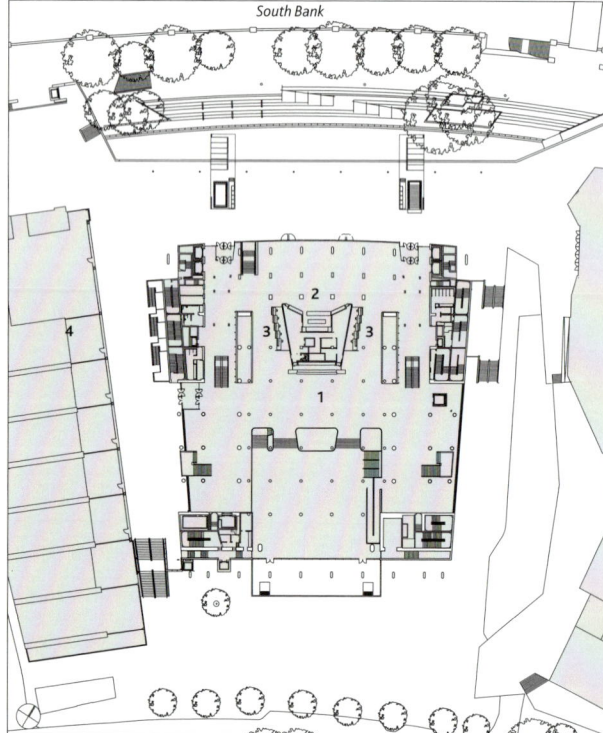

1 foyer
2 tickets
3 cloakroom
4 Liner Building

◀ View from cafe to the Thames terrace
▶ Restored staircase and carpet
▶ The renewed foyer buzzes with activity when in use

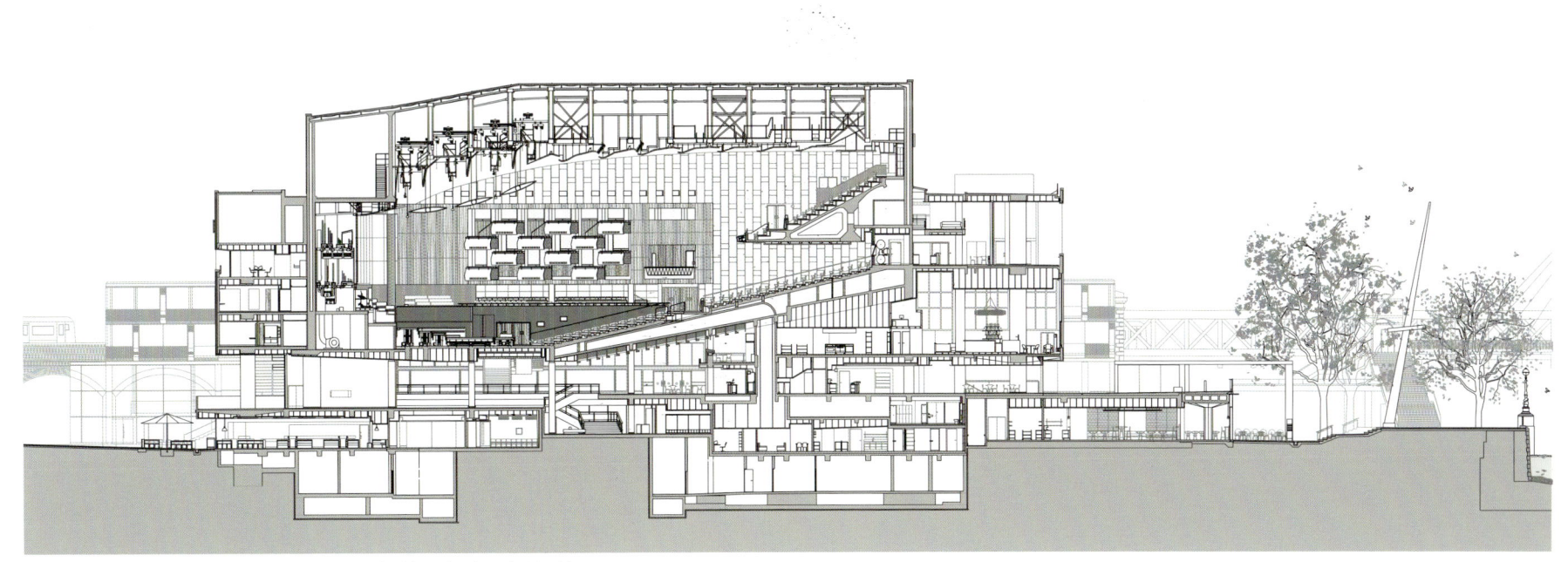

Section through the main auditorium and new terraces and public realm along the River Thames

95

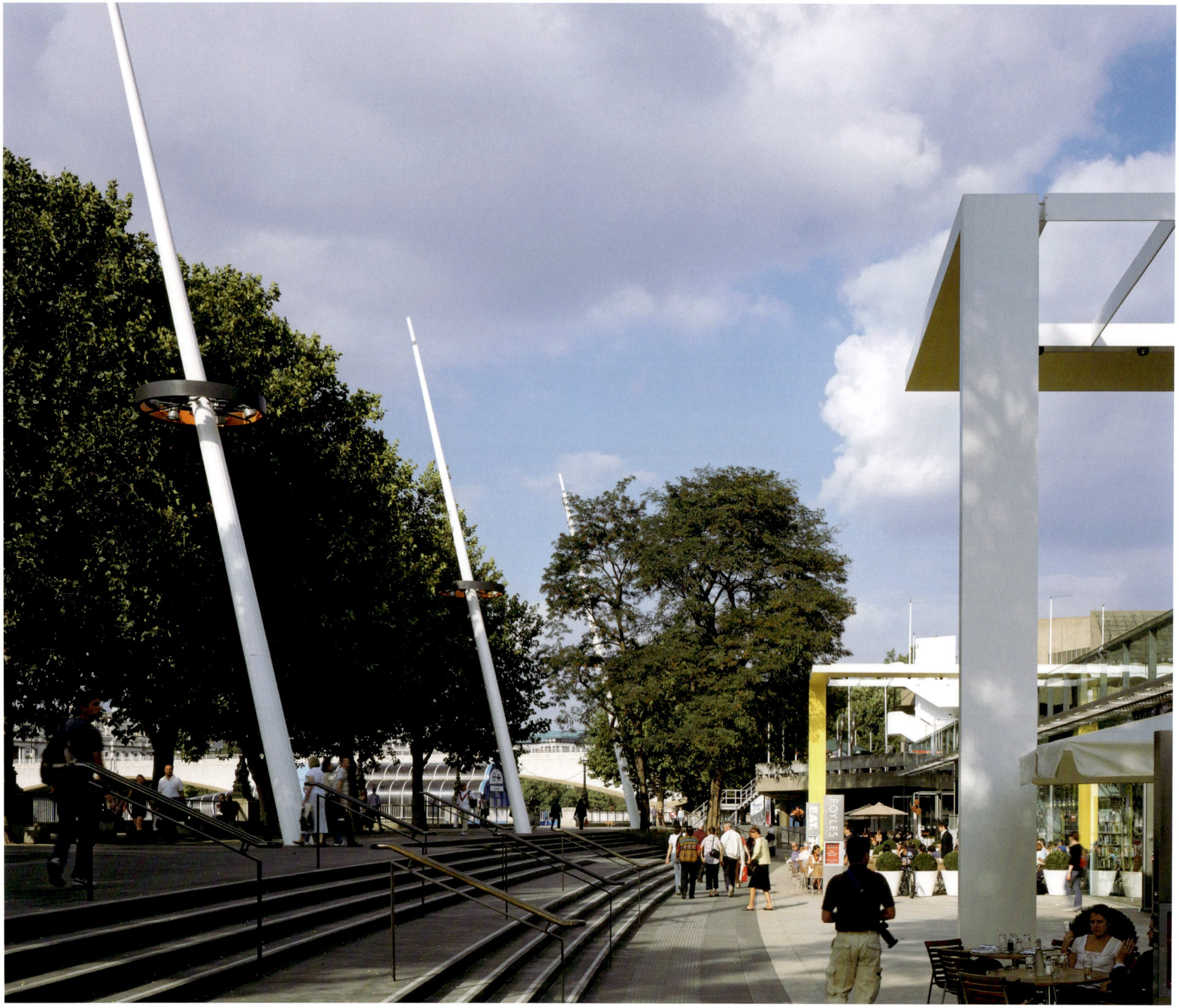
EAT.
FOYLES

In the foyers, the removal of ad-hoc offices reclaimed a significant part of the original space, and also facilitated the reinstatement of the remarkable original pattern of circulation. This reversed the decline begun by the 1960s extension of the building towards the river, worsened by the arrival of some Greater London Council offices from County Hall in 1986 and completed by the yearly attrition of pragmatic adjustments.

The new project re-establishes the significance of the pivotal raised ground floor by restoring Leslie Martin's high-level and low-level entrances, which deliver all visitors to the point within the foyers, below the expressive sweep of the raised auditorium 'egg', from where the circulation routes unfold.

The renewed primacy of this level also resuscitates the building's open relationship with the city, which was one of its most endearing characteristics. The confident optimism that characterised the 1951 Festival of Britain exhibition waned and it was perhaps inevitable that the Festival Hall's extrovert youth was subverted by the earnest social modernism of the 1960s South Bank, exemplified by the Hayward Gallery complex. However, the rejuvenation of the Queen's Walk along the Thames and the establishment of a footbridge link around Hungerford Bridge provided a context that the original building might almost have anticipated.

Two moves allowed the Festival Hall's relationship with this context to be realised. First, the creation of a new home for the Southbank Centre administration, moved from the foyers to what became known as the 'Liner Building' alongside the Hungerford Bridge rail viaduct. And second, the fulfilment of Leslie Martin's original intention – that both the riverside and the Belvedere Road side of the Festival Hall would be characterised by venues rather than entrances. This idea has supported a confident festival-like relationship with the river with a lively environment of restaurants and bars, while the Liner Building has made a new 'street' out of an unprepossessing route past service yards and the raised railway.

The significance of the Royal Festival Hall to London has never been in doubt, but now its auditorium and foyers are once again worthy of its status. Perhaps its future will be defined as much by the renewed relationship with the city it serves as its musical offerings.

◀ *Pedestrianised riverfront with new restaurants and shops*
▶ *Cafes, restaurants and shops enliven the external terrace*

**LINER BUILDING
ROYAL FESTIVAL HALL**
Lambeth, London
1999–2007

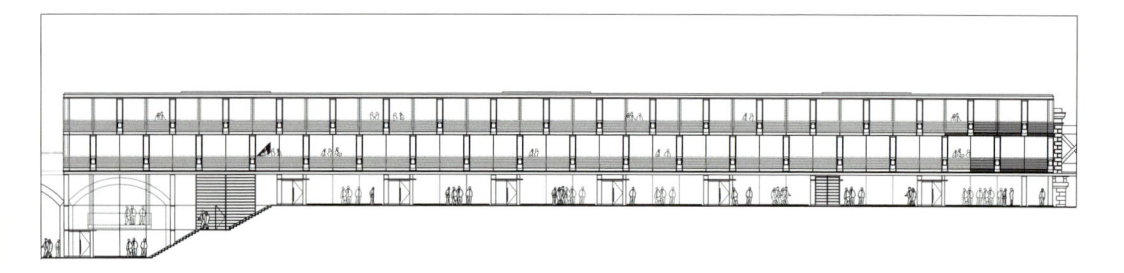

Built primarily to accommodate the Southbank Centre offices that had colonised parts of the Royal Festival Hall, the Liner Building thereby unlocked the strategic problem of refurbishing the concert hall. The unusually long and narrow building, 112 by nine metres, occupies the site of an existing service road sandwiched between the railway viaduct approaching Hungerford Bridge and an external raised foyer-level terrace.

The building is arranged on four levels. The lowest, ground floor provides a new artists' entrance and back-of-house space that links beneath the raised terrace to the Royal Festival Hall. Above, at terrace level, a line of new shops faces the original high-level entrance to the foyers, helping to animate the space. Above, the top two floors accommodate the offices of the Southbank Centre.

While the Liner Building was conceived primarily to solve a practical issue, the addition also delivers several urban benefits. It has established a lively new street on the mid-level step of the busy pedestrian route from Hungerford Bridge to Belvedere Road and Waterloo Station; it shields the public space from the noise of the trains on the Hungerford Viaduct; and, at night, the oblique view of its lighting installation (recalling the playful quality of the 1951-era temporary facade) brings a sparkle to the Festival Hall's foyer entrance.

▲ *The Liner Building and Royal Festival Hall frame a new route to the river front*
▶ *View from the South Bank towards Upper Ground*
▼ *Elevation aligning the route from Belvedere Road to the river walk*

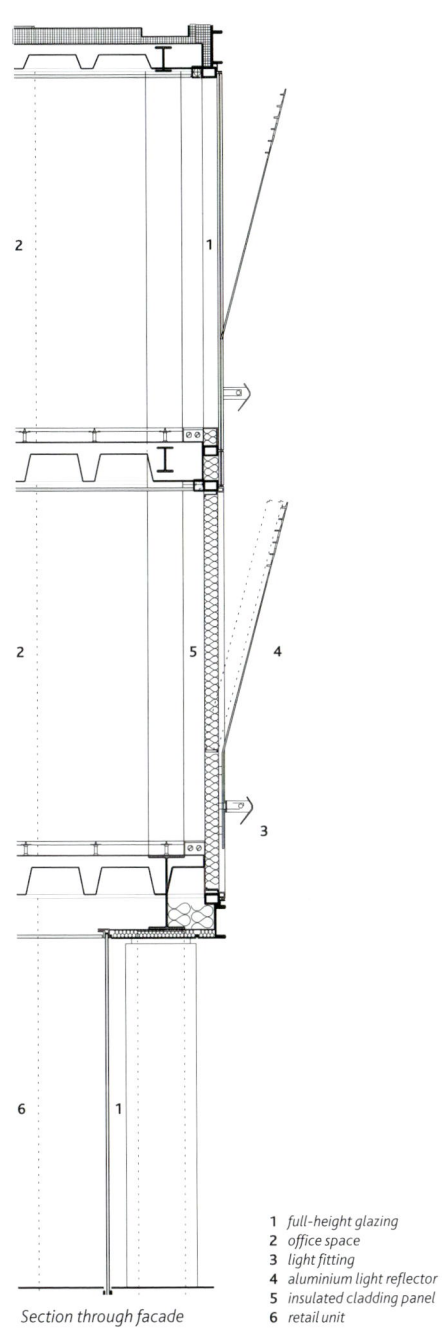

Section through facade

1 full-height glazing
2 office space
3 light fitting
4 aluminium light reflector
5 insulated cladding panel
6 retail unit

**CANTEEN
ROYAL FESTIVAL HALL**

Lambeth, London
2006–07

A second venue for the Canteen, the award-winning restaurant that launched in London's Spitalfields area in 2005, has been integrated within the newly refurbished Royal Festival Hall. The restaurant is on the previously underused south side of the building, facing onto the new Southbank Centre Square, a key addition to the public realm on the busy pedestrian route between Waterloo Station and the Thames that forms a performance space and destination in its own right. The restaurant helps animate the new square with the provision of up to 100 covers beneath an array of large umbrellas.

Inside, the main dining area is aligned by two full-length counters – a kitchen preparation area and servery, and a bar – with seating clustered between them in a regular arrangement of signature 'Canteen booths'. The sculptural ceiling, which references the original elegant plasterwork of the Royal Festival Hall, adds lightness and volume to the deep plan.

The selection of materials and fixtures, also influenced by the 1950s building, helps create an aesthetic in keeping with the client's wish for a 'democratic, welcoming and elegant' restaurant.

▼ *Terrace and entrance on Belvedere Road*
▶ *Interior of the restaurant with booths*

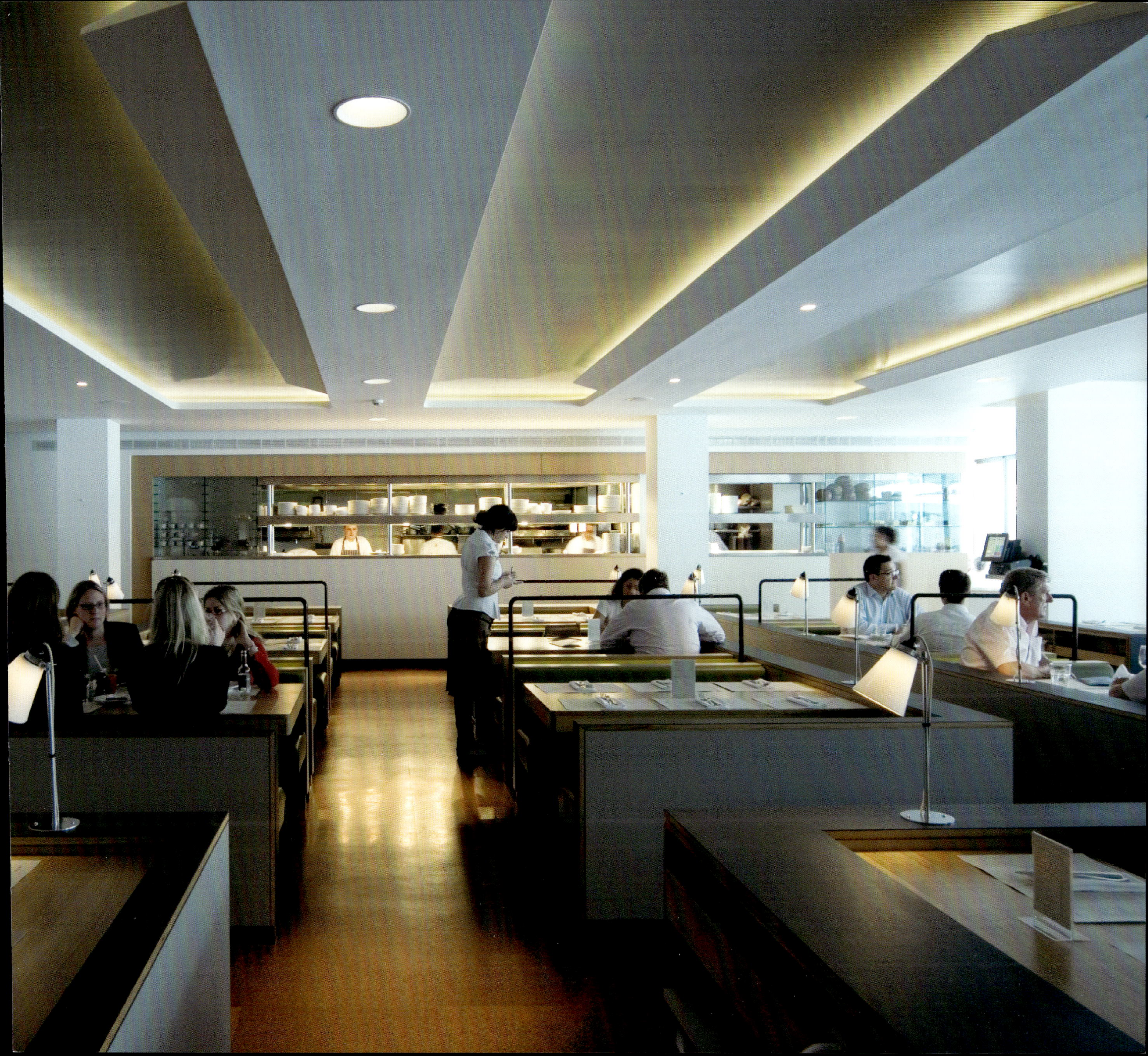

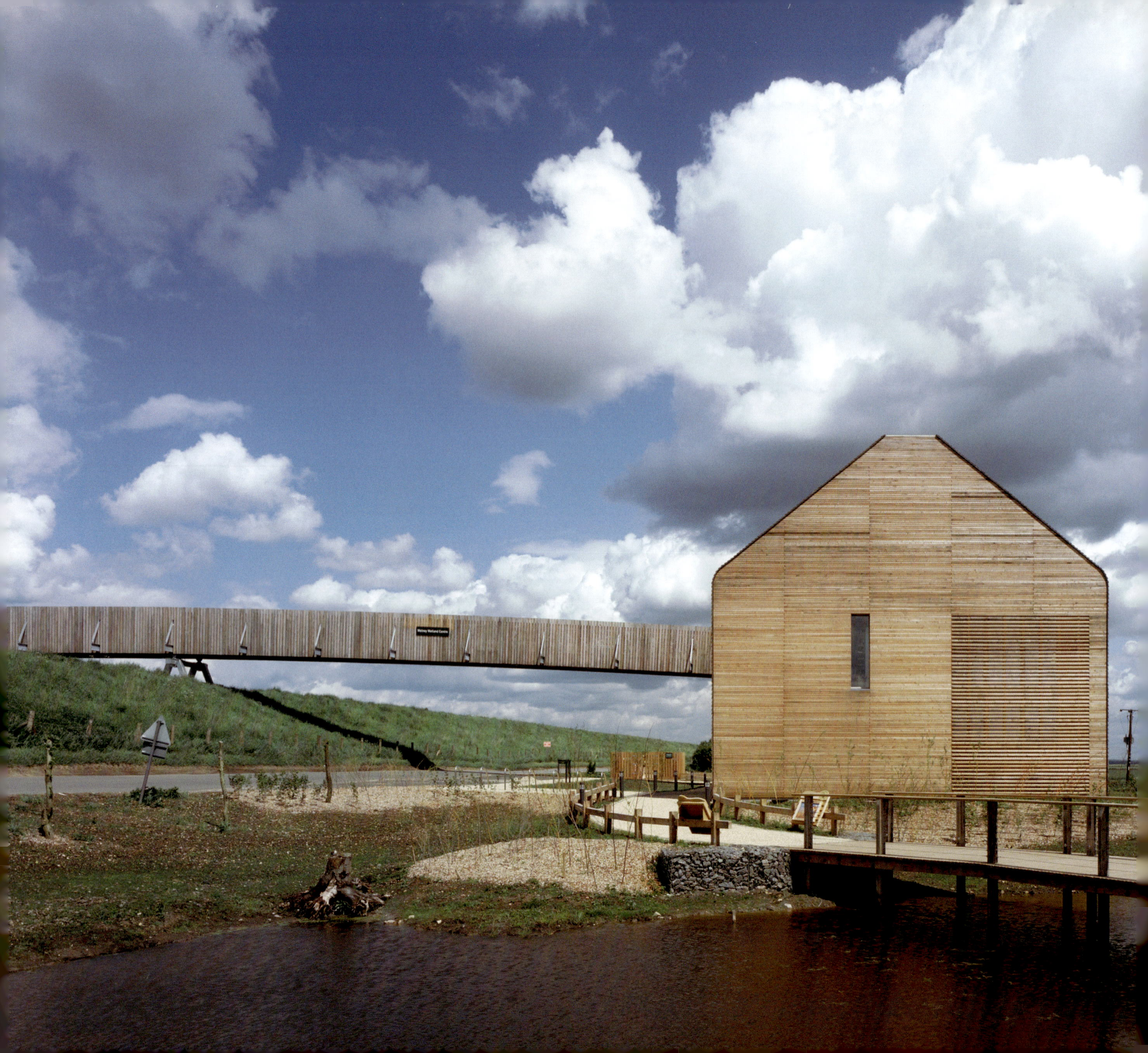

VISITOR CENTRE AND FOOTBRIDGE

Welney
2004–06

The Wildfowl & Wetlands Trust, a charity that helps conserve wetland areas, is responsible for nine Wetland Centres around the UK, including Welney, south of King's Lynn in the Norfolk Fens. The intention with this project was to improve facilities for Welney's growing number of visitors both in terms of amenity and information.

The new building contains an exhibition and education space, a shop, a cafe, meeting rooms and office accommodation. It also

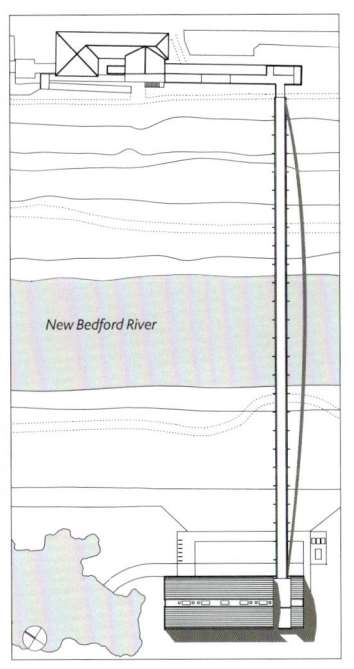

The new bridge spans between the visitor centre and the main hide

◀ *South-west elevation*
▶ *The first-floor cafe overlooks the fenland landscape*

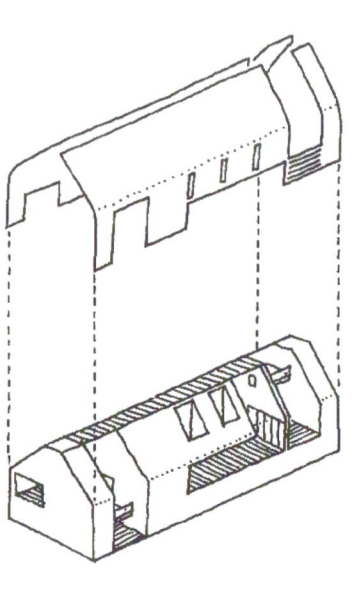

forms part of a route that leads up to and over a new bridge across the Hundred Foot Water, a raised fenland drainage channel, to the birdwatching hides beyond.

While the timber-clad gable clearly signals the centre to arriving visitors, its overall form is intended to harmonise with the wider landscape setting. Recalling East Anglian barn structures and visible across miles of open fenland, its construction and composition represent the apparent contradiction, readily acknowledged by the Wildfowl & Wetlands Trust, of an organisation that seeks to both promote and protect.

The design approach, developed with the client, was to make a self-assured building that would find a natural place in the landscape and which explored ecologically responsible construction methods. Both the structure and cladding are made from certified timber, including timber-skinned panels filled with blown recycled paper insulation. The Siberian larch cladding is sawn rather than planed, so that rainwater runs easily over its swept eaves to ground level, where it is collected in reed beds, filtered and reused. A concrete base and first floor provide a thermally absorbent core on which the timber structure sits, enclosing the roof-lit and top-ventilated principal spaces and providing access to the second-floor footbridge.

The simple, barn-like form of the building is 'eroded' on its south side, to incorporate a series of large windows and terraces that overlook the farmed fenland landscape, but closed on its north side to avoid disturbing the wetlands, which can be viewed only from carefully disguised hides across the water.

IQ BUSINESS PARK
Farnborough
2003–07

The IQ Business Park occupies part of the site of the historic Royal Aircraft Establishment (RAE) facility, adjacent to Farnborough Airport in Hampshire.

Dominating the site is a significant section of the 1910 Airship Hangar frame. This listed structure forms a powerful east-west axis for the masterplan to which the two new office buildings defer with; placed at one end of the hangar's skeleton, they define a new square that introduces a civic dimension to the development. On arrival in the historic quarter, this arrangement frames the view of the restored Gadel listed wind tunnel.

These paired buildings at 200 and 250 Fowler Avenue have simple orthogonal plans providing uninterrupted open-plan office space with central cores, each with a

1 *The Hub*
2 *Fowler Avenue buildings*
3 *car park buildings*
4 *re-erected hangar*
5 *wind tunnel*

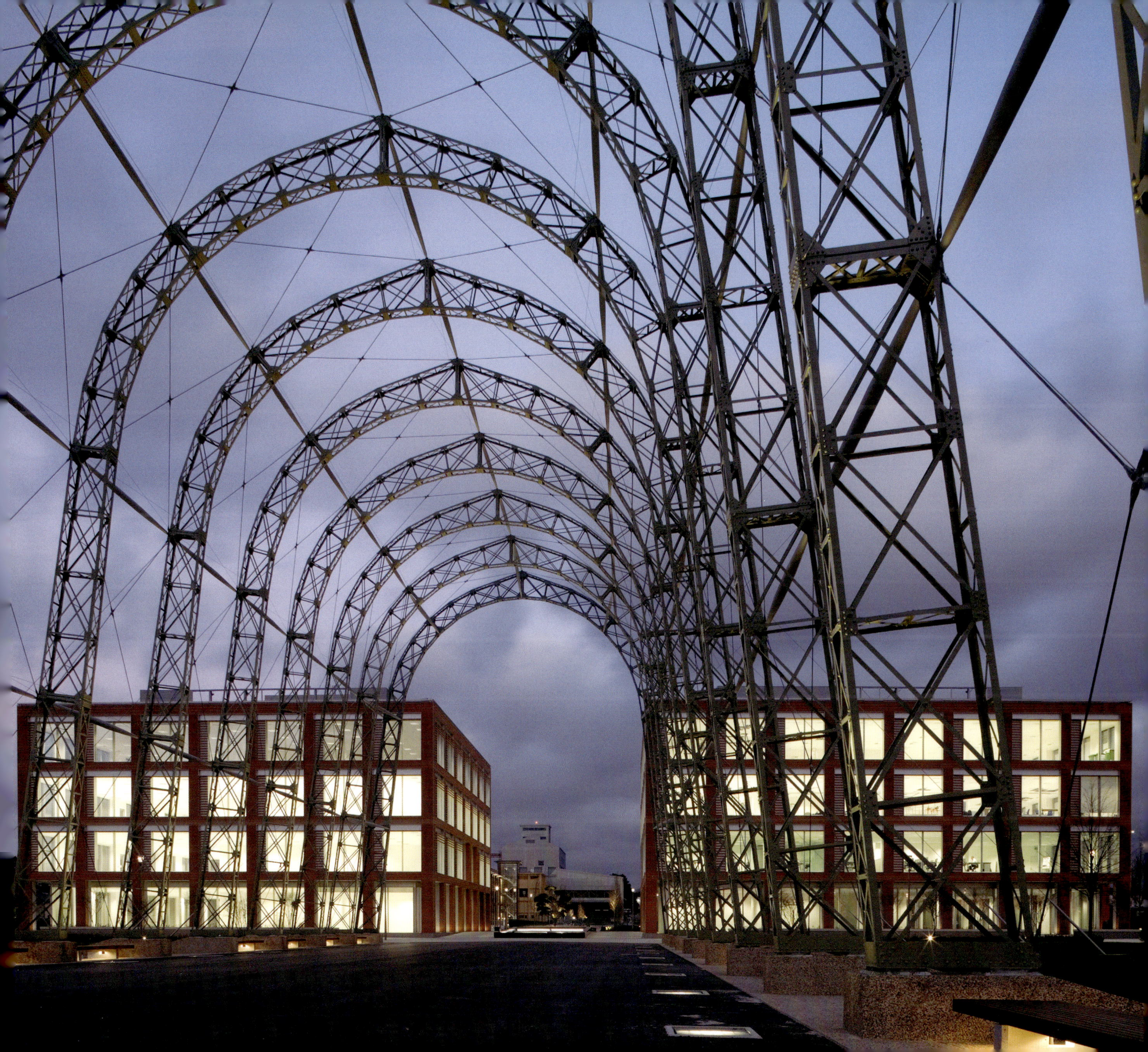

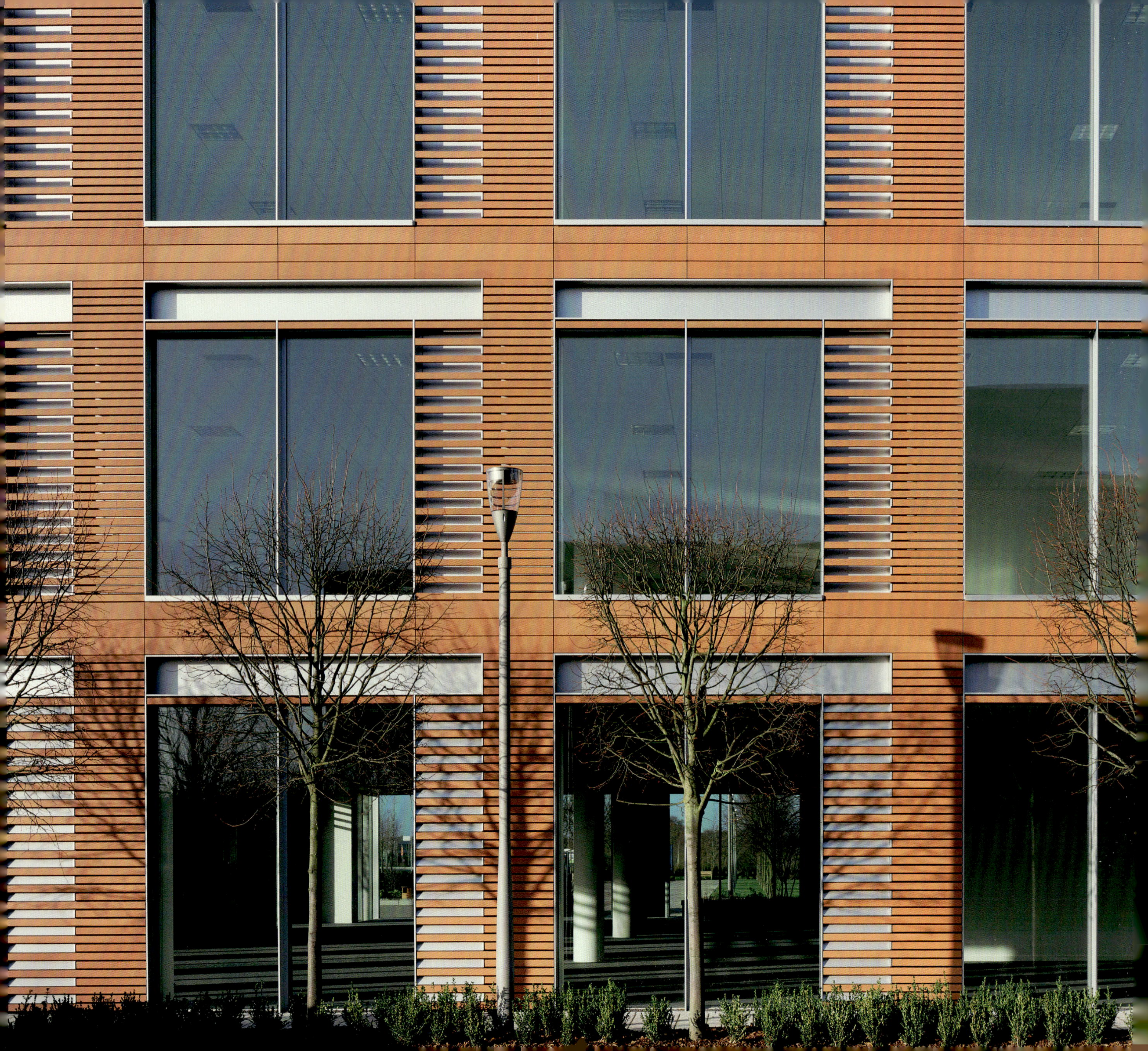

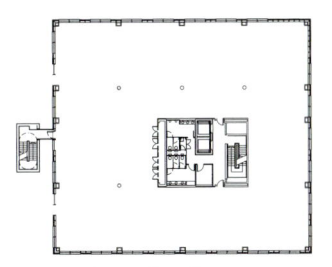

Typical upper floor plan

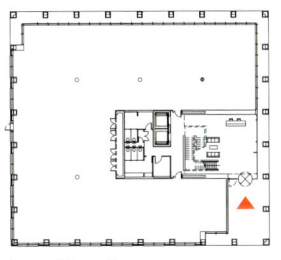

Ground floor plan

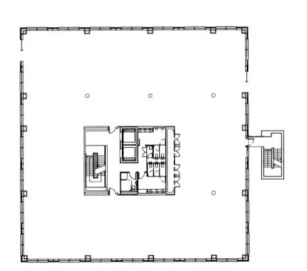

single external fire escape stair. Their entrances, orientated to face one another, open onto double-height spaces with central accommodation stairs. Externally the buildings are clad in terracotta with deep reveals and infill panels of aluminium and glass to provide a solid contrast to the open silhouette of the hangar.

◀ *Facade detail*
▲ *External staircase detail*

▲ *Internal floorplates are column-free*
▶ *Entrance facade of the Hub building*

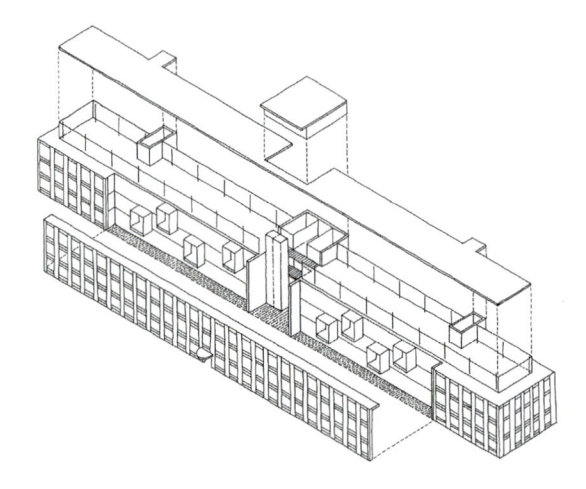

Also surviving from the 1940s is the 125-metre-long, steel-framed, brick-clad and symmetrically planned building, which is now known as The Hub. This flexible structure began as a hospital and later became a weapons research centre. Its column-free structure has been renovated to provide light, flexible open-plan office space capable of subdivision. A later lightweight attic storey has been removed and the central core remodelled to bring light into the centre of the plan, producing a triple-height space with internal horizontal circulation routes radiating outwards. The ground floor is now converted to a heritage centre, café and conference centre. These semi-public functions are accessed from a new internal street along the building's southern facade, seperate from the pedestrian plan of the overall site.

To ensure the clarity of this plan, two multi-storey car parks with simple reinforced concrete-framed structures are set out as a series of staggered decks to accommodate an efficient one-way circulation pattern. Semi-mature hornbeam trees and evergreen hedges soften the paved areas and integrate the car parks within the landscape that defines the masterplan.

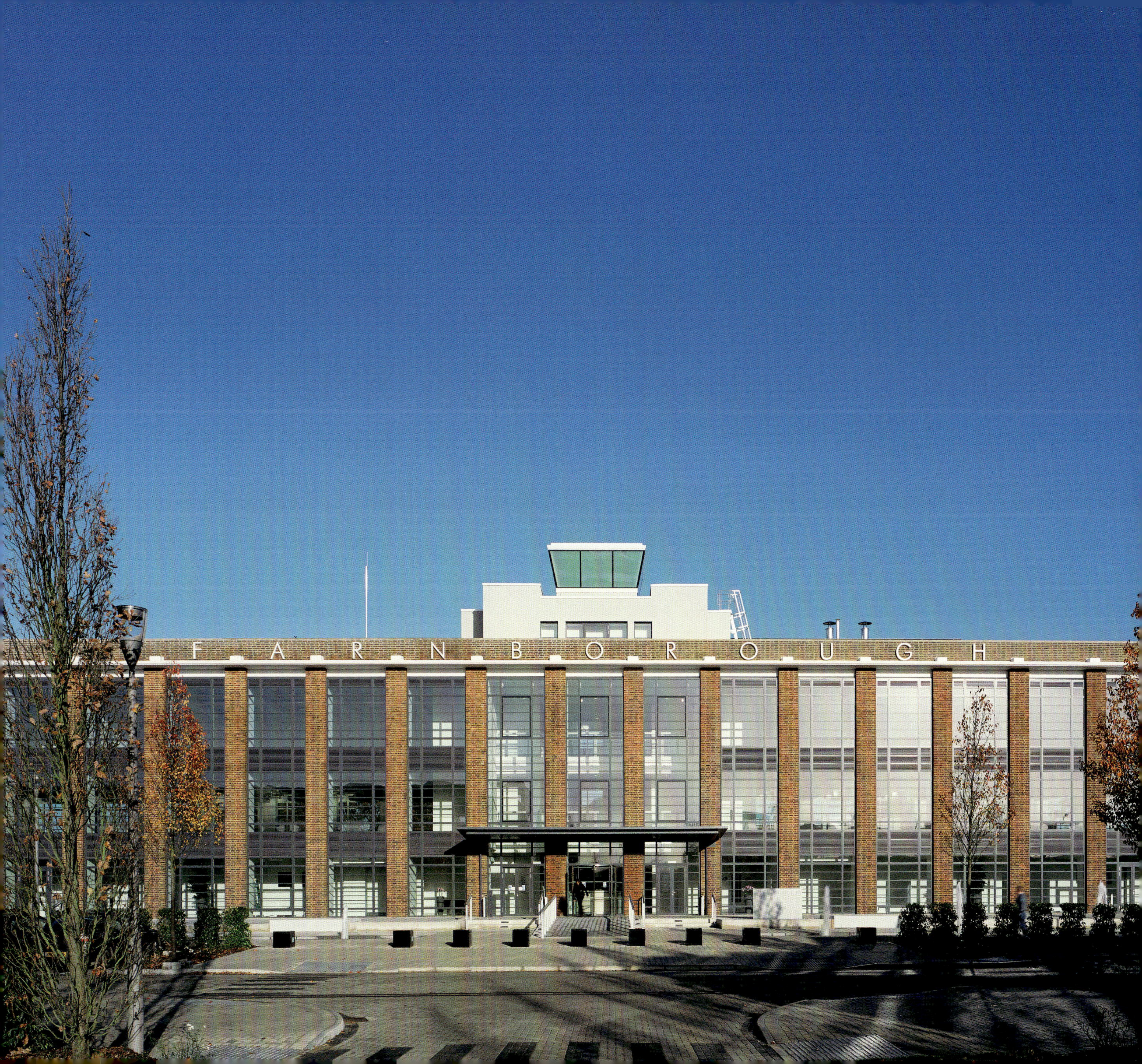
F A R N B O R O U G H

PLANETARIUM
ROYAL OBSERVATORY
NATIONAL MARITIME MUSEUM
Greenwich, London
2004–07

Separated by a narrow pathway from the main Royal Observatory buildings and the much-visited Prime Meridian – the historic line of zero longitude that divides the world's east and west hemispheres – the South Building, completed in 1899 by William Crisp, had never felt an integral part of the museum complex.

However, the plan to construct a new planetarium provided an opportunity to transform the South Building into a centre for Modern Astronomy as well as to unify the whole observatory site.

Situated at the heart of Greenwich Park and within the UNESCO World Heritage Site of Maritime Greenwich, the project was defined by the sensitive relationship between landscape and building. Rather than perpetuating recent moves towards a 'garden' character for the southern site, the new landscape comprises a gently inclined paved square that provides step-free access to the main entrance to the South Building. This tilted plane also forms the roof of the extensive underground service accommodation and foyer space associated with a new 80-seat planetarium.

Consequently the only part of the planetarium above ground level is the enclosure to the projection dome, a sculptural metal object

1 *new planetarium cone*
2 *William Crisp's South Building*
3 *Altazimuth Building*

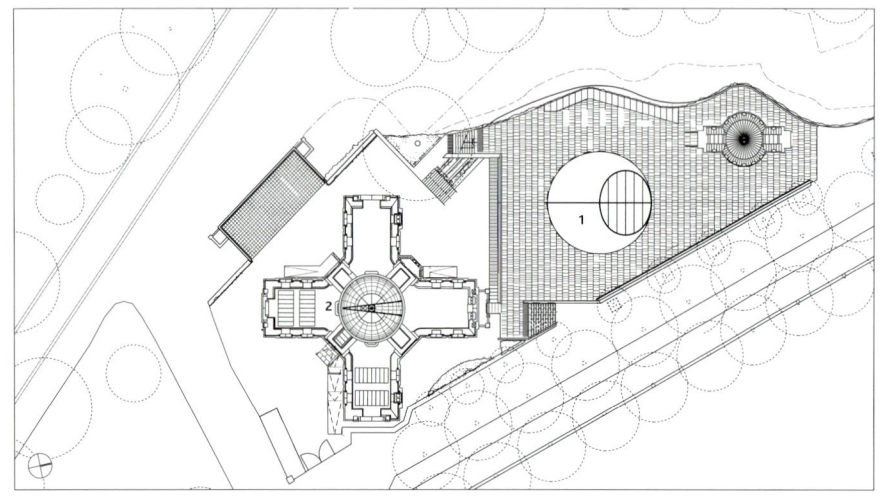

Lower ground floor plan

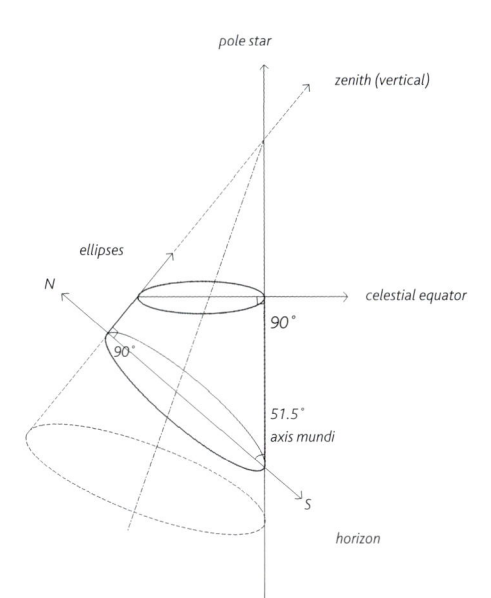

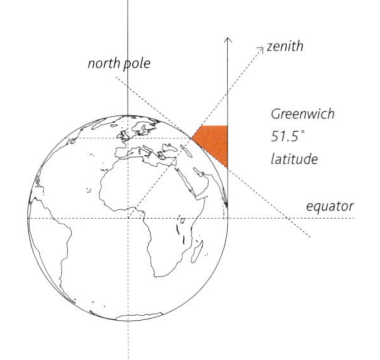

pole star

zenith (vertical)

ellipses

N

90°

90°

celestial equator

51.5°
axis mundi

S

horizon

north pole

zenith

Greenwich
51.5°
latitude

equator

that seems at home among the instruments and telescopes of the historic site. Internally the vulnerable perforated metal dome is spherical but a spherical outer enclosure would have been both difficult to construct and acoustically unsuitable. Instead, a truncated cone, circular in plan and asymmetrical in section, was devised with the observatory's senior astronomer.

The conical form (conical geometry describes the orbits of planets, asteroids and comets) is tilted so that one side is vertical (a radius of the earth, pointing to the zenith of the night sky) while the other is inclined towards the Pole star, forming the 51.5-degree angle of the Greenwich latitude, and thus parallel with the earth's axis. The cone is truncated at right angles to this edge, resulting in a mirrored plane, parallel with the equator, that reflects only the northern hemisphere of the night sky. The geometric form therefore not only encloses the projection dome, allowing access space around it, but also represents its astronomical purpose.

The geometry was also 'developable', meaning it could be constructed from a single flat sheet. It was therefore made from an 8mm-thick bronze plate, constructed, welded and patinated on site, using shipbuilding technology.

The resulting 'instrument' is circular in plan and sits comfortably between two elaborate nineteenth-century

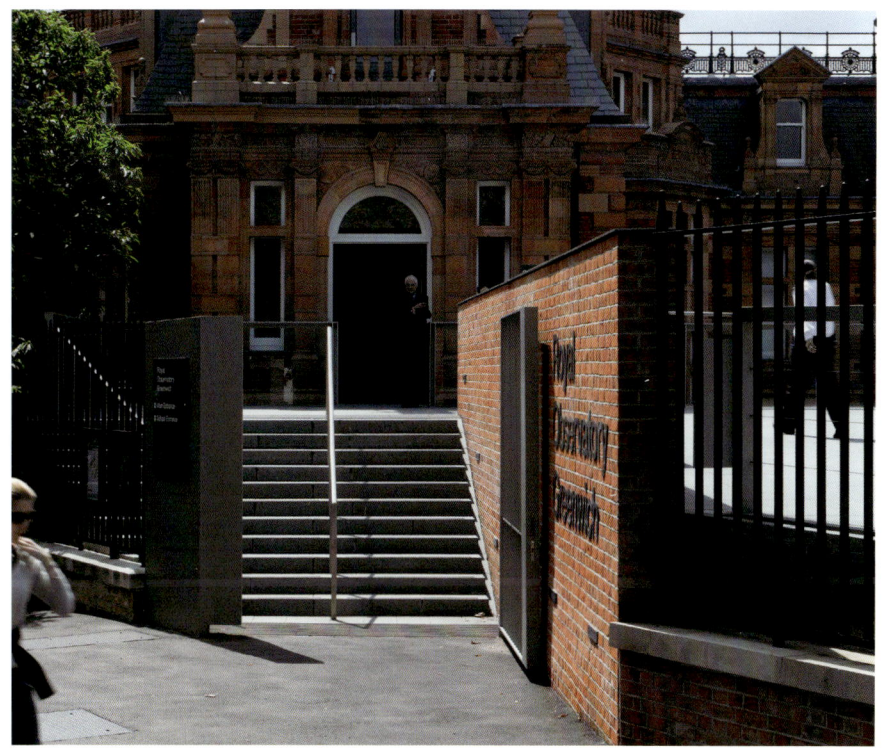

◄ Planetarium from lower ground
► Planetarium cone with Altazimuth behind and new entrance from Greenwich Park
▼ Cross section through planetarium

South Building   new planetarium   Altazimuth Building

115

buildings, the South Building and the Altazimuth, whose solar observatory was restored as part of the project.

The lower and higher points of the tilted, truncated cone mediate between their neighbours' relative heights. As a sculptural object in the landscape, the structure also resolves two apparently conflicting local geometries: that of the park, set out by Charles II and inspired by André Le Nôtre with an axis (Blackheath Avenue) perpendicular to the Thames and bisecting Inigo Jones' Queen's House; and that of the north-south meridian, with which the other observatory buildings align.

The new landscape forms a threshold to the South Building, drawing it into the group of historic observatory buildings. Its internal transformation was accomplished by removing a solid brick 'plug' at the centre of its cruciform plan that had been redundant since the telescope was removed in the middle of the last century. This was replaced by a light, open spiral staircase giving access to a series of galleries and education spaces in the wings.

In essence, three interventions – landscape, 'instrument' and stair – have facilitated the transformation of the southern part of the Royal Observatory from a little-visited garden and staff building into one of its most prized assets.

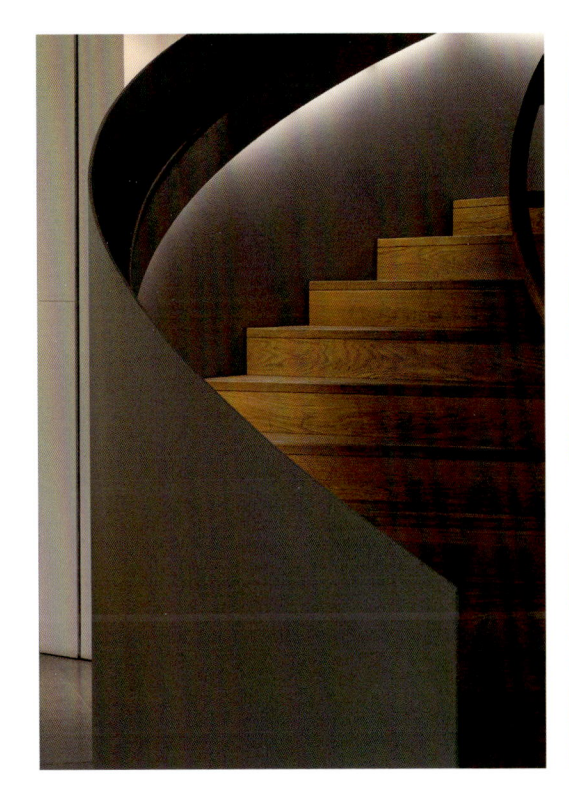

◀ Stair at the centre of the South Building
▲ Exhibition room from the stairs and the new library and boardroom

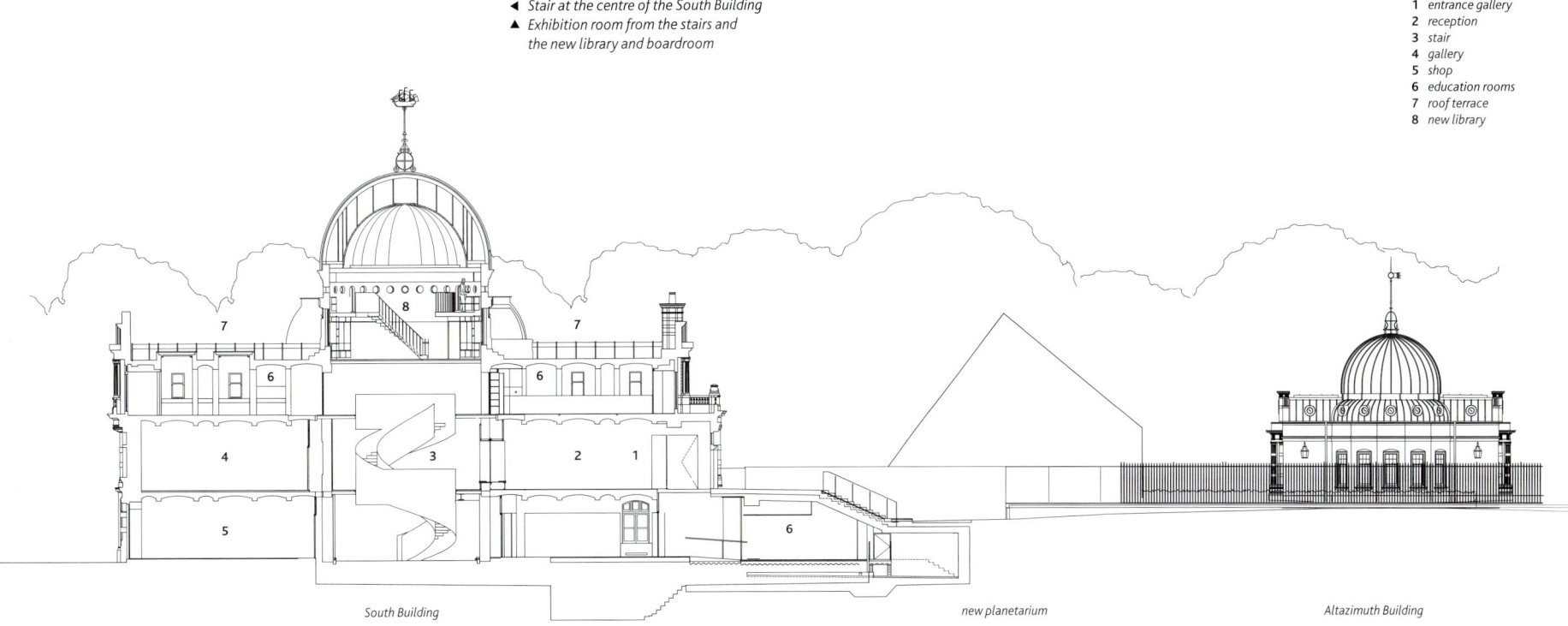

1 entrance gallery
2 reception
3 stair
4 gallery
5 shop
6 education rooms
7 roof terrace
8 new library

South Building   new planetarium   Altazimuth Building

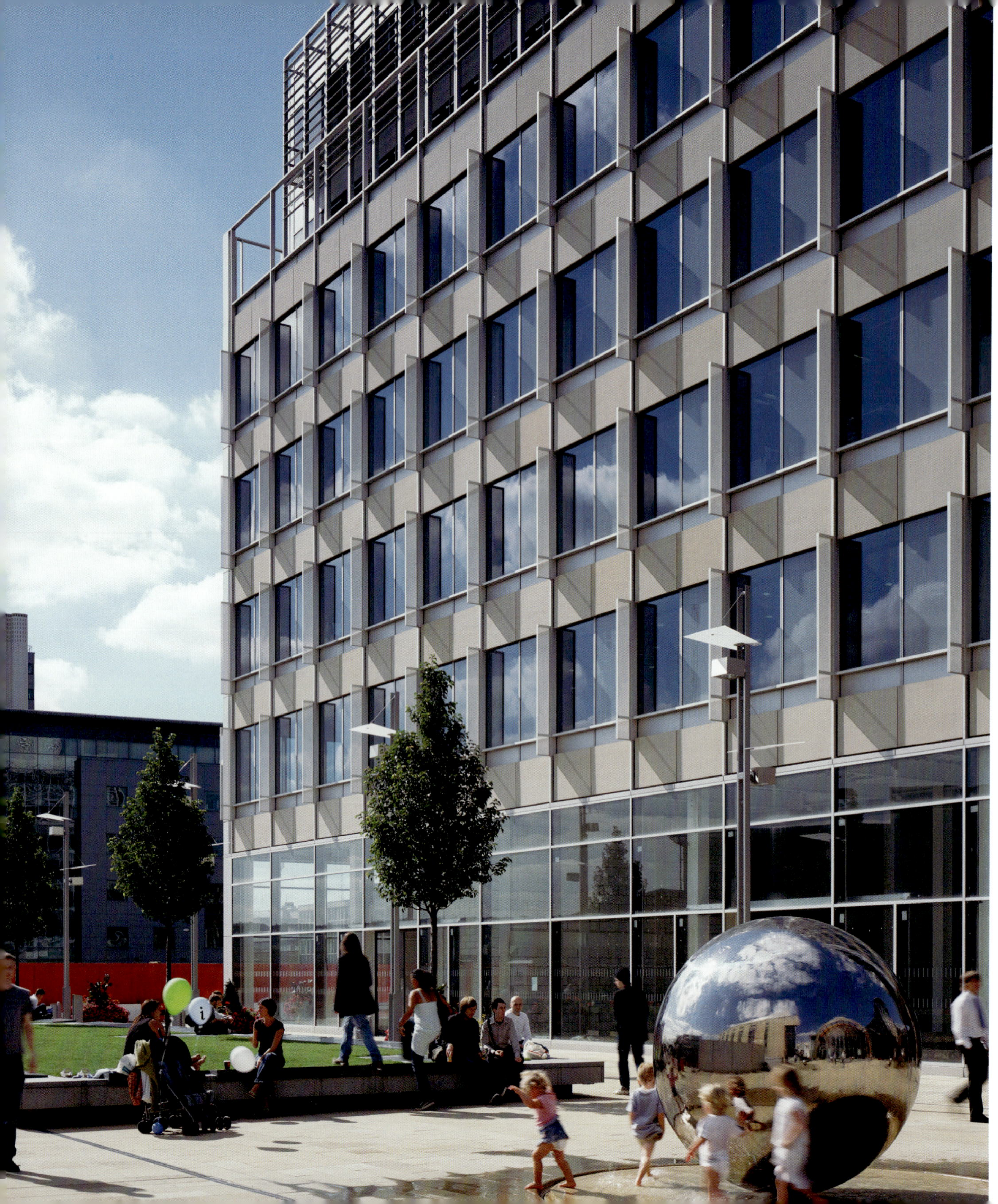

HEART OF THE CITY
Sheffield
2003–07

Between 2004 and 2016, the £130m Heart of the City redevelopment created a series of new public spaces and buildings in Sheffield city centre. The programme led from Allies and Morrison's appointment in 1994 to develop a masterplan, itself following the city council's decision to demolish its own civic offices. The 1960s behemoth contributed little to the public realm, and its removal provided an opportunity to re-imagine radically the character of the city centre, as well as to improve its pedestrian links to the station.

A key aspect of the project was dealing with the barrier of Arundel Gate – a 1960s dual carriageway created as part of the city's inner ring road – both by considering new ways in which it might be crossed and by encouraging future buildings to turn to face it, rather than backing on to it, as was originally envisaged.

The 1994 masterplan defined a series of tasks that were to be addressed by subsequent developments. These included establishing a stronger connection between the station and city centre; increasing accessibility across Arundel Gate; introducing a public realm link between Tudor Square and the Peace Gardens; reinstating a clear urban structure with smaller, individual buildings on the site of the 1960s civic offices; and re-inventing the Peace Gardens as a major public space. The objectives

1 1 St Paul's Place
2 2 St Paul's Place
3 Charles Street car park
4 office
5 apartments
6 hotel
7 new public realm

▲ Peace Gardens
◀ St Paul's Place

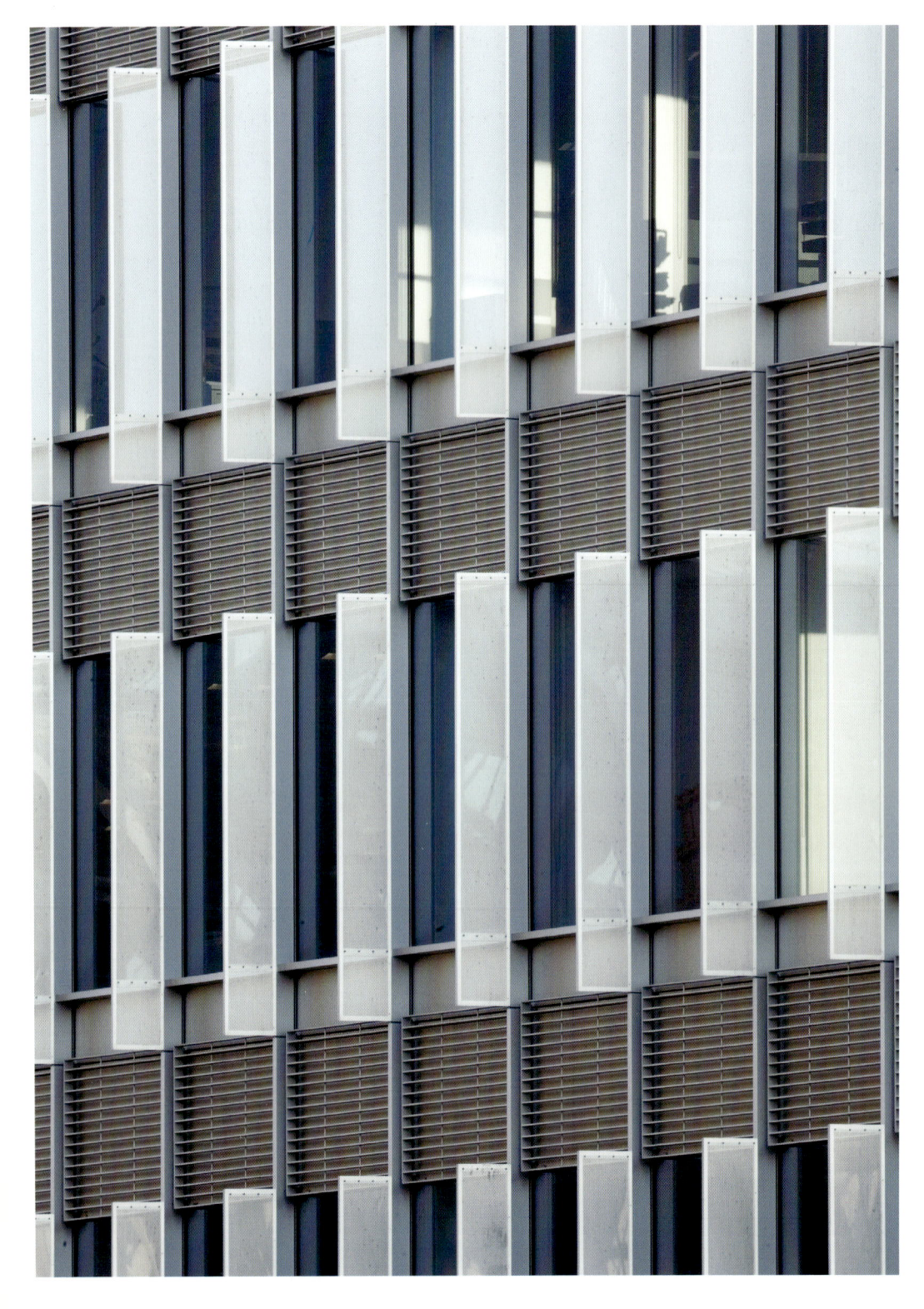

were defined in such a way that they could be brought forward as separate initiatives as they became viable. Allies and Morrison's involvement continued with the planning and design of St Paul's Place, immediately west of the new Winter Garden. (The proposed external public realm connection had been rendered as a dramatic covered space by architect Pringle Richards Sharratt). This more detailed plan replaced the civic offices with a pattern of urban blocks that re-established the former street pattern and facilitated movement across the site.

The new buildings – a combination of office, residential and hotel use with shops, cafes and restaurants on the ground floor – were configured around a second new public space to the east of the Peace Gardens, which was itself terminated with a new multi-storey car park, conceived as a significant civic building in its own right. The initial two office buildings and the car park building were designed by Allies and Morrison.

◀ 1 St Pauls Place east facade
▶ 1 St Pauls Place west facade

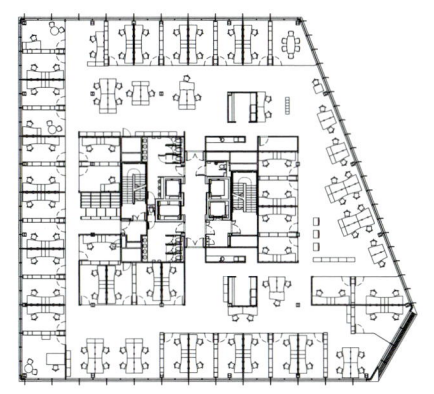

Typical upper floor plan

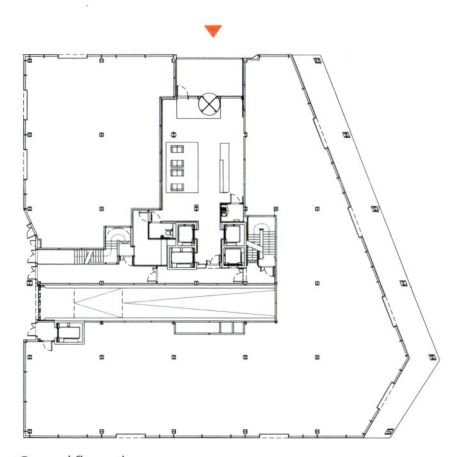

Ground floor plan

121

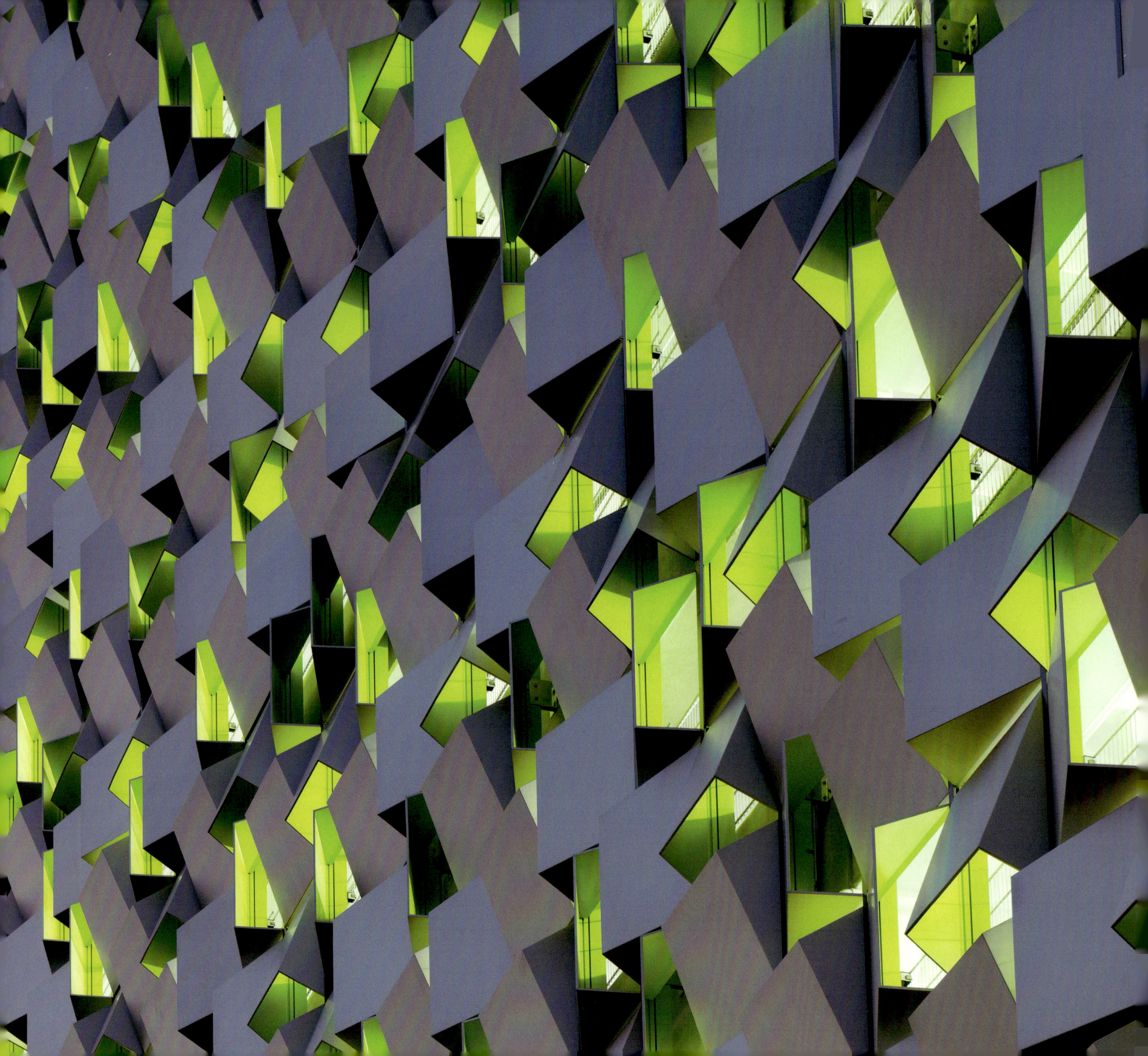

CHARLES STREET CAR PARK
Sheffield
2003–07

Occupying the south-east corner of the site, and performing an important role in the new urban fabric, the Charles Street multi-storey car park was afforded the same attention to detail as the other buildings within the masterplan.

The car park is arranged as a single continuous ramp, its floors hidden behind a screen of folded, anodised aluminium panels. Each panel is formed as a square with two folded triangular sides that produce a tilted face. The panels are mounted in a composition of the four possible orientations on vertical mullions

▶ *Car park in the city context*
▲ *Full-size mock-up of the facade elements*
◀ *Car park facade by night*

Cross section through car park screen

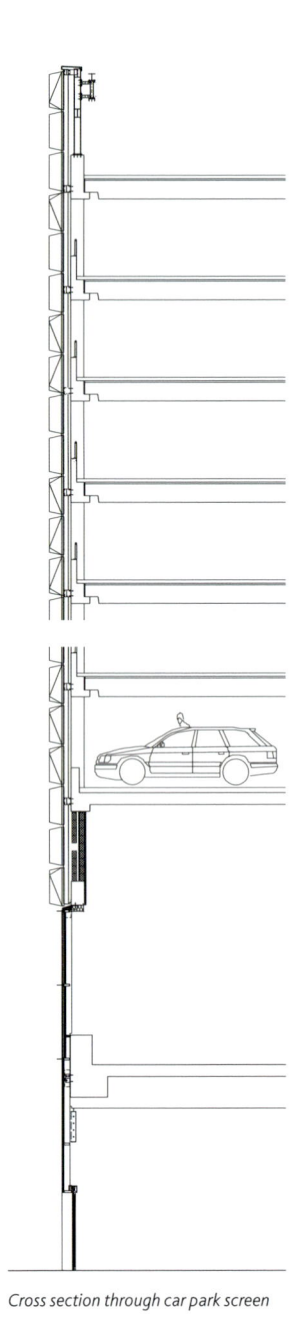

124

mounted onto a standard frame. This simple system results in a variety of open ends and tilted faces which produce a varied pattern of light reflectance across the elevations, an optical effect enhanced by the use of colour on the inner faces of the panels.

The appearance of the panel system differs significantly between day and night. By day, a monochromatic pattern is achieved across the elevations, changing as daylight fades. By night, the interior lighting bleeds between each panel and creates a random composition of light and dark across the surface.

From within the car park horizontal views are glimpsed between the top and bottom of the panels, with more substantial portrait views through the open slots at the sides.

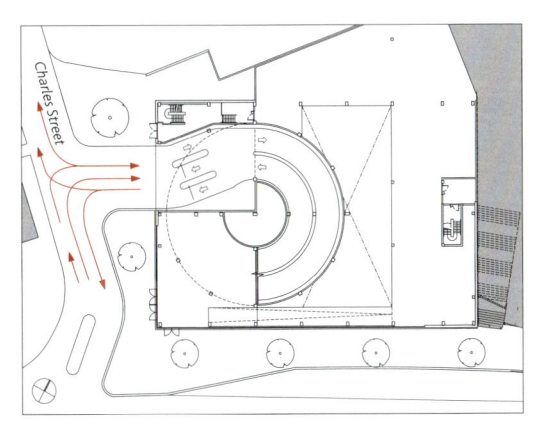

Ground floor plan

◄ *Car park facade by day*
► *Car park and ramp*

PARADISE STREET LIVERPOOL ONE

Liverpool
2005–08

Allies and Morrison was among the 25 architectural practices commissioned to design individual buildings at Liverpool One, the major retail, leisure and residential project between Lime Street Station and the Albert Dock, intended to spearhead regeneration of the city centre. Conceived by BDP, the Liverpool One masterplan rejected the convention of a central internal mall in favour of a network of external streets and spaces designed to integrate with the surrounding urban fabric while also recovering aspects of the earlier historic street pattern.

Occupying an entire urban block, Allies and Morrison's Paradise Street building plays a key role in establishing the new street pattern, as well as generating an important new pedestrian route linking the centre of the city to the river. Aligned with the existing thoroughfare of College Lane, this route takes visitors from ground level on Paradise Street, up stairs and escalators, first to a semi-external cinema foyer (the cinemas themselves, in an adjacent building, are approached via a high-level bridge) and then to a new west-facing terrace lined with restaurants. From here the route continues across more bridges into Chavasse Park, a new public landscape created on the roof of the multi-storey car park, before returning to ground level on the banks of the River Mersey.

The ascent from ground to third floor is one of the most dramatic aspects of the building, with escalators forming a direct route, while above them a sequence of stairs zigzag their way across the space as they

◄ *Concept model*
▶ *Zigzag stair soffit*

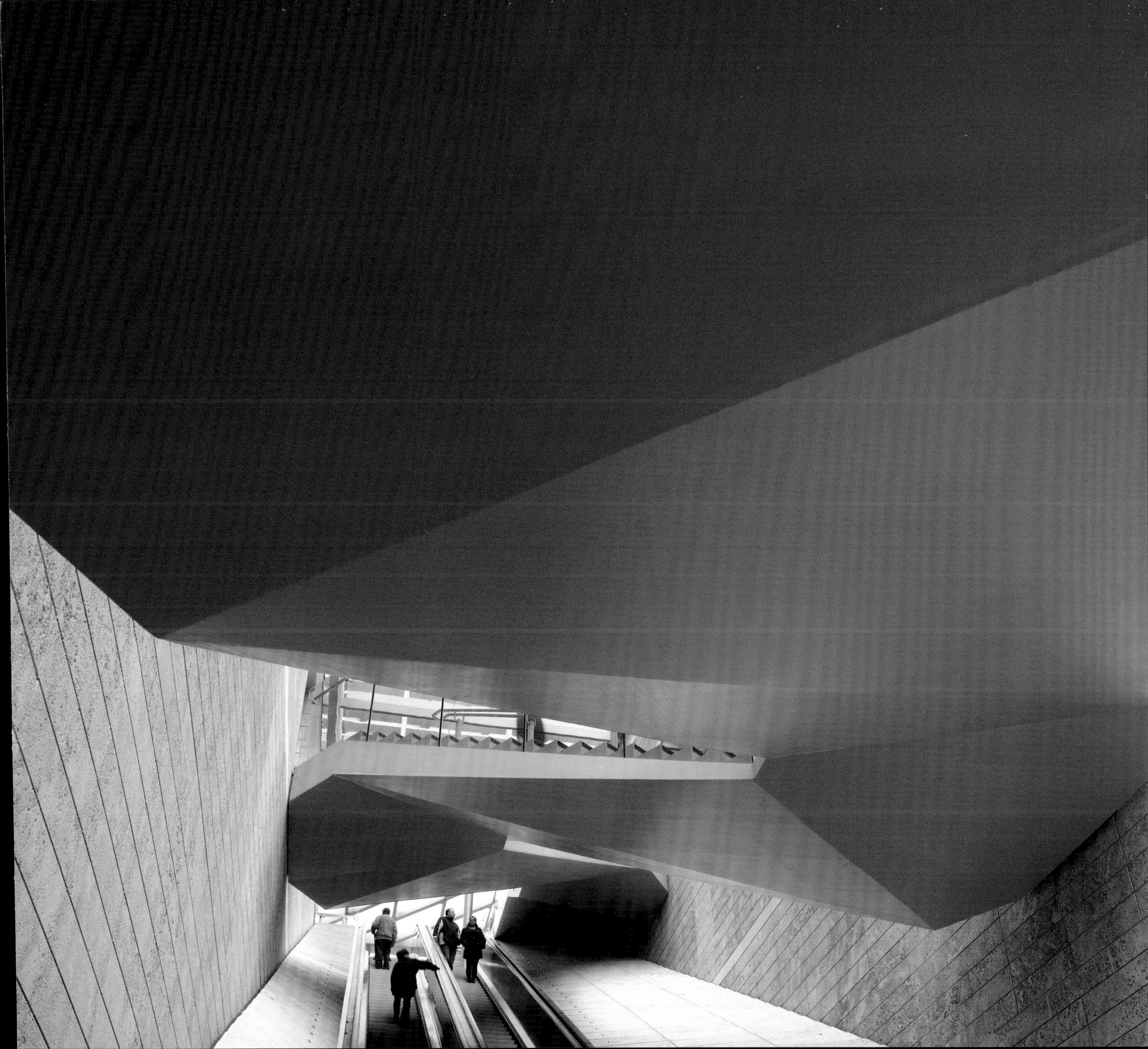

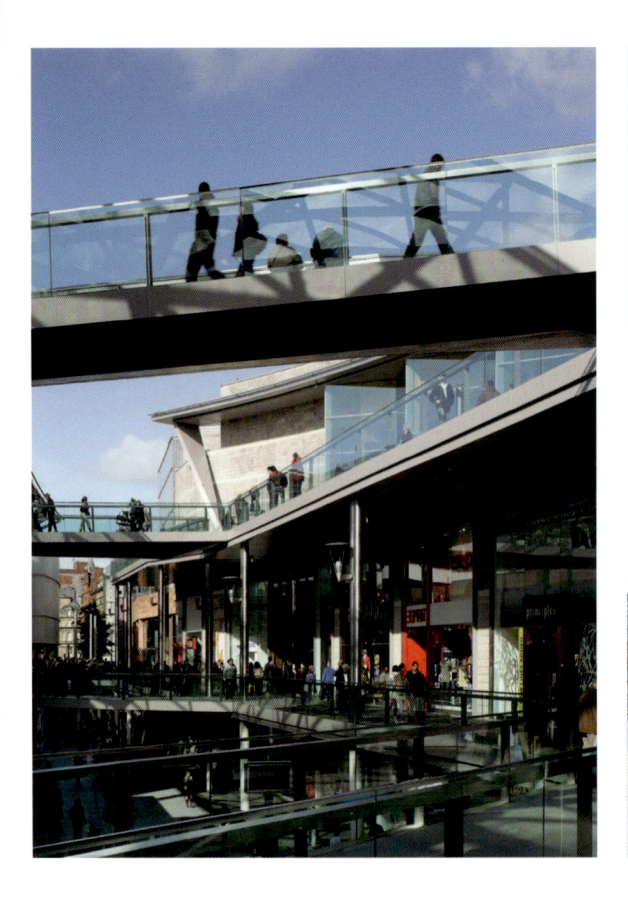

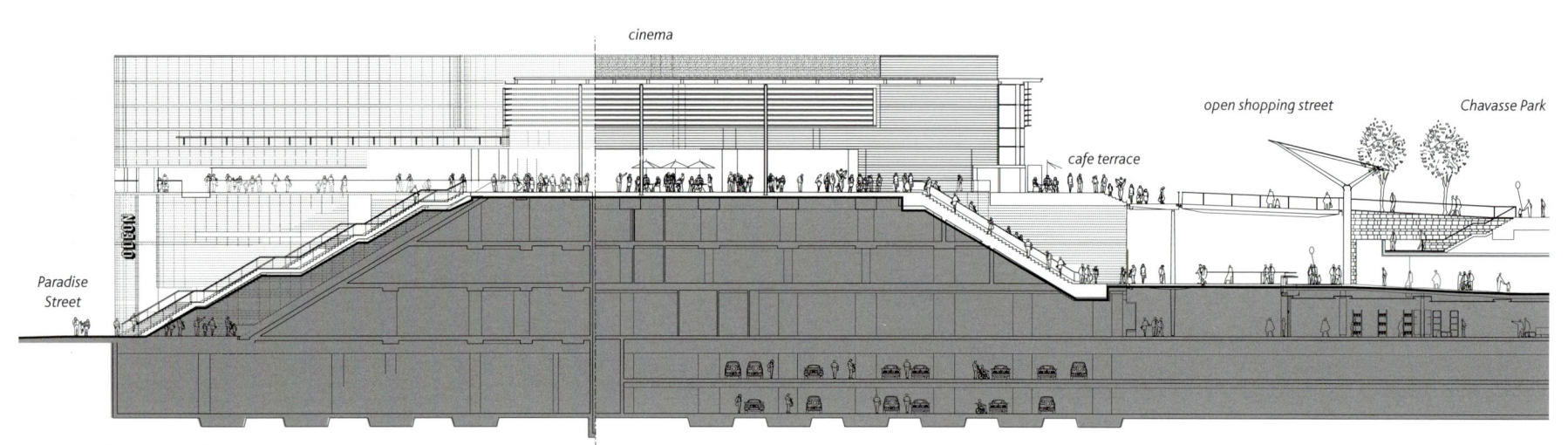

Long section showing the retail concourses and parking

generate sufficient length to achieve the required change in level.

The complex configuration of the site envisaged by BDP's masterplan – in which none of the four perimeter edges aligned – required an architectural response that accommodated all these conditions. A similar flexibility was required in the building's sectional design to allow for a series of set-backs that would retain strategic views across the site to some of the city's landmark buildings.

A clear distinction was made, both in material and scale, between the three facades that face towards the city and the fourth that addresses the

◀ *Bridges, galleries and the upper terrace level*
▶ *Zigzag stair*

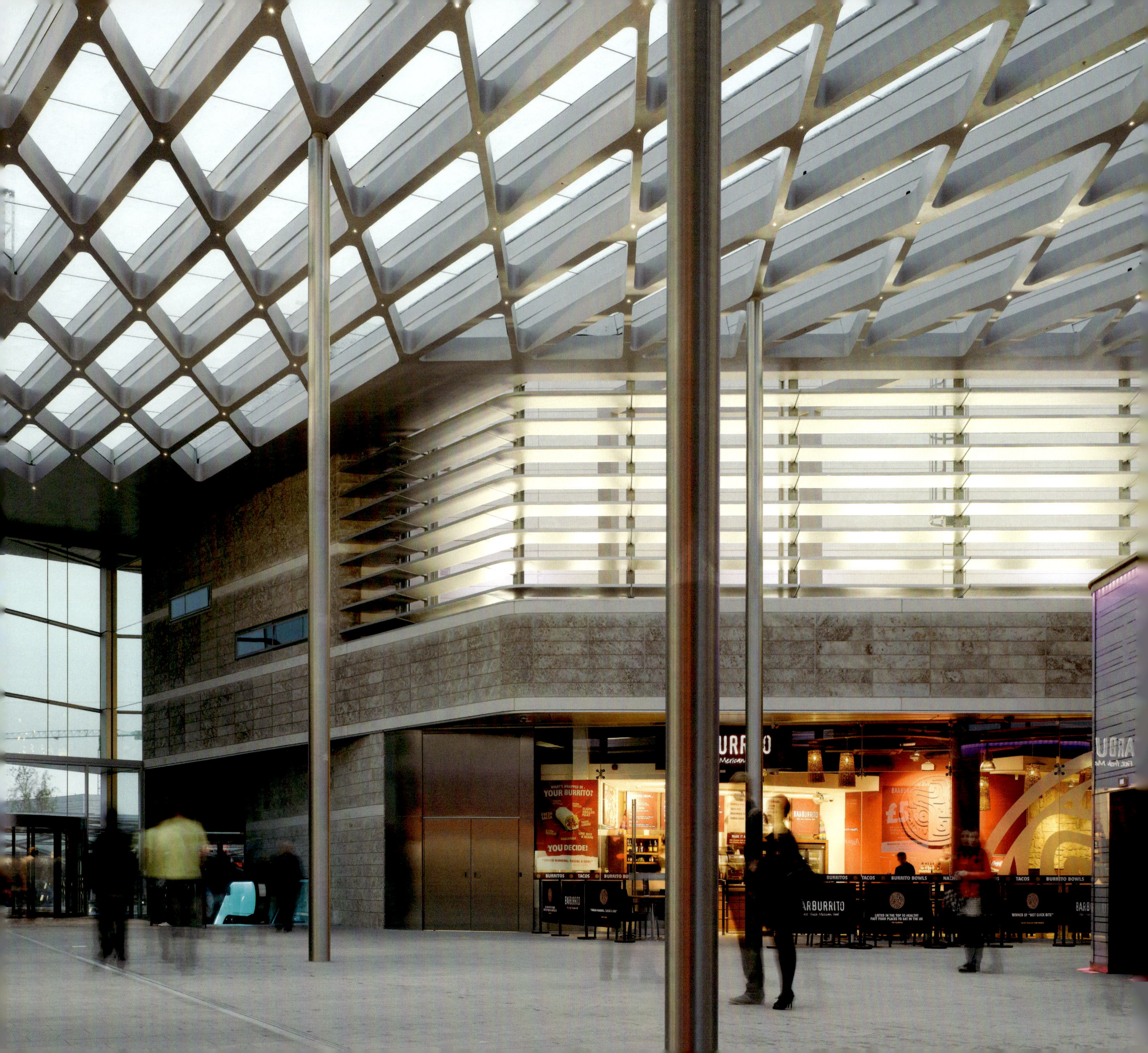
YOUR BURRITO?
YOU DECIDE!
BURRITOS
TACOS
BURRITO BOWLS

park. A series of horizontal bands of masonry create a continuous surface which, when required, can 'peel apart' to accommodate changes in form and cross-section. These surfaces extend into the 'crevasse' occupied by the escalators and stairs and continue to the cinema foyer. The facade that faces the park is by contrast largely glazed, its concave form determined by the elliptical geometry of the park, while its faceted glass bays reflect the configuration of the various cafes and restaurants within.

The building is arranged over five levels, with ground floor shops facing onto the surrounding streets, more shops at an upper raised level extending from the existing street to the north, and the cinema foyer and restaurant occupying the top of the building.

The cinema foyer is roofed by a glazed steel lattice structure supported on freestanding columns. The parallelogram-shaped geometry of the lattice derives from the larger geometry of the site.

◀ *Cinema foyer*
▶ *Frontage to Paradise Street*

ONE VINE STREET

Westminster, London
2004–08

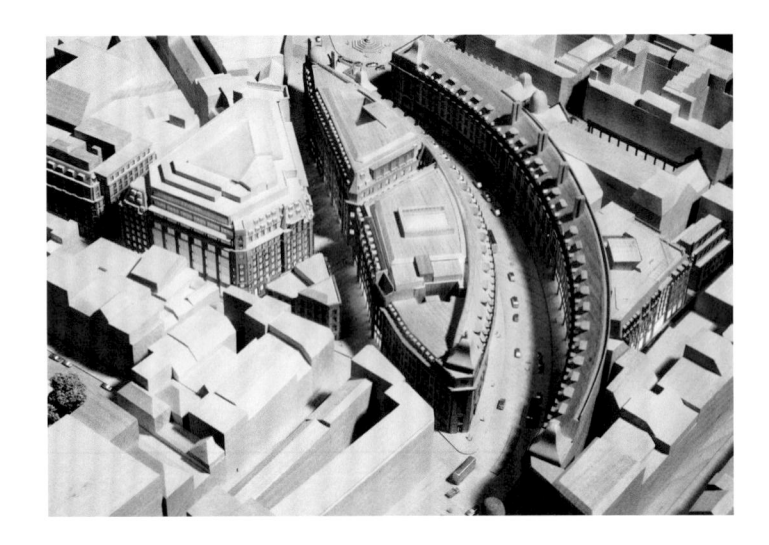

One Vine Street forms part of The Crown Estate's Regent Street portfolio, which comprises 25 blocks on the east and west sides of Regent Street, from Piccadilly Circus to Portland Place. The development forms part of Allies and Morrison's masterplan for the 'Quadrant'.

The building's curved frontage faces Regent Street on the north-east side. To the west it faces Swallow Street, the alignment of which predates the construction of the Nash crescent to Piccadilly Circus, and to the south, Vine Street. At street level the building is separated from its easterly neighbour by the diminutive Man-in-Moon Passage.

The reinstatement of the block included the retained facades to Regent Street (numbers 83-97) and Swallow Street (16-20), both of which were grade-two listed. Within, the building has been transformed into an integrated mixed-use scheme comprising a large retail unit on Regent Street, with five floors of offices above arranged around a central atrium. Seven two- and three-bedroom residential apartments are located on the fifth floor within the mansard roof. Including major improvements to Swallow Street, the scheme creates a new public space linking Regent Street with Piccadilly.

New elevations, partly constructed in Portland stone, extend and conclude the backs of the Regent Street buildings and establish a 'front' at the corner of Swallow and Vine Streets. Large windows are inserted into the facade at ground level for the new retail units, which help to invigorate the public realm. Large regular window openings, set within the stone frame of the upper floors, are lined on two sides

One Vine Street   retained facade   Piccadilly   St James's Church

▲ Entrance
▲ Swallow Street facade
◄ Model showing the Regent Street masterplan
► Facade detail of Swallow Street elevation

with sections that both register the incision into the surface more precisely, and produce an inflection within each bay towards the corner. In order to maintain a sense of scale that harmonises with the range and style of buildings on the west side of Swallow Street, the new elevation is further defined and subdivided by changes in the planes of masonry and glazing along its length.

The corner marks a compositional focal point in the development, defines the location of the new entrance and establishes an axis directed towards Piccadilly. The reception is set back from the building line, creating a simple canopy. Above this the Portland stone frame forms a distinctive corner. At the top of the wall the frame is void, forming a terrace, and above a mansard roof, constructed in traditional materials using dressed slates, contains large dormer windows. At the corner these are linked so as to form a glazed screen that acts as a lantern to the street.

Strips of birch, interspersed by lights, provide a backdrop to the reception area. Alison Turnbull, commissioned to install an artwork in the reception foyer, added coloured filters to a number of these lights to extend her influence throughout the circulation spaces.

◀ *View from Vine Street*
▶ *Ground floor atrium and office floors*

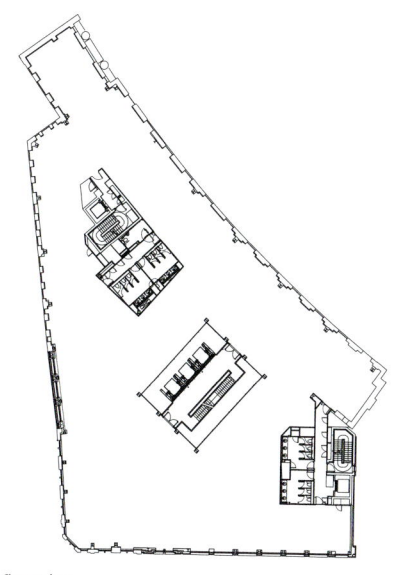

Typical office floor plan

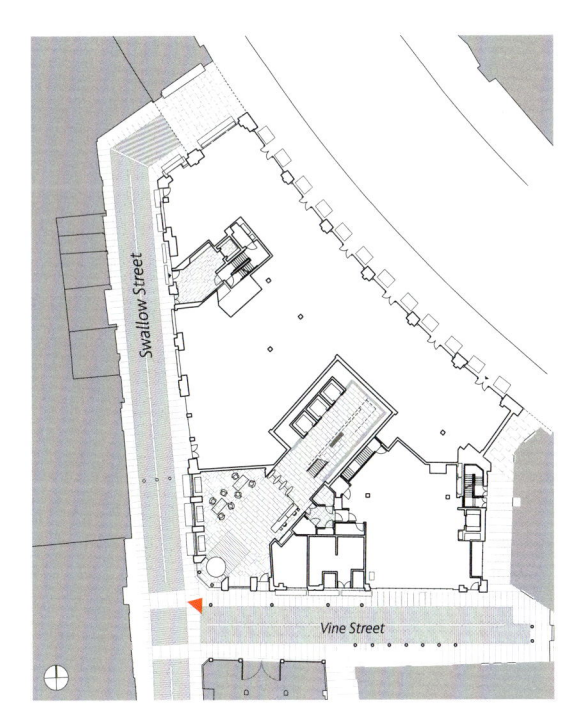

Ground floor plan

135

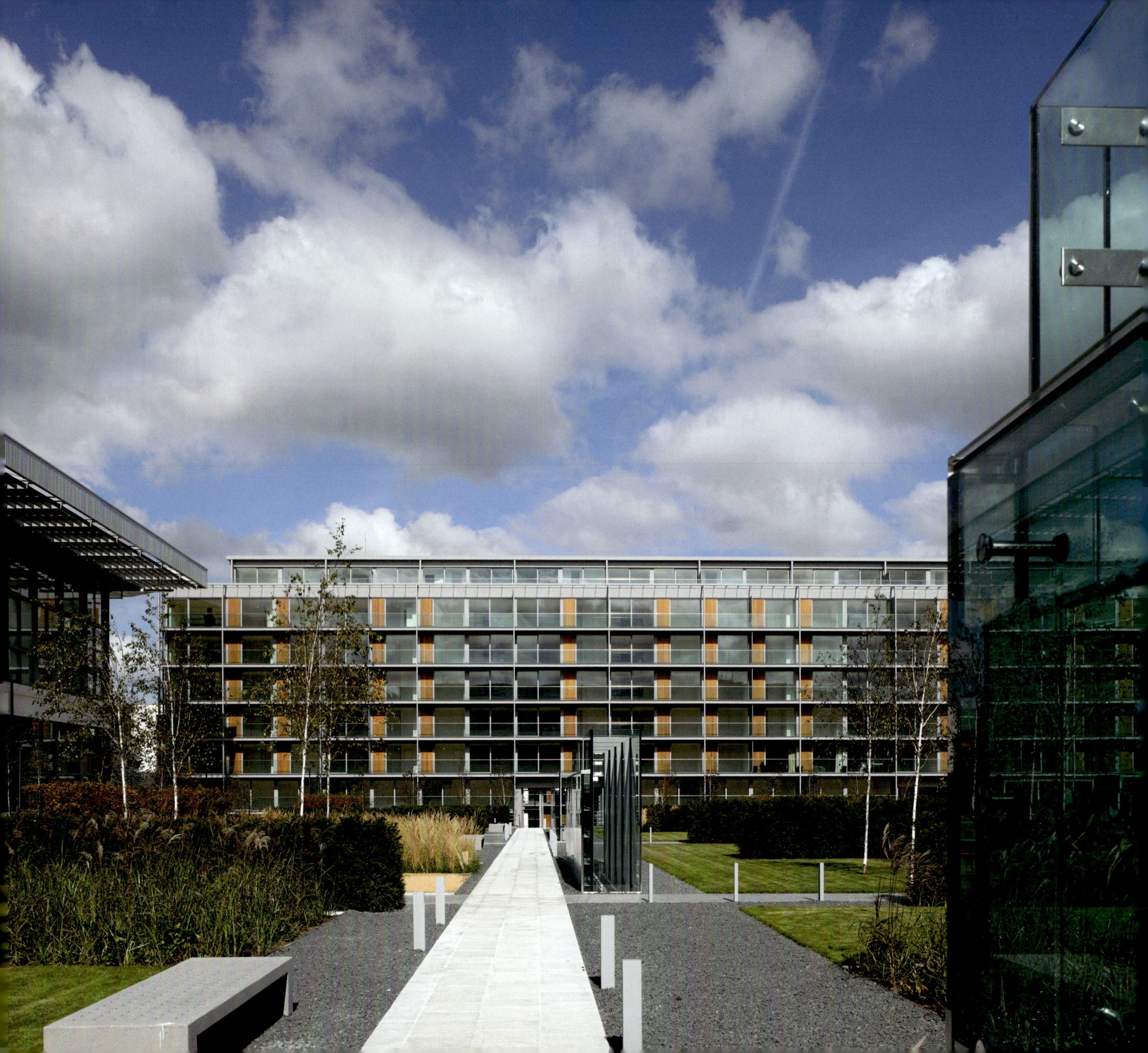

HIGHBURY SQUARE

Islington, London
2005–09

The historic Highbury home of Arsenal Football Club has been retained as a local landmark and integrated into the surrounding urban fabric by adapting the East and West Stands for residential use and replacing the North and South Stands with new apartment buildings, while retaining the former pitch as a shared garden.

Arsenal's decision to move to the larger Emirates Stadium nearby at Holloway posed the question of what should become of its former stadium, a reservoir of memories for the club and its supporters. Embedded in a typical London neighbourhood of Victorian terraces and some post-war blocks of flats, the location was clearly a suitable site for residential development. But the stadium's 1930s art deco east stand – one of the first purpose-built football stands in the world – was grade-two listed and worthy of retention.

1 converted East Stand
2 converted West Stand
3 south block
4 north block
5 new garden
6 courtyards
7 mews

▲ Original stadium in its residential context
◀ Communal garden on site of original pitch

137

There are numerous examples in ancient history of stadium buildings being adapted to accommodate new uses. One of Rome's great public spaces – the circus-shaped Piazza Navona – was created at the end of the fifteenth century on the remains of the first-century Stadium of Domitian. Similarly, the Piazza dell'Anfiteatro in Lucca echoes the elliptical footprint of the second-century Roman amphitheatre, while the amphitheatre at Arles was, until its reclamation as an arena in 1830, put to use as a fortified town of 200 houses. And even today, the Theatre of Marcellus in Rome is still colonised by apartments dating from the sixteenth century. The challenge at Highbury was how to acknowledge the cultural significance

◀ *Refurbished and reconfigured stands*
▶ *The pitch forms a new urban landscape*

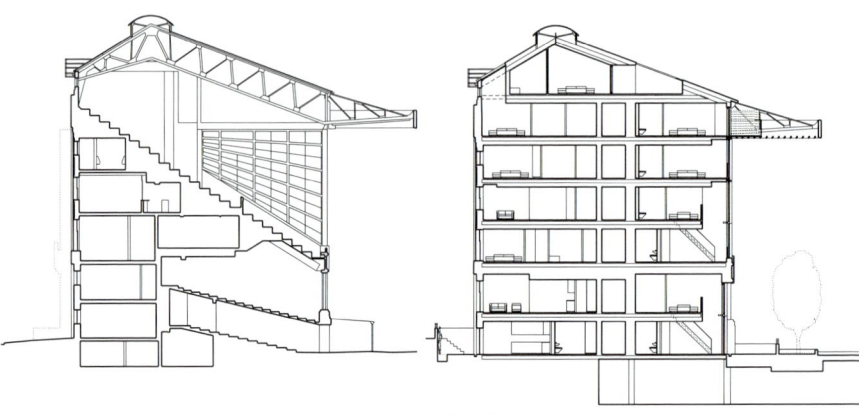

Original cross-section   *Adapted cross-section*

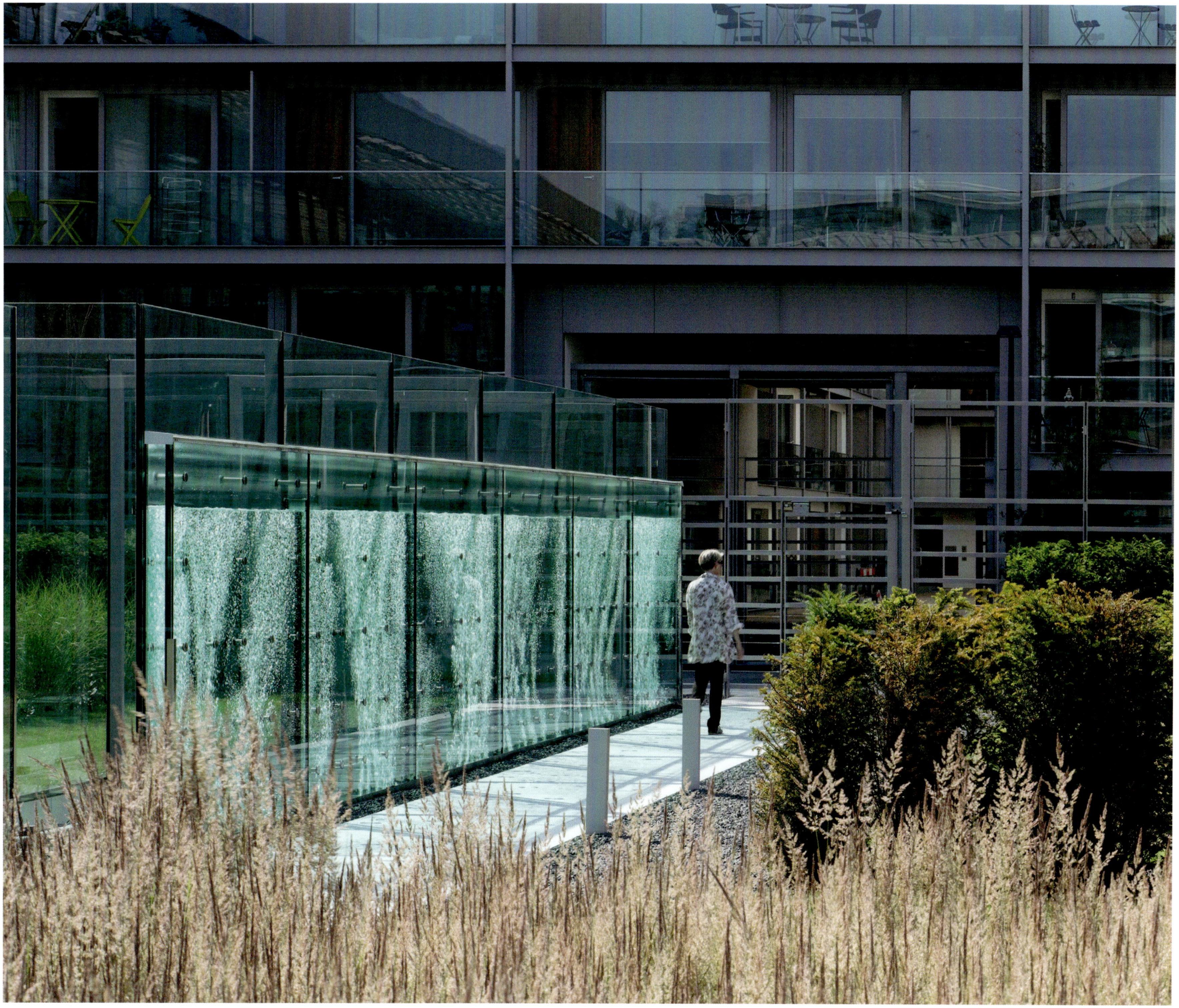

of the redundant structure, a local monument that had played an important role in the identity of the area since its opening in 1913, while converting it to residential use.

There was also the issue of scale. How could such a large building retain its status and at the same time be assimilated into the much smaller scale of the local residential streets and squares? In this respect the morphology of the stadium – a series of substantial, inward-looking structures grouped around the central space of the pitch – was regarded as an opportunity. Rather than just keeping the fabric of the single listed East Stand, Allies and Morrison argued for the retention of the whole geometry and setting of the pitch.

It proposed retaining – and inserting new apartments into – not just the listed East Stand but also the later,

▶ *Courtyard*
▶ *Residential facade*
▶ *Ground floor maisonette*

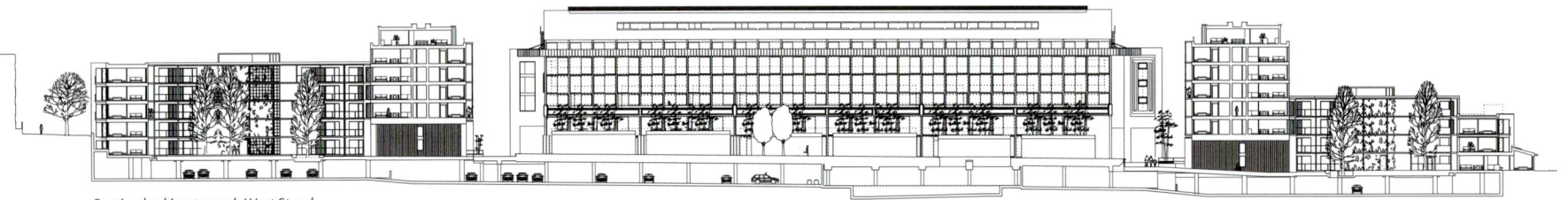

Section looking towards West Stand

Section looking south through East and West Stands

141

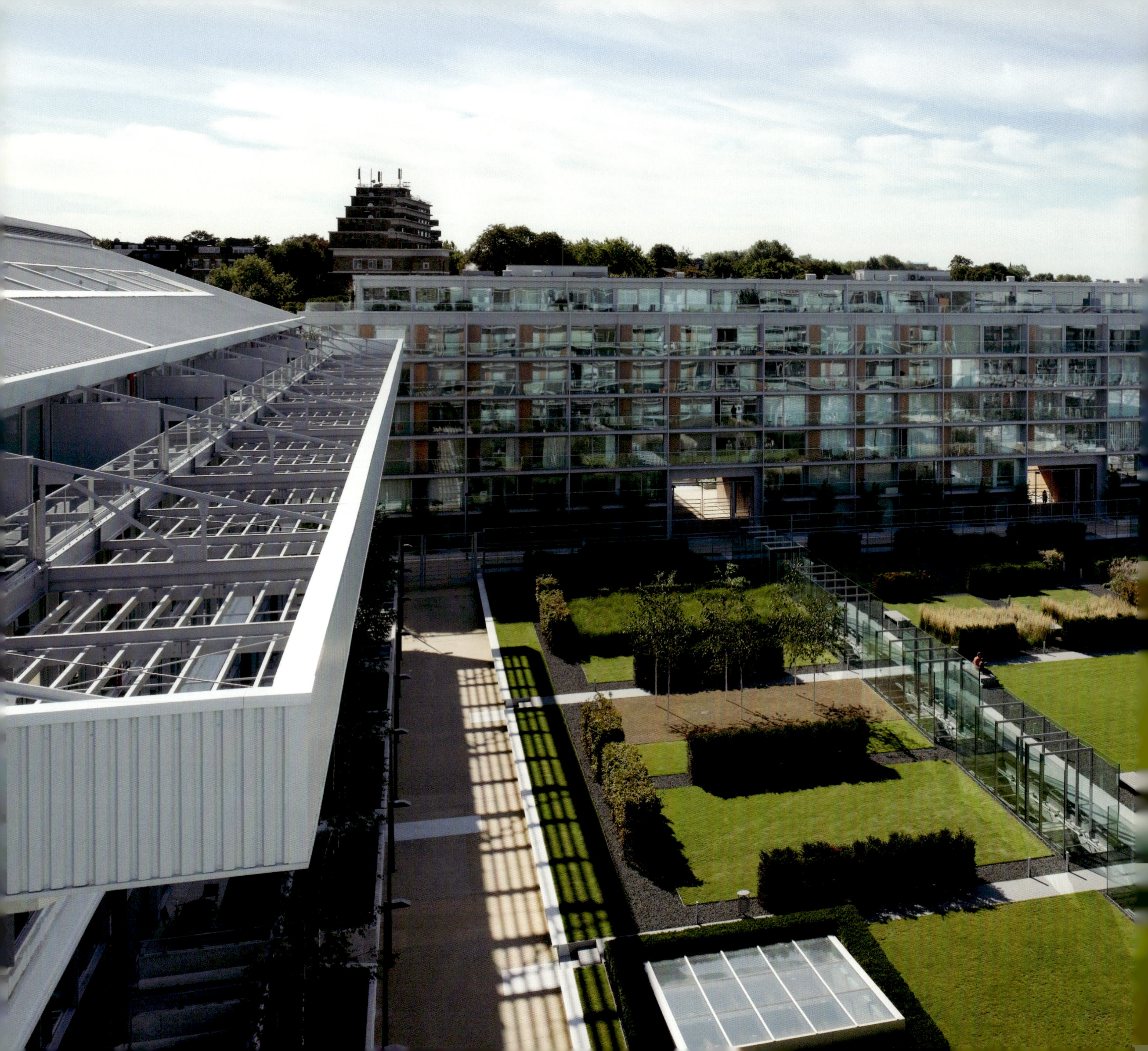

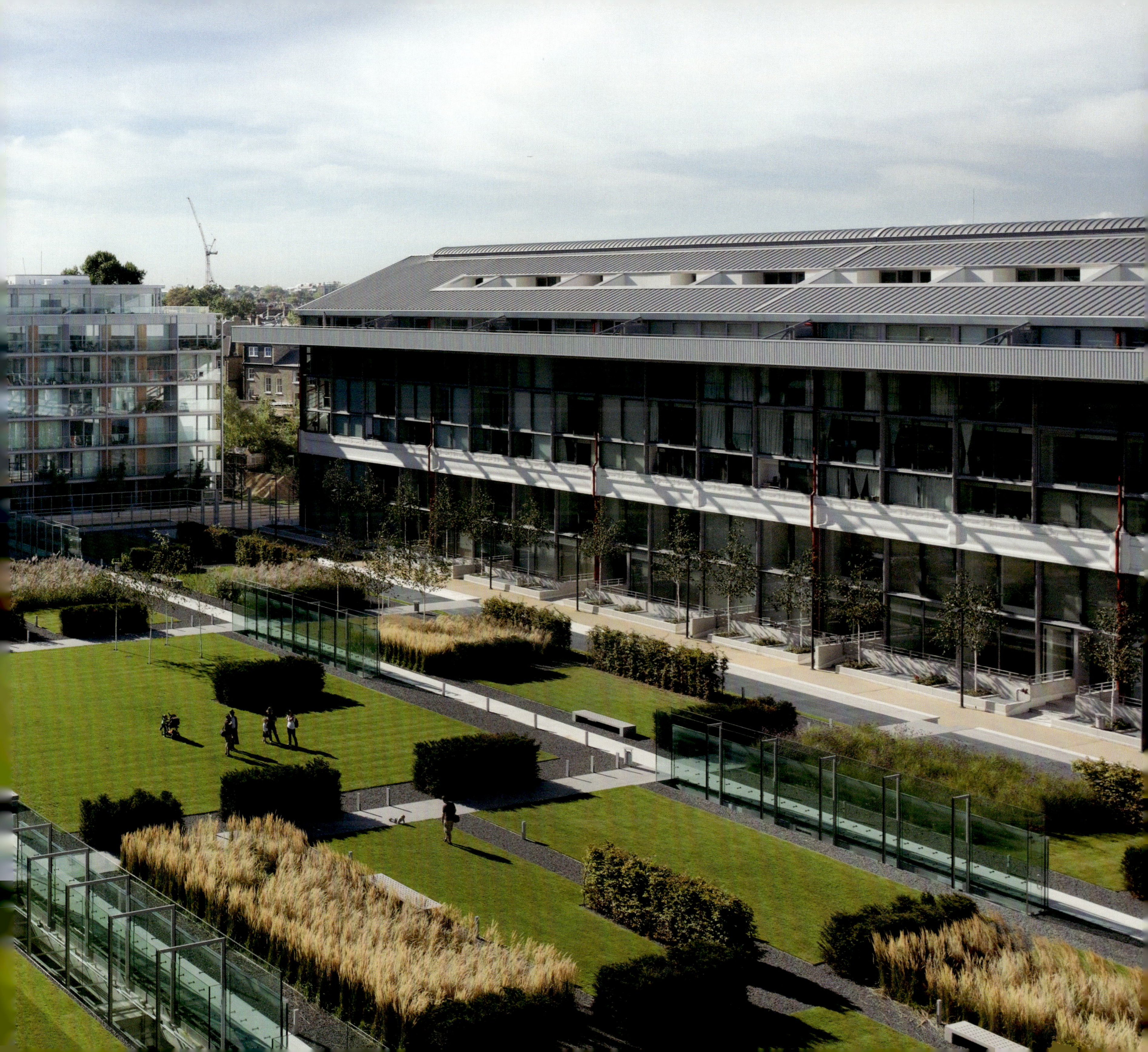

unlisted West Stand, while adding new, similarly scaled buildings to the north and south to complete the enclosure to, and preserve the memory of, the pitch.

The former pitch was configured by landscape designer Christopher Bradley-Hole as a new garden, like a traditional London square, that is shared by all the residents. Glass shafts punctuate the landscape, delivering natural light and ventilation to the subterranean car park hidden beneath its surface. The new space also fulfils a wider role within the city, providing a new pedestrian route between Avenell Road and Highbury Hill.

While the pitch – now the new garden – retains its role as the focal point of the site, a dense urban residential community has been created around it. The scale of the development is substantial, and the character of the buildings – reflecting the scale of the existing stands – is open and expansive. Behind the buildings to the north and south of the pitch, two clusters of lower blocks are arranged around intimate courtyards, their facades marked by the continuous balconies that front

◀ *Residential buildings along Avenell Road*
▶ *Entrance to the former stadium*
▶ *Mews houses*

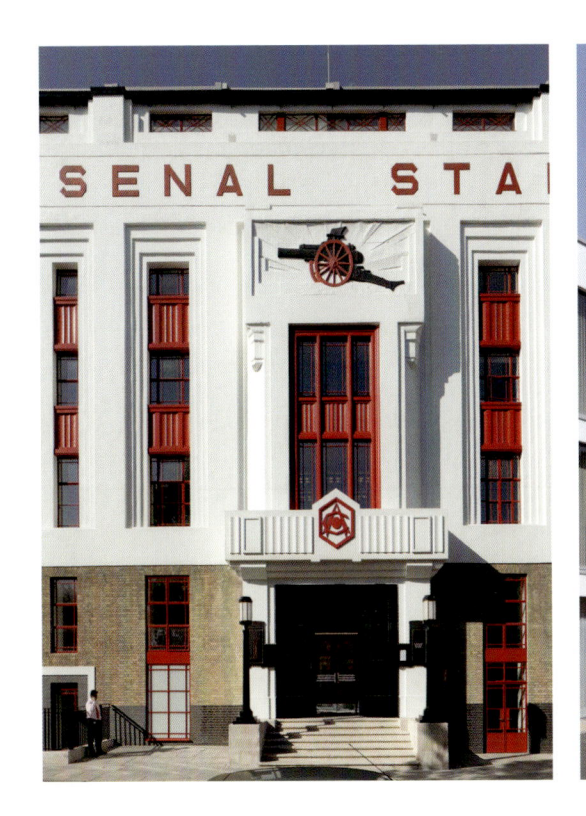

all the dwellings. Beyond these, a range of smaller buildings adjust the scale of the development to the surrounding streets, one adopting the form of a mews, and another re-establishing the line of a terrace.

The individual buildings differ according to their place within the overall scheme, responding in scale, composition and rhythm to the character of their particular context. For example, while the buildings facing the open space of the garden are predominantly glazed with strong horizontal proportions, the facades to the street are brick with a regular grid of openings, and the elevations to the mews are more formal and finished in white render. This strategy of introducing variety helps blur the boundary between new and old, allowing the continuum of the city to reassert itself across the site.

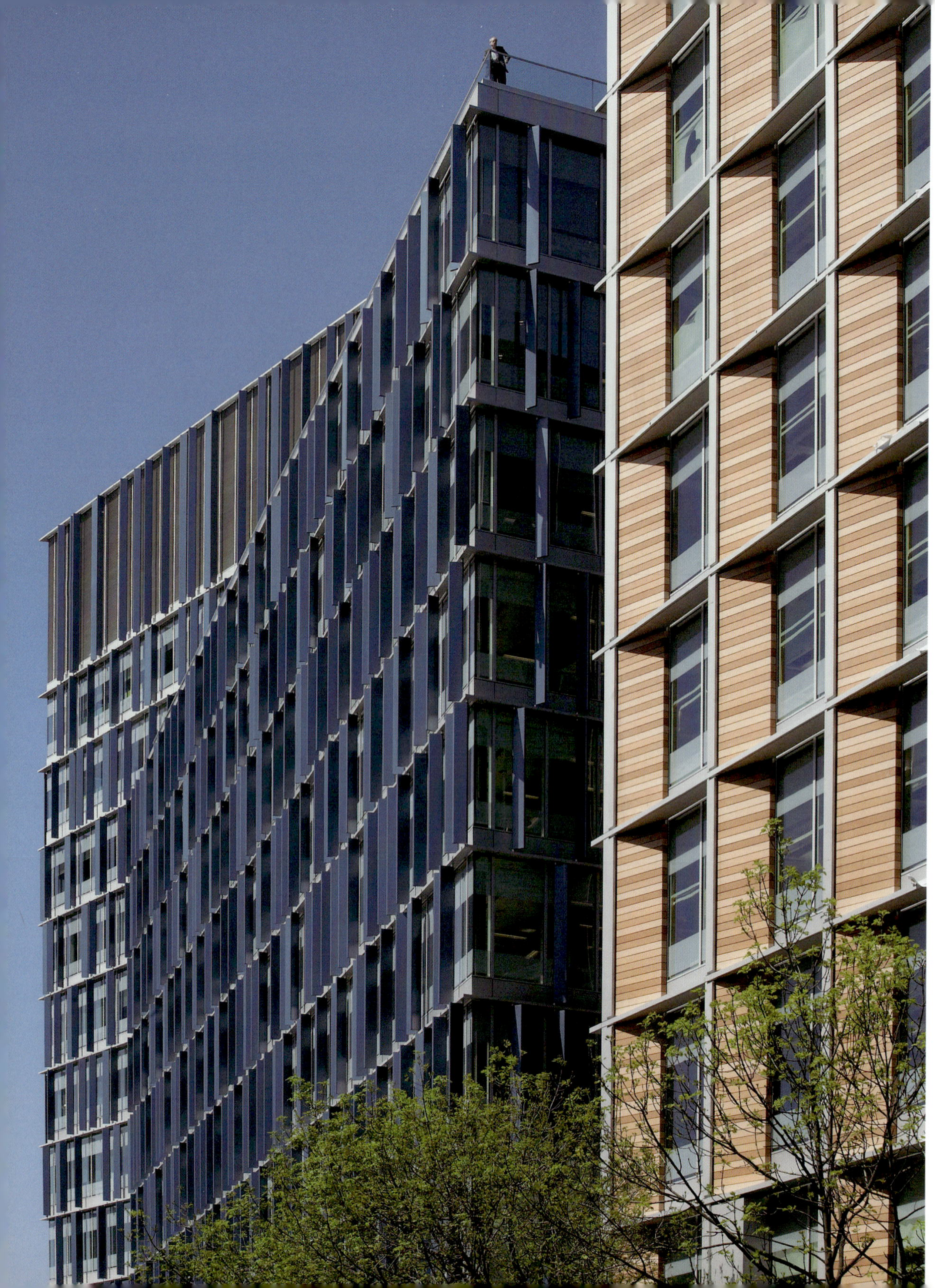

BANKSIDE 123

Southwark, London
2000–11

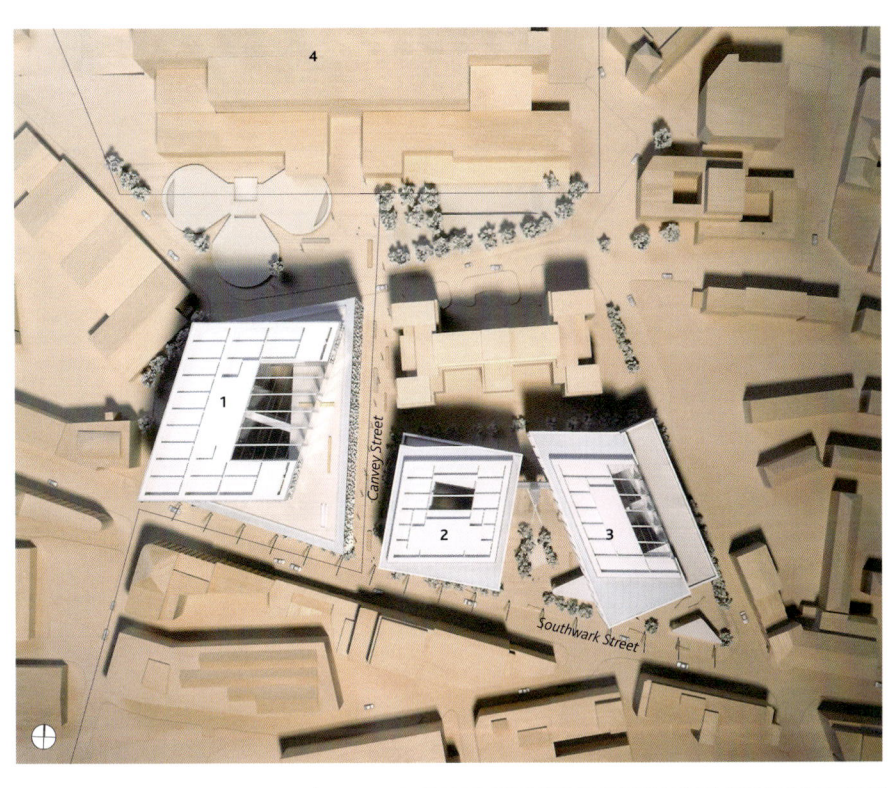

Comprising three substantial office buildings on Southwark Street, this development is an early example of the regenerative effect of the opening in 2000 of both the Tate Modern art gallery in the former Bankside Power Station and the pedestrian Millennium Bridge. The fragmented, informal group of buildings replaced St Christopher's House, a singular, unloved 1960s linear building that contributed neither permeability nor activity to the street.

A new north-south public route was cut through the site, breaking down the scale of the urban block and enabling a new pedestrian link from Southwark Street through to St Paul's Cathedral to the north. On the west, east and north sides of the site, the new development aligns with the existing streets but on Southwark Street a series of south-facing public spaces has been formed. The easternmost space, originally designated to provide a home for the

1 *Bankside 1 (Blue Fin Building)*
2 *Bankside 2*
3 *Bankside 3*
4 *Tate Modern*

▲ *Model of new proposal facilitating routes from Southwark to the South Bank*
◀ *The former St Christopher's House blocking the permeability to the River Thames*
◀ *Bankside 1 (Blue Fin Building) and Bankside 2 facades*

Architecture Foundation in a building designed by Zaha Hadid, now provides a small garden.

To the west side, the Blue Fin Building (Bankside 1), the largest in the development, draws together the geometries of the pre-nineteenth century fabric of Bankside and the mid-nineteenth century alignment of Southwark Street. Its massing is arranged in three parts. The top, a parallelogram, acknowledges the geometry of the older street pattern; the middle follows the site boundary; and the two-storey base recalls the top. The ground level is set back on the northerly elevation to generate an entrance porch facing Tate Modern and, more dramatically, on the south to provide a link to the entrance of its neighbour – Bankside 2. The three parts appear to 'fuse' together on the south-west corner where a dramatic prow announces the route to Tate Modern from Southwark Station.

The facades of Bankside 1 are characterised by a syncopated arrangement of vertical blue external louvres or 'fins', marshalled by clear horizontal 'shelves' at each floor level. Positioned in a varied arrangement of angles and intervals, the slender fins provide dappled shade to the otherwise fully-glazed building envelope, and produce an opaque facade when viewed obliquely from the surrounding streets.

◀ *View of roof terrace towards Tate Modern*
▶ *The new Canvey Street*
▶ *Approach from Southwark Street*

149

Inside, the 4,000-square-metre floor plates look onto a central atrium that is traversed at each floor level by wide, angled bridges. These link directly to the timber-faced lift core that rises through the 13 storeys of the building to a capacious rooftop terrace with spectacular views over the city. The arrangement allows for the potential letting of floors to different tenants.

The ground floor office entrances are integrated into the continuous shop fronts that wrap around the base of the buildings. With its new landscape of granite paving, trees, lighting and benches, the development proved instrumental in the subsequent regeneration of the Bankside district.

◀ *Blue Fin Building interior*
▶ *Bridges across the atrium*

10th floor plan

Ground floor plan

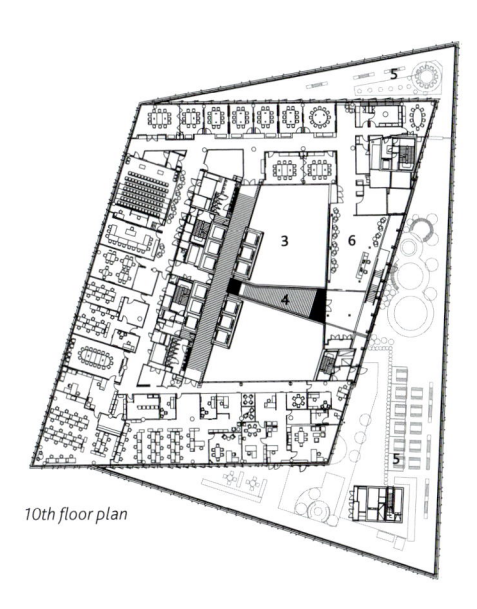

1	entrances	**5**	roof terrace
2	reception	**6**	service yard
3	atrium	**7**	shops and cafes
4	bridge	**8**	gym

151

Typical upper floor plan

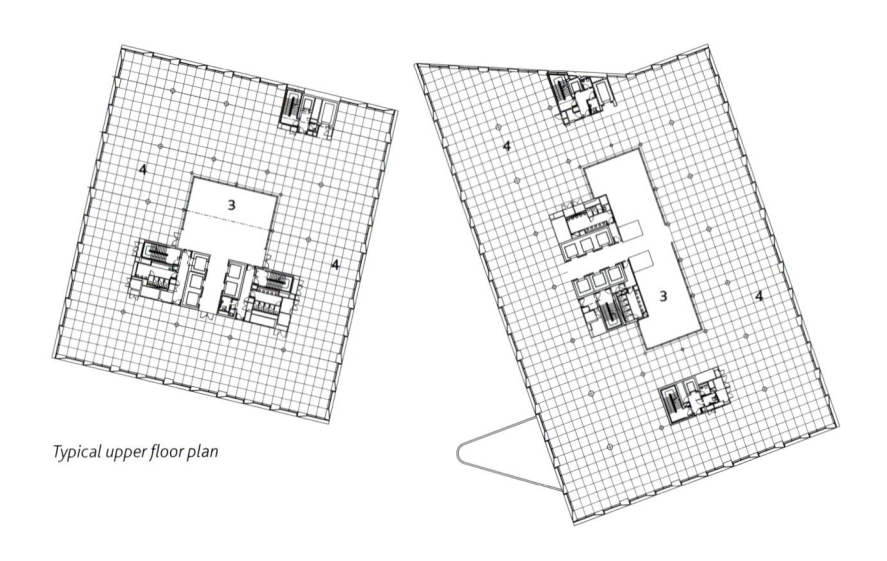

Bankside 2 and 3 were conceived as a pair. The buildings were designed to be separately let or, as subsequently happened, joined by a bridge that would form the backdrop to a new public space between them. Both are planned around a diminutive atrium and both reflect the tripartite arrangement of Bankside 1. Rather than repeating the light veil of fins of the larger neighbour, however, the facades are more robustly composed with a square grid of variegated terracotta panels angled to the line that bisects the wedge-shaped space between them. These panels follow identically in exact sequence around each of the two buildings but in opposite directions so that the detail inflects to the space they share. The effect of this inverse repetition is that while one building displays its horizontal terracotta patterning, the other reveals its perpendicular and naturally anodised aluminium surface.

Ground floor plan

1 *entrances*
2 *reception*
3 *atrium*
4 *office floor*
5 *large retail unit*
6 *small retail unit*
7 *service yard*

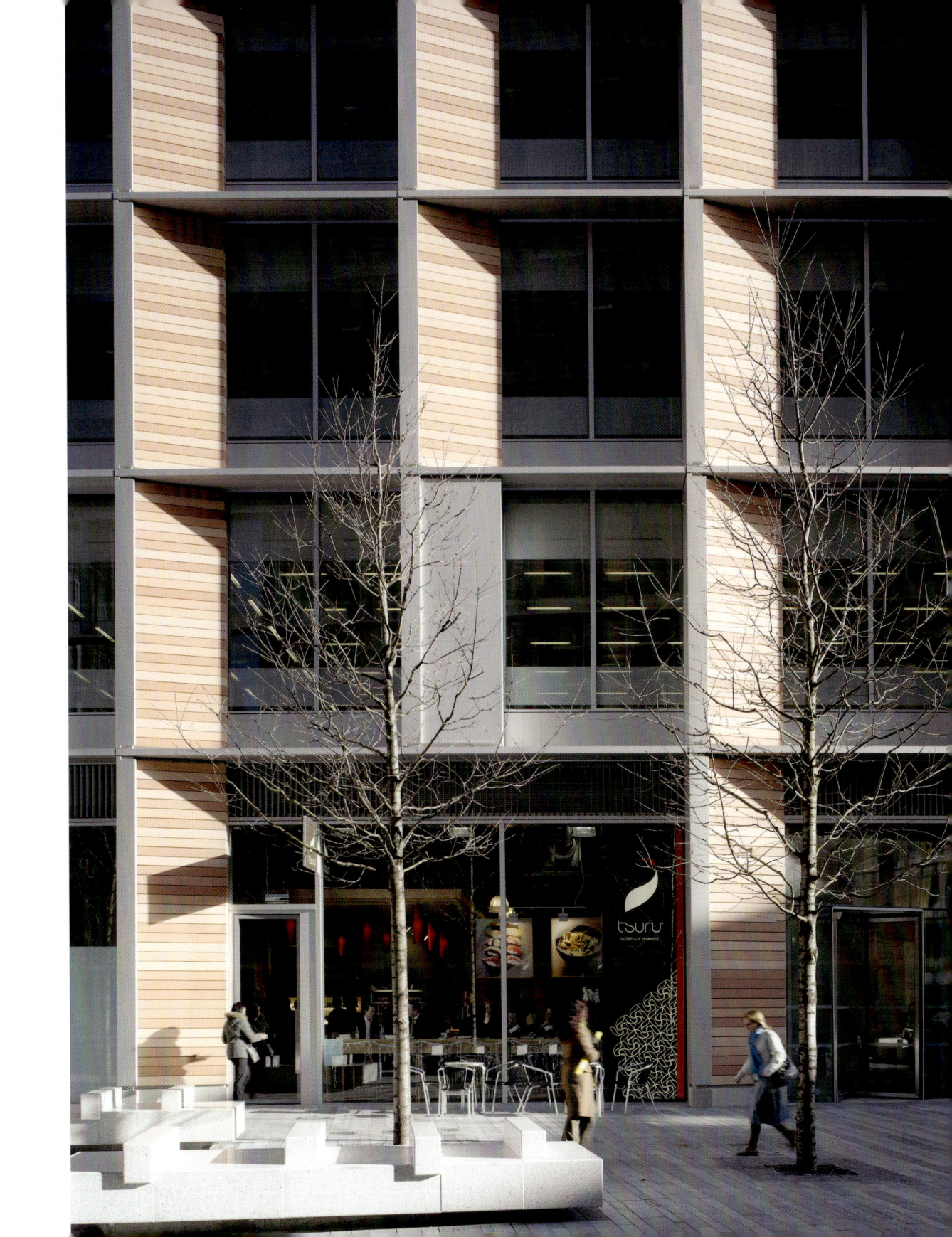

◀ *Asymmetrical window reveals highlight aluminium or terracotta on different facades*
▶ *Facade detail of Bankside 2 with ground floor retail units*

BOFORS TOWER

Dunkirk, Kent
2008–09

Bofors Tower, a grade-two-listed former anti-aircraft gun emplacement in Kent, was restored to provide a residential dwelling for Allies and Morrison partner Robert Maxwell and Frances Eustace. Constructed in 1940 to defend the key wartime radar station at Dunkirk, the abandoned structure consisted of two abutting concrete and brick buildings, each with its own staircase, and containing spaces that had the potential for conversion into accommodation. Set within a coppice and broadleaf wood on a hilltop, the building has raised views towards the river Swale, the Isle of Sheppey and the Thames Estuary.

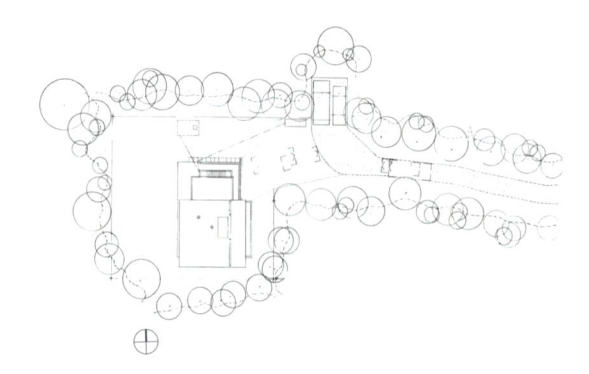

◄ *Staircase and oversailing roof*
► *West elevation*
▼ *West elevation before renovation*

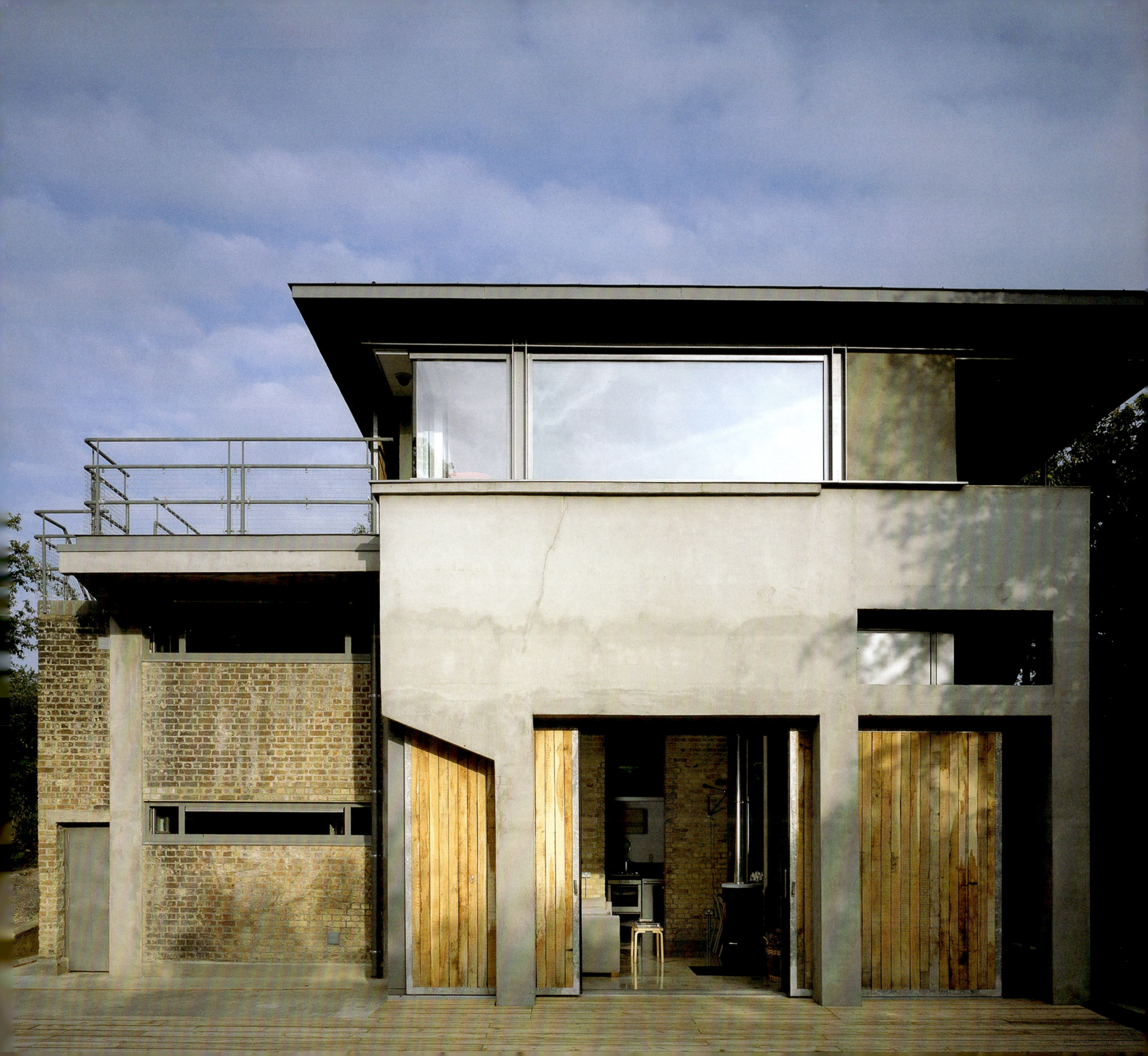

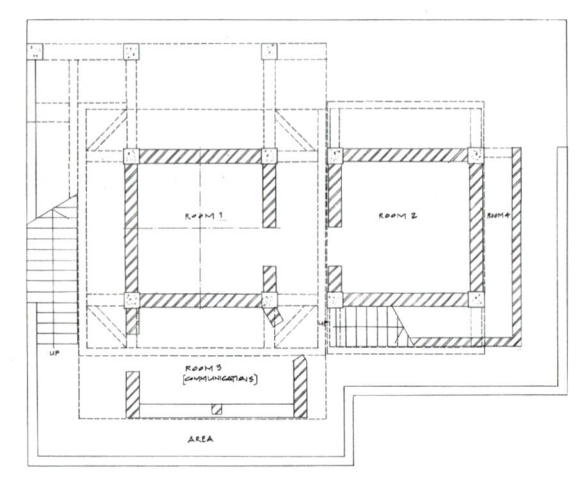

Ground floor plan before renovation

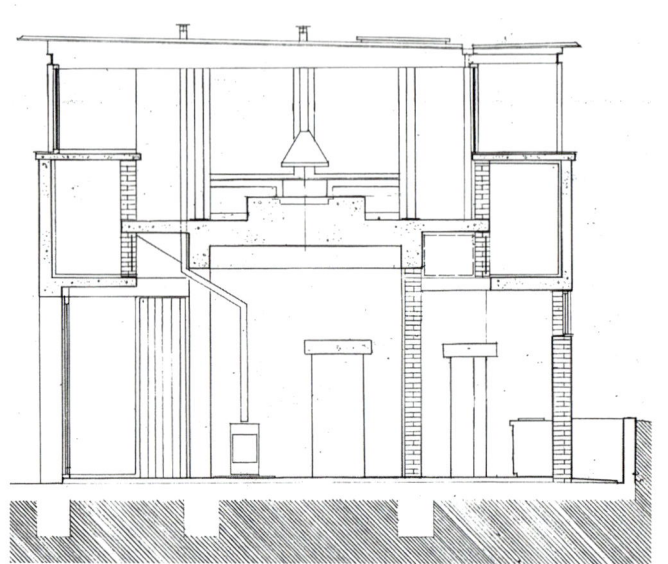

Cross section

The conversion retains the majority of the existing fabric and protects the original concrete roof from further weather damage. The new interventions include zinc and render facing to the external walls and timber panels and glazing set back within the existing frame. A new flat roof, supported on slender steel columns that align with the existing structure, oversails the main block on all sides and provides protection to the retained external south stair. Large glazed sliding doors, protected by separate panels of sawn green oak boards, open the interior spaces to a ground level external deck and the roof terrace.

The original gun emplacement remains legible within the completed building which now provides an idiosyncratic yet comfortable dwelling in its isolated and picturesque woodland setting.

◄ *Ground floor kitchen*
◄ *Upper floor with terrace*

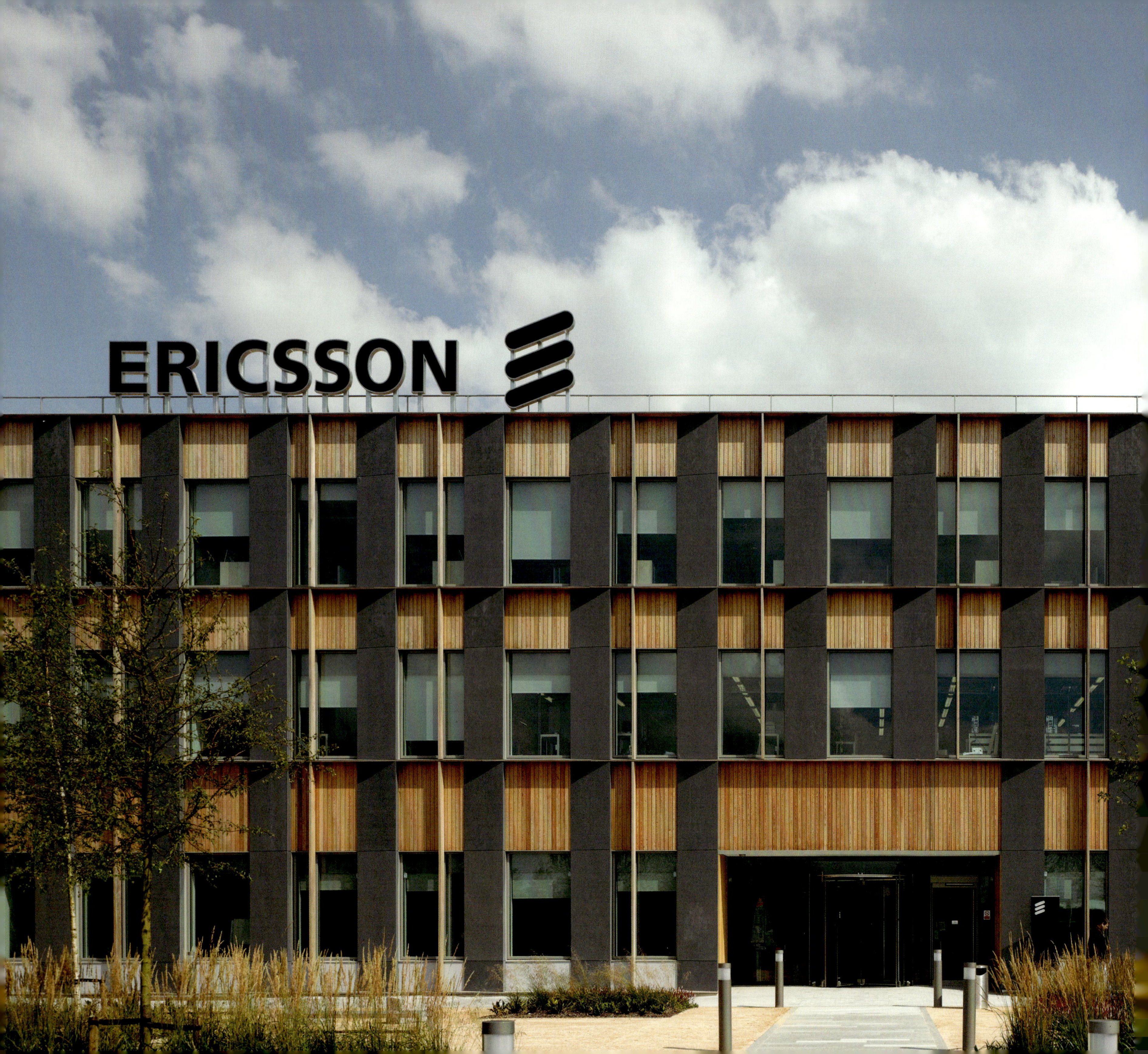
ERICSSON

ERICSSON HEADQUARTERS
Ansty Park, Coventry
2006–09

Two buildings form the first phase of a masterplan to develop part of the former RAF Ansty airfield, six miles west of Coventry, as a business park. The three-storey buildings, each identically planned around an atrium, accommodate 15,000 square metres of research and development facilities for the Stockholm-based telecommunications company Ericsson. In accordance with the overall landscape plan for the business park they are placed at right angles to one another so as to define a series of garden squares. With entrances facing the more major square and the staff restaurant opening to a shared garden, a hierarchy of spaces is formed to which the facades of the two buildings respond.

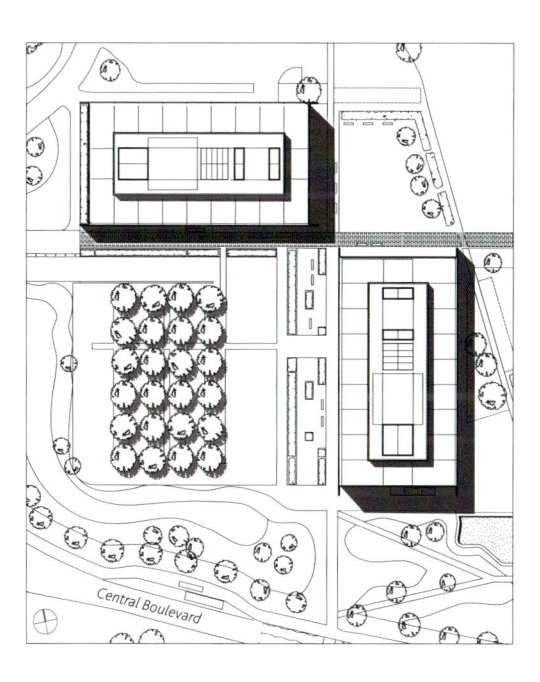

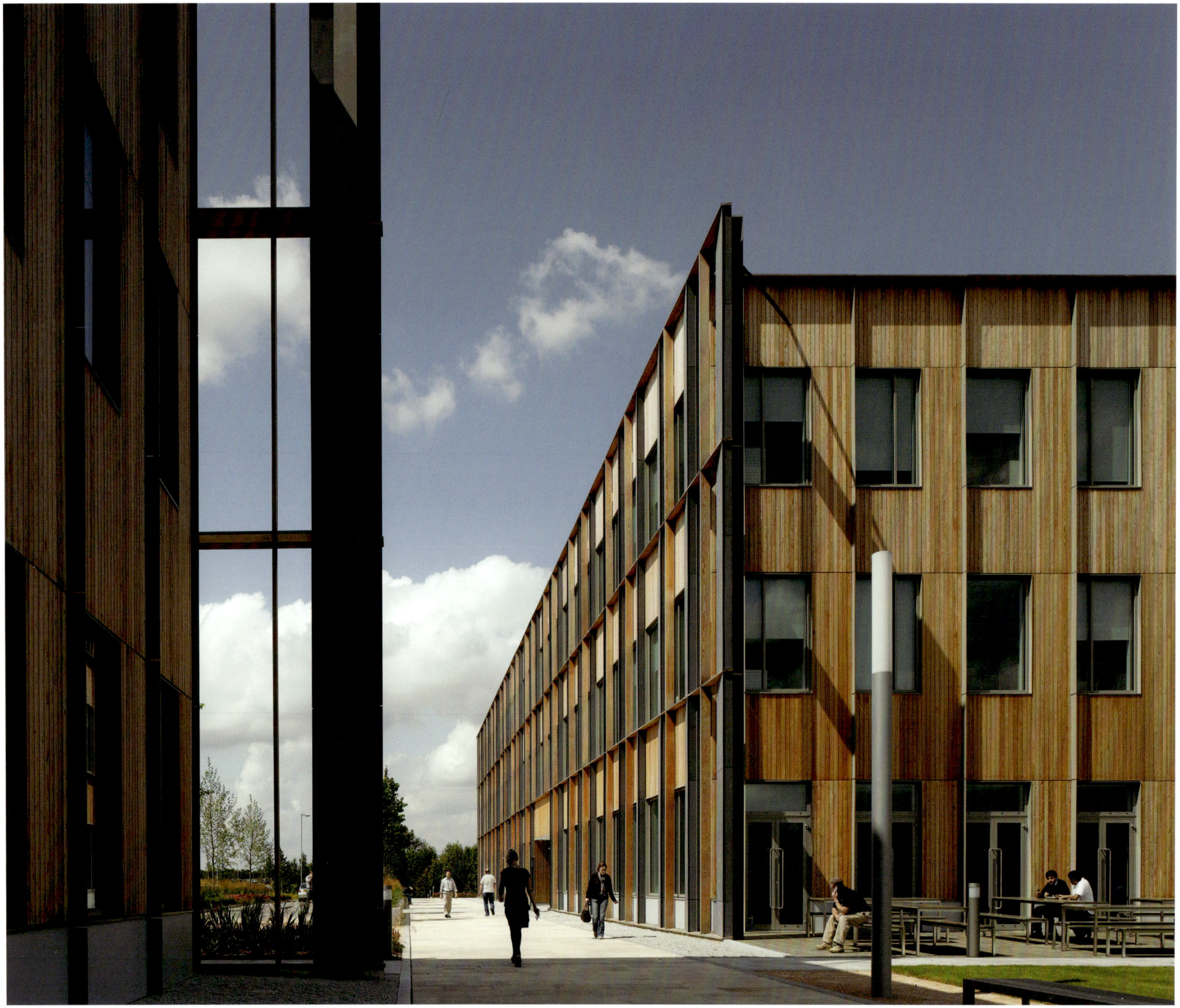

Timber is used extensively, both inside where the atria and main stairs are lined with thin, closely-spaced Siberian larch slats, and outside where the buildings are clad in untreated Douglas fir vertical boarding.

The elevations are composed in layers. The inner layer throughout is a repeating pattern of 1.5-metre-wide, floor-to-ceiling windows on a three-metre grid. Set in front of the window plane is a layer of timber boarding articulated by slender projecting timber 'mullions' that reach full height from the ground plane to the cornice. Added depth and significance is accorded to the two primary facades with an oversailing layer of angled fibre-cement panels on a counterpointed three-metre rhythm.

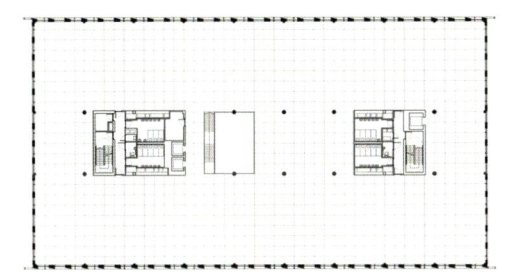

Typical floor plan

◀ *Public realm between the office buildings*
▶ *Interior staircase detail*

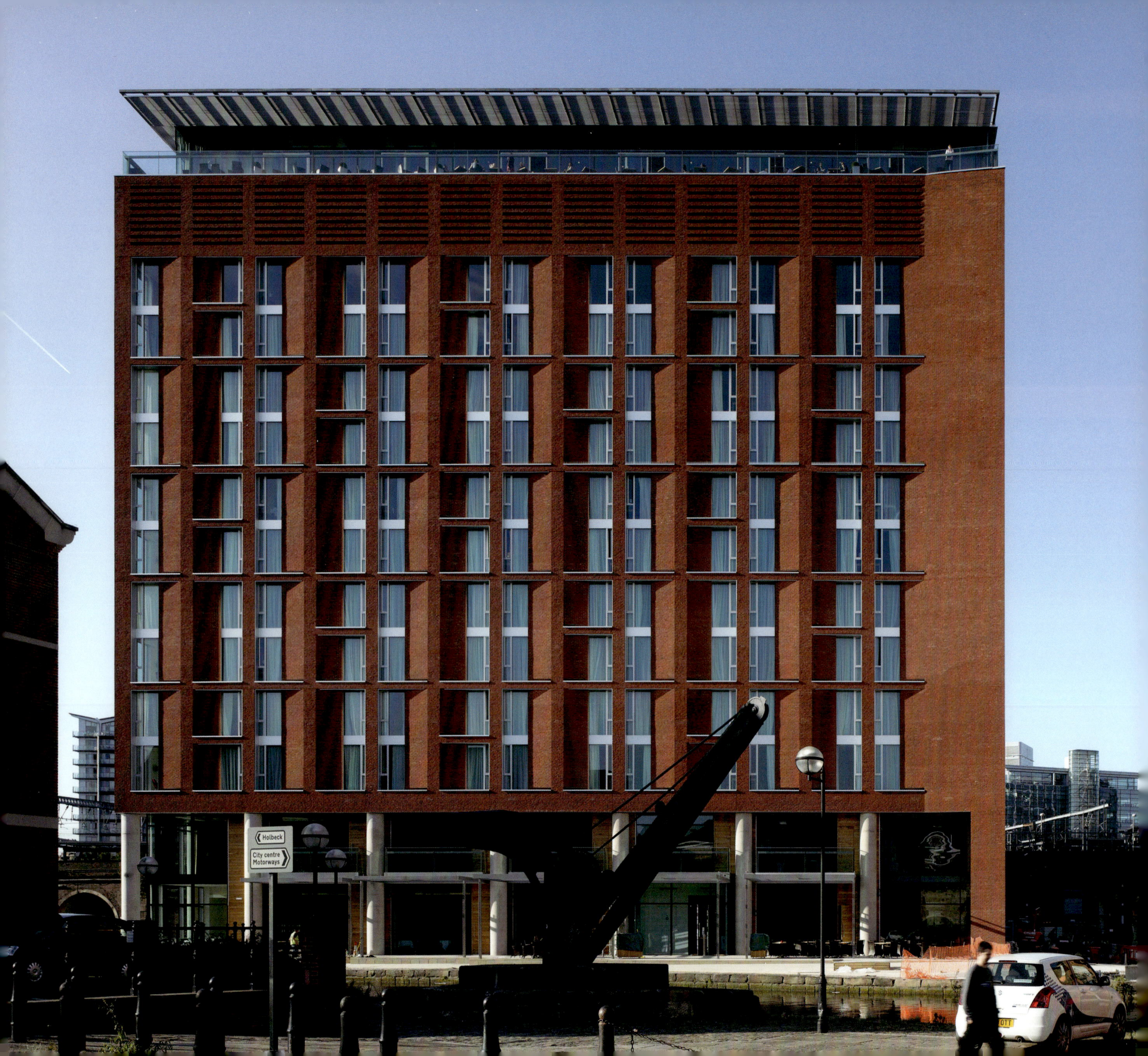
Holbeck
City centre
Motorways

MINT HOTEL

Granary Wharf, Leeds
2005–09

The site of Granary Wharf, already flanked by the River Aire, was further cut off from the centre of Leeds by the arrival of the canal and railway in the middle of the nineteenth century. Redevelopment of the site offered the opportunity to reintegrate the area with the city centre and provide a key point of connection with the surrounding conservation area of Holbeck Urban Village.

The masterplan for Granary Wharf identified potential locations for three buildings, with guidelines that they should be of a scale and character appropriate to the industrial history of the site. It also proposed that about two-thirds of the site should be allocated to public open space. Allies and Morrison was appointed to design one of the three buildings—a new hotel—at the centre of the site.

The design of the hotel responds to its location in three principal ways: through its orientation and configuration on the site; in its use of materials; and in the robustness of its form. The red brick facades – reminiscent of nineteenth-century mills and warehouses – adopt a tripartite devision into of bottom, middle and top, with a composition of double-storey openings intersected by deep orthogonal, or splayed, reveals that cut into the surface and allow light and shadow

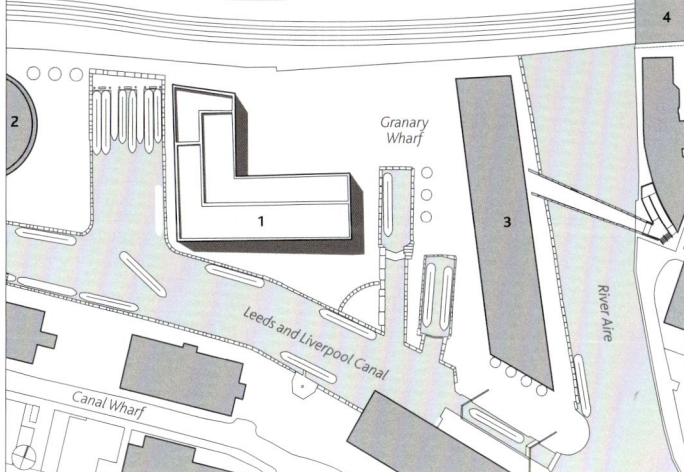

◀ *main facade following a tripartite arrangement*
▶ *View from the Leeds and Liverpool Canal*

1 *hotel*
2 *Candle House*
3 *Waterman's Place*
4 *Leeds Station*

to produce an effect ranging from transparency to opacity.

At the base of the building the masonry is replaced by tall in-situ concrete columns which emphasise the relationship between the ground-floor cafe and restaurant and the waterfront. At the top, above a floor of plant, the building terminates with a deep cornice in the form of a brise-soleil shading the south-facing rooftop bar.

While the primary orientation of the building is towards the canal to the south, the entrance is located on the north side within a freestanding steel and glass pavilion, held within the L-shape of the plan.

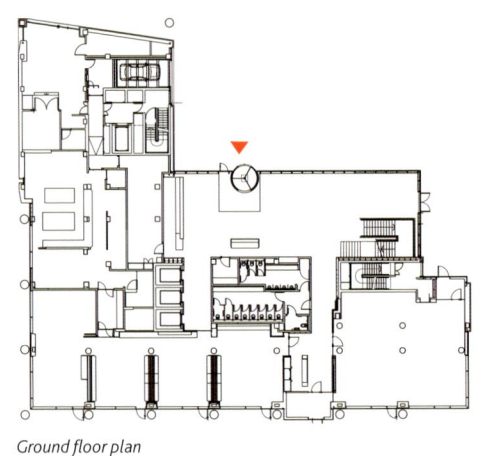

Ground floor plan

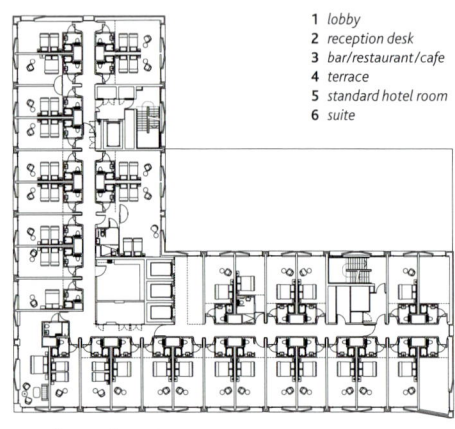

Typical upper floor plan

1 lobby
2 reception desk
3 bar/restaurant/cafe
4 terrace
5 standard hotel room
6 suite

▶ *Ground floor lobby*
◀ *Entrance foyer with reception*

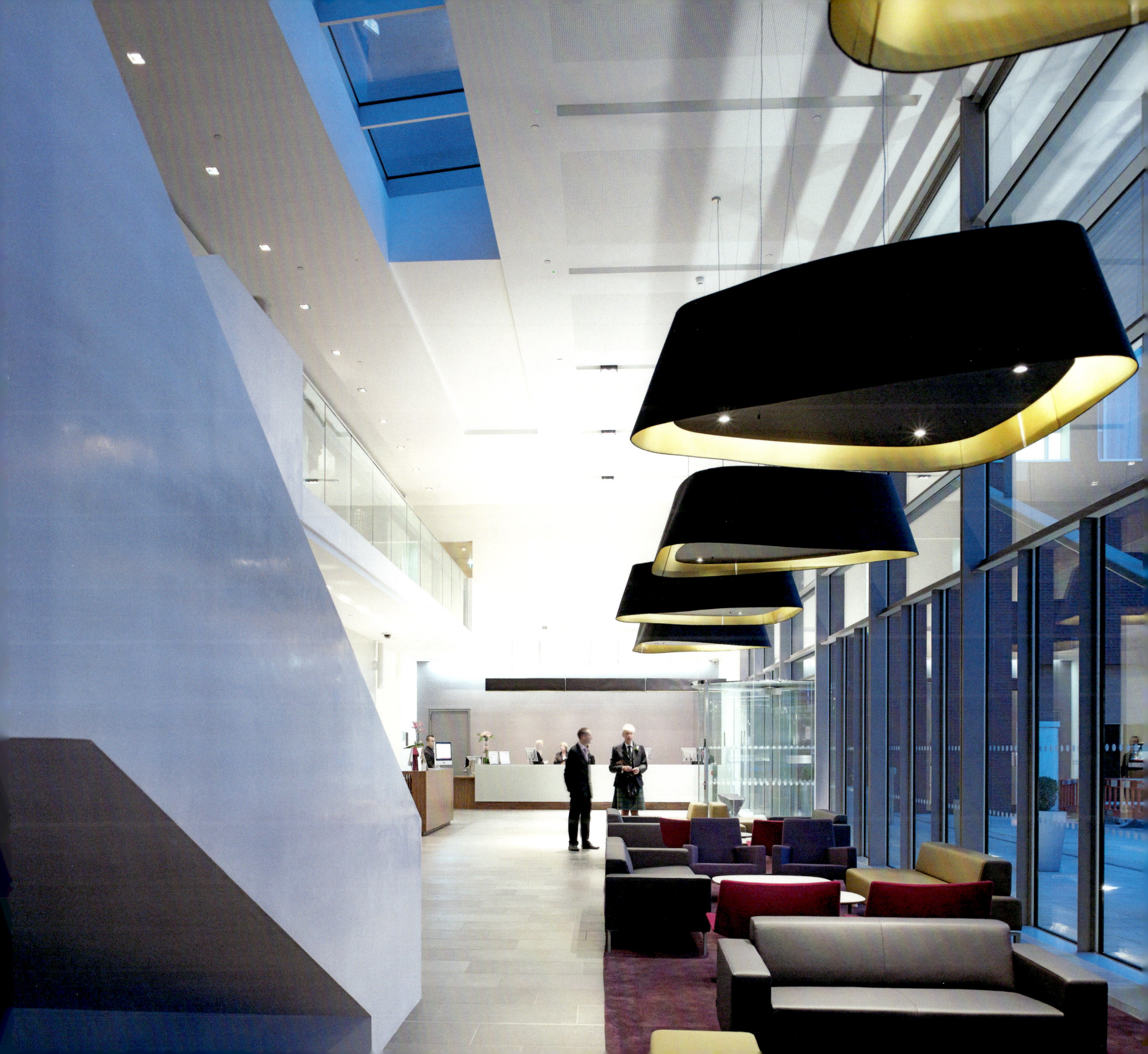

STUDENT HOUSING AND HOTEL

Southwark, London
2006–10

This student housing and hotel project, built on the site of a former car park, forms an integral component in the recovery of a lost London street. The reinstated Great Suffolk Street joins the network of routes between Southwark Station and Tate Modern, and so represents a significant contribution to the regeneration of the Bankside district.

The project accommodates 230 students in two separate structures, a six-storey building with shops at

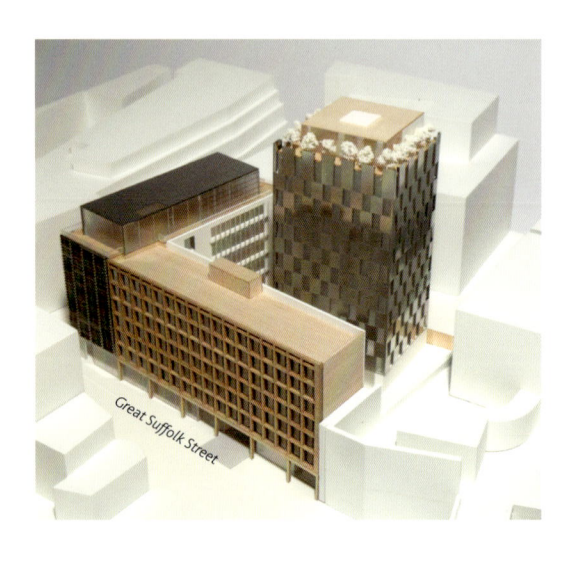

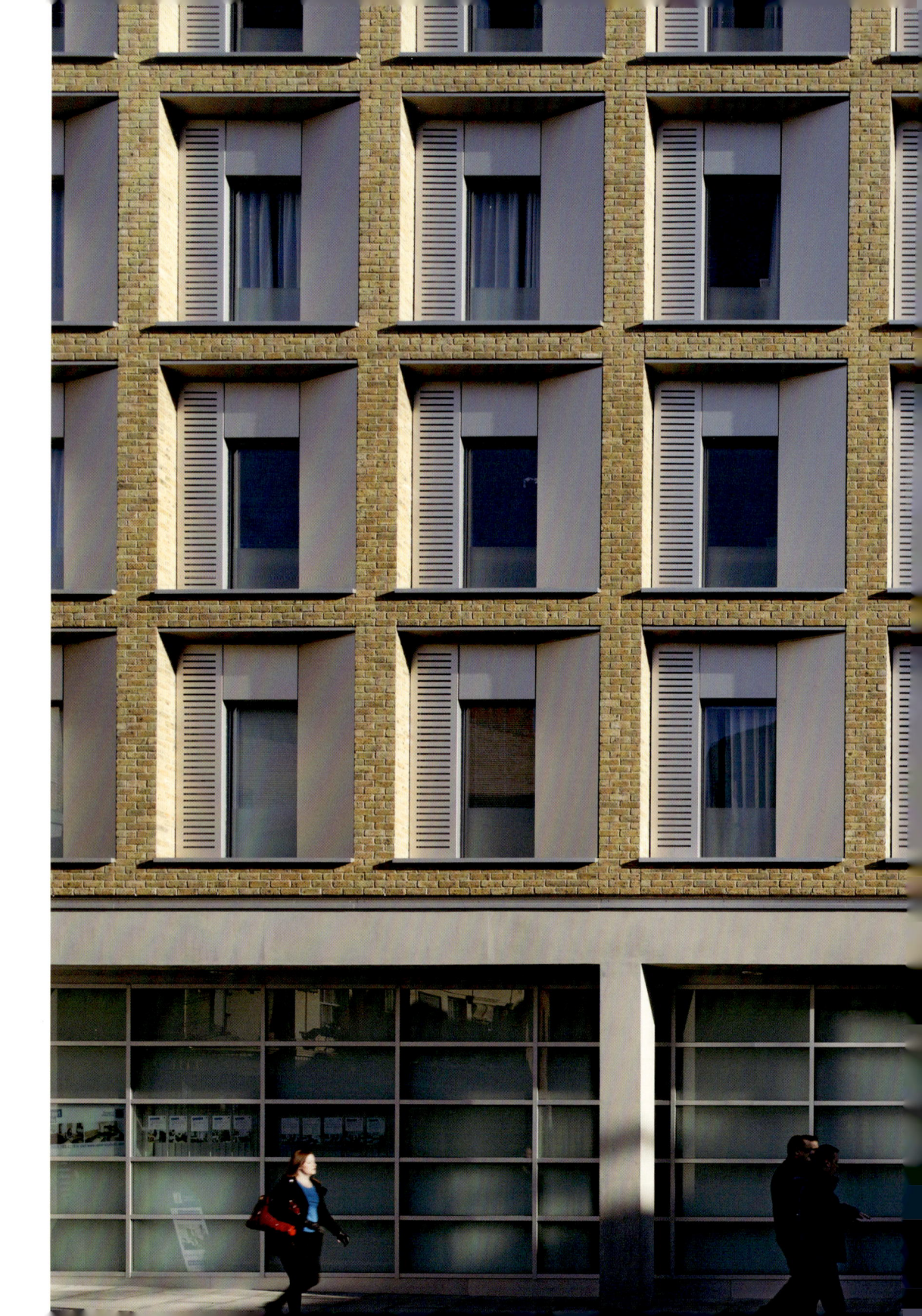

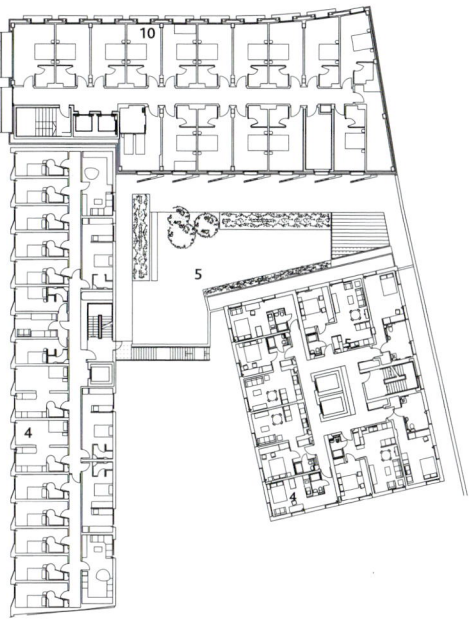

Typical upper floor plan

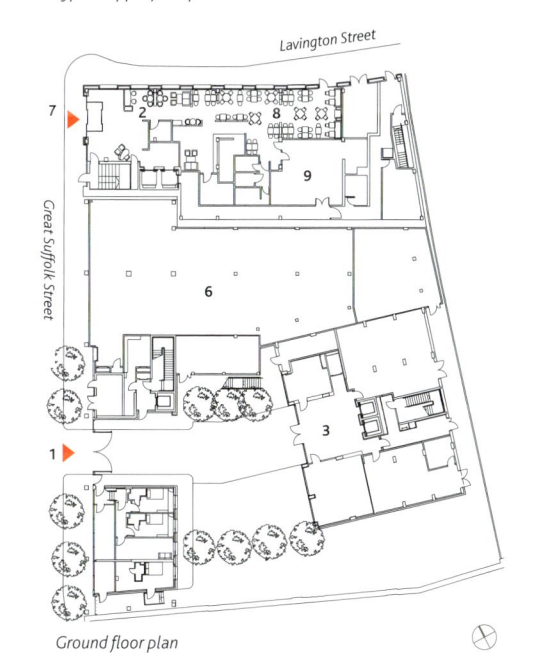

1 student housing entrance
2 reception
3 foyer
4 student room
5 terrace
6 retail unit
7 hotel entrance
8 restaurant
9 kitchen
10 hotel room

Ground floor plan

167

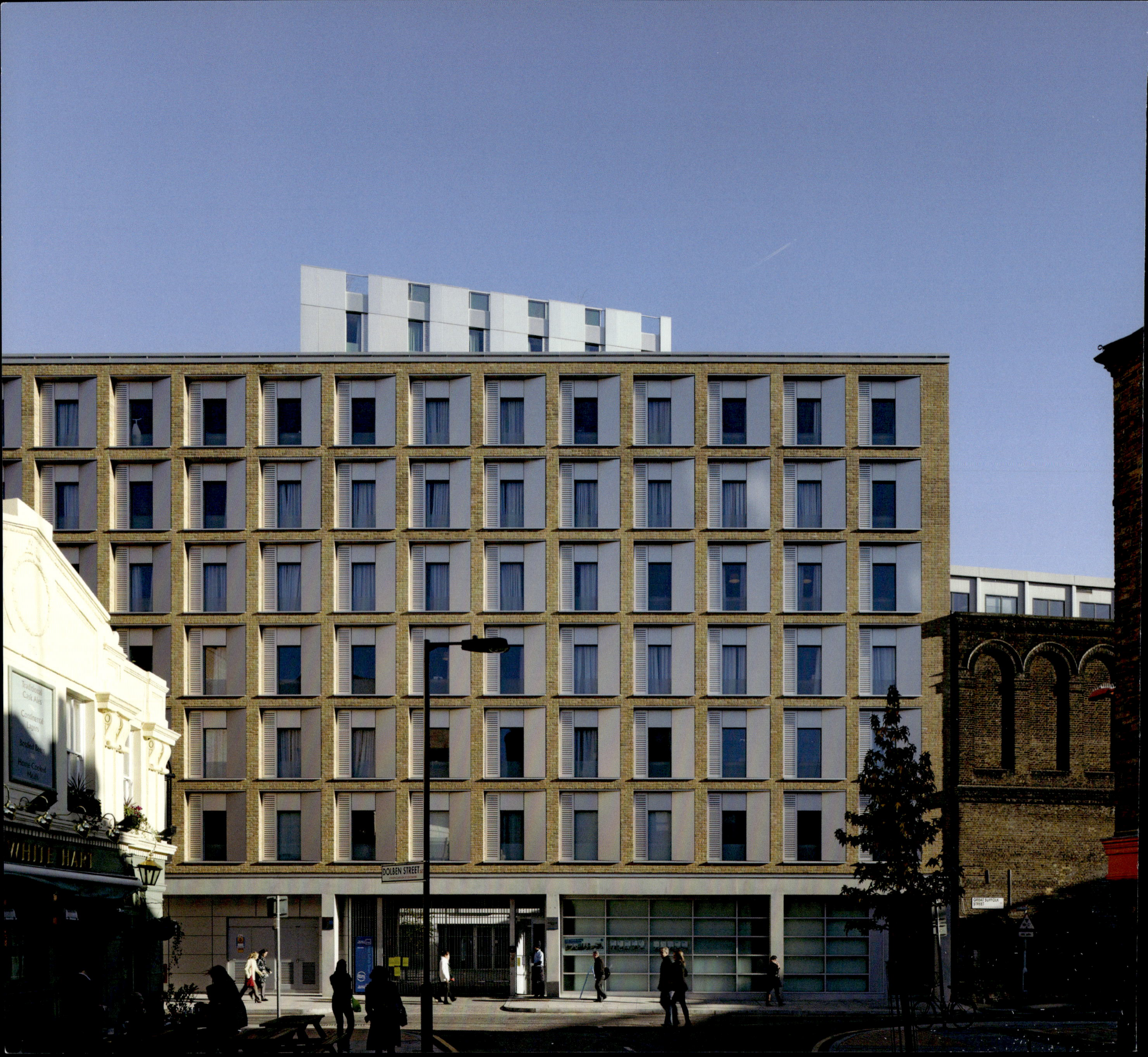
DOLBEN STREET

ground level that follows the line of the existing street, and a 13-storey tower within an inner courtyard.

The square tower is capped by a common room that opens onto a roof terrace. Set at an angle to the lower building, it is clad in an alternating chequerboard composition of glass and anodised aluminium panels that flows seamlessly around its corners in a continuous surface. The lower building, formed of prefabricated rooms, is also clad in anodised aluminium panels but set within a delicate brickwork frame. The more modelled, asymmetrical arrangement of these panels, inclined in plan to

◀ *Main facade on Great Suffolk Street*
▲ *Delivery of prefabricated rooms on site*
▶ *Courtyard facade*

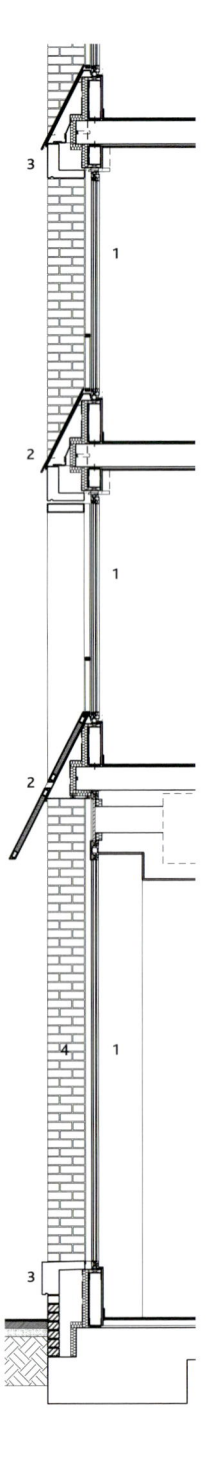

1 double-glazed aluminium windows
2 pre-weathered pigmented metal cill
3 reconstituted stone lintel
4 facing brick

allow southerly light into the rooms, leads to a distinctive but informal composition that reinforces the character of the new street. On the approach to Tate Modern, the facade appears to be composed entirely of brick, whereas from the other direction the aluminium is dominant.

The hotel occupies the corner site at the junction of Great Suffolk Street and Lavington Street, and shares a party wall with the student housing. The entrance on Great Suffolk Street gives access to the reception, guest restaurant and circulation core. Levels one to six each accommodate 16 rooms arranged on either side of a central circulation corridor.

Above, set back from the main facade, two further storeys with 26 rooms are configured as a zinc-clad roof pavilion.

The design of the hotel seeks to extend the enigmatic quality of the adjacent brick Victorian warehouses through simple massing, restrained materials, deep window reveals and expressed lintels, cills, copings and cornices.

◀ Hotel elevation on Lavington Street
▲ View along Great Suffolk Street
▲ Courtyard with student housing and the hotel

RIVER SOAR FOOTBRIDGE
Leicester
2010

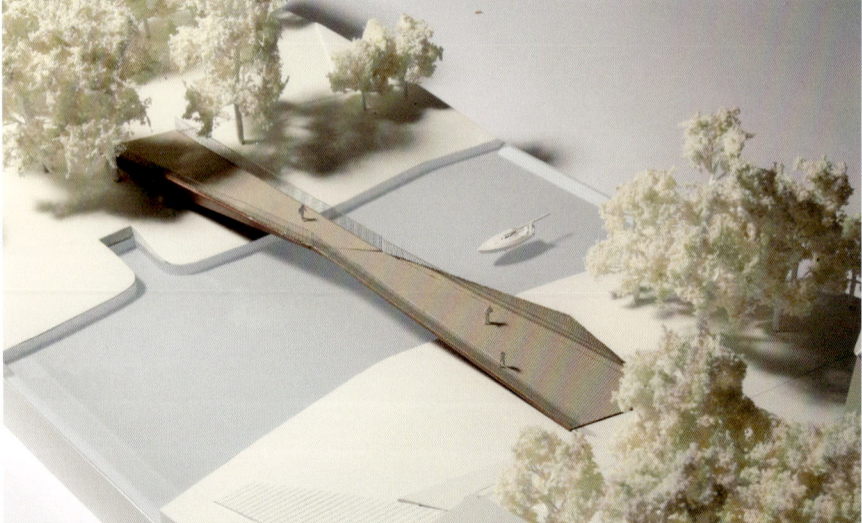

This competition proposal is for a foot and cycle bridge across the River Soar at Abbey Meadows in Leicester, adjacent to a former water tower on Wolsey Island and the National Space Centre. Designed with structural engineer Price & Myers, it is envisaged as a restrained response to the arcadian landscape that aligns the river as it flows gently through the north of the city.

Rather than a single structure, however, the proposal comprises two linked bridges that carry the landscape across the river within the simplest of folded enclosures. Both bridges are cantilevered from single piers on each bank. Their spans, deepest at the piers, extend to a minimal depth as they touch at the middle of the river. Here they provide the necessary headroom to allow for the passage of barges along the river while also forming a continuous timber deck for pedestrians to cross.

Each bridge has two parts: an 'outside', comprising a simple weathering steel plate, folded to form the asymmetrically cantilevered structure; and an 'inside', with a timber deck folded to touch the rim of the steel plate on one side but extending on the other to form a handrail, which at night provides a continuous lighting strip.

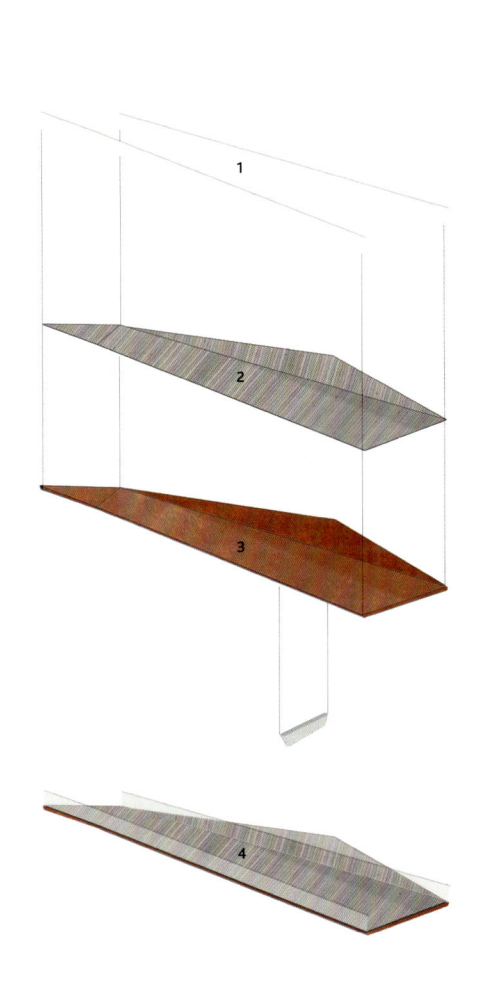

Isometric drawing showing individual
elements of the bridge

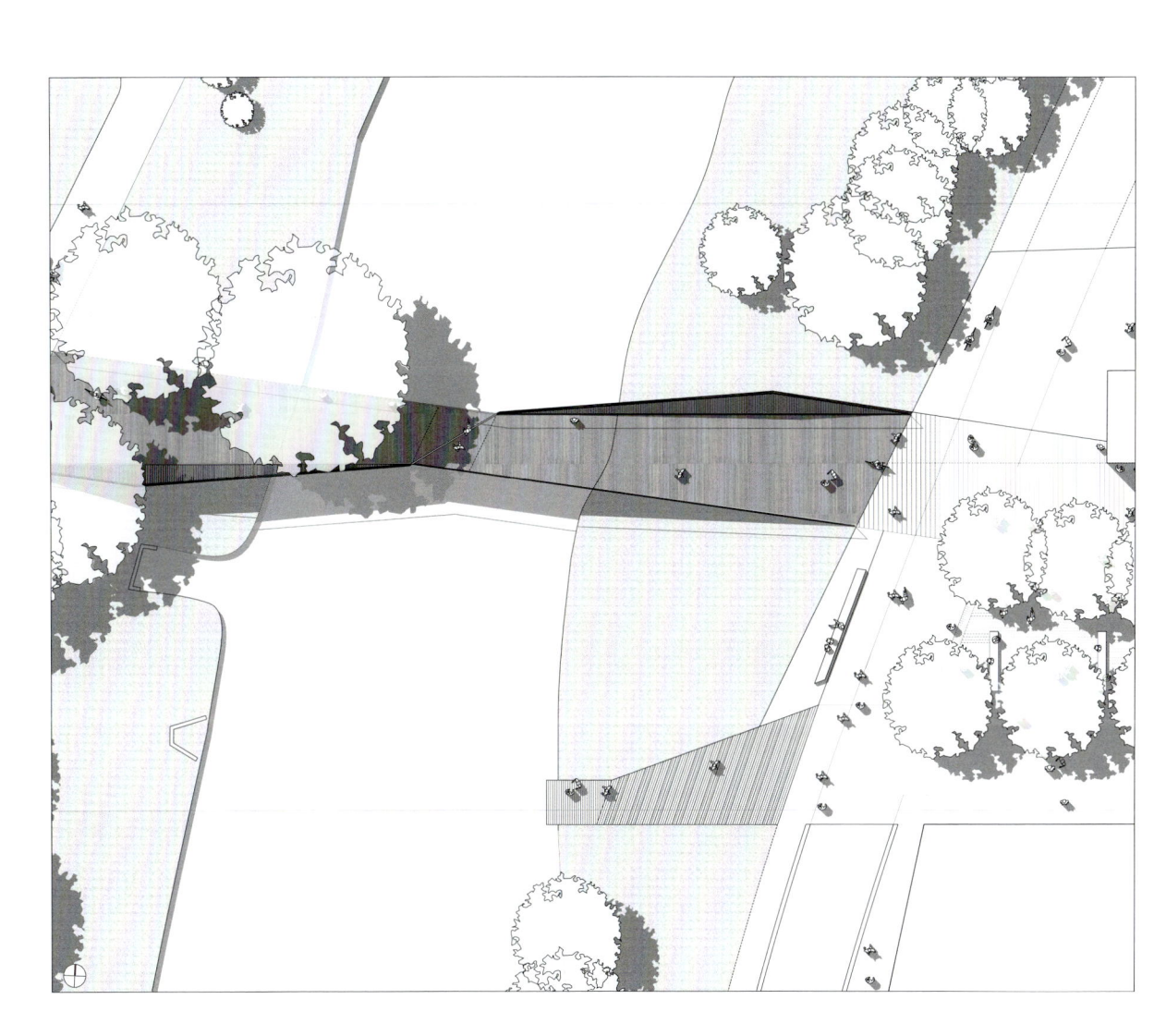

1 balustrade
2 timber desk
3 folded steel plate
4 concrete prop

173

120 MOORGATE
City of London
2010

This proposed nine-storey, 15,000-square-metre office building was designed for a site at the corner of Moorgate and South Place, where it would signal the 'entrance' to the City of London from Islington.

The prominence of the angular form is enhanced by a 'fold' in the Moorgate elevation. The increased legibility this affords reveals a basic compositional order – a tripartite division of two-storey retail base, flat-fronted office facade and steeply inclined roof – that reflects that of its southerly neighbour, Edwin Lutyens' Britannic House.

The elevational asymmetry of 120 Moorgate derives from the angled cornice, where the 'facade' becomes 'roof', as it negotiates the height differences between its South Place neighbour and Lutyens' building.

This composition is in two parts. An inner volume, structured by the rigorously repetitive order of its office planning discipline, is shaped by its planar relationship to its external context into a crystalline form. The envelope, conceived as a delicately etched metal plate, is folded precisely around the inner volume. The counterpoint of inner grid and external plane is referenced in the complexity of its pattern; a complexity further elaborated by smaller, repeating folds that provide solar shading to the roof, and by the chequerboard composition of the facade, in which white cast glass panels resonate with the Portland stone of its neighbour.

▲ Junction of Moorgate and South Place
▶ Etched metal facade model
▶ Elevation of Moorgate facade

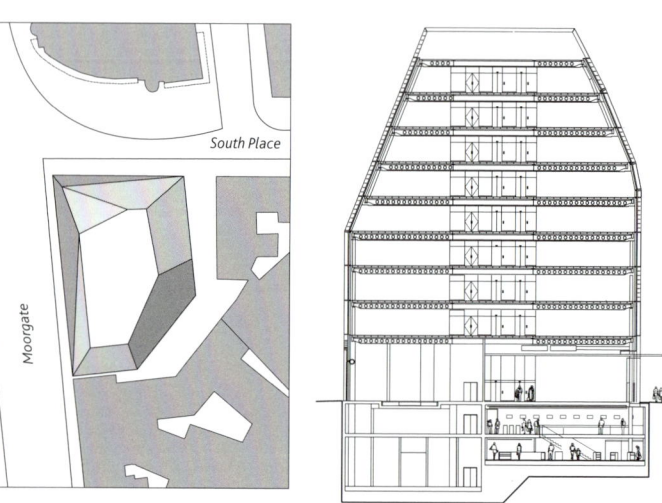

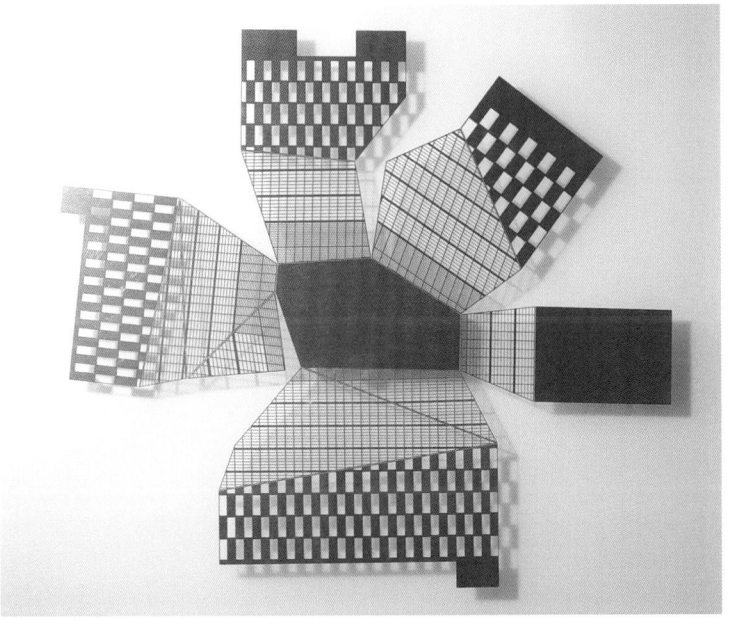

1 metal brise soleil
2 aluminium louvres
3 cast glass
4 retail ventilation zone
5 retail glazing

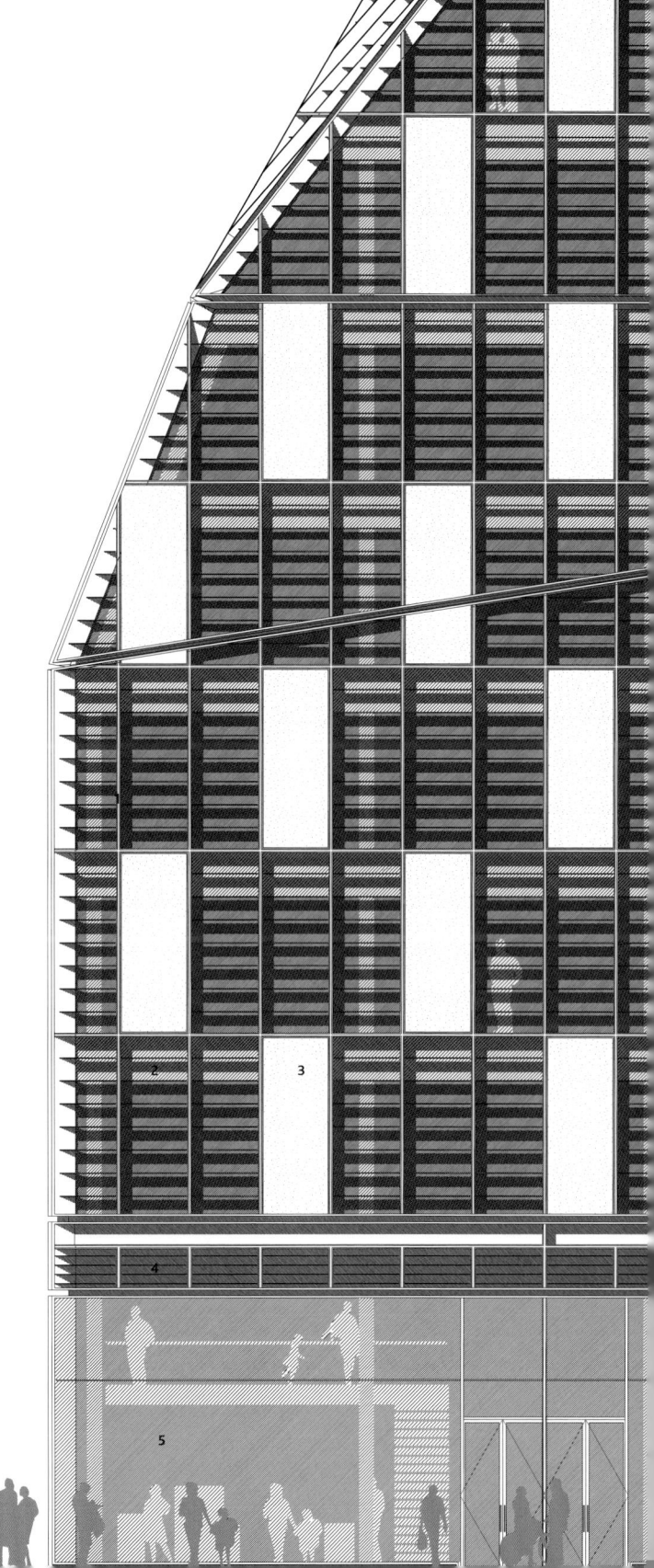

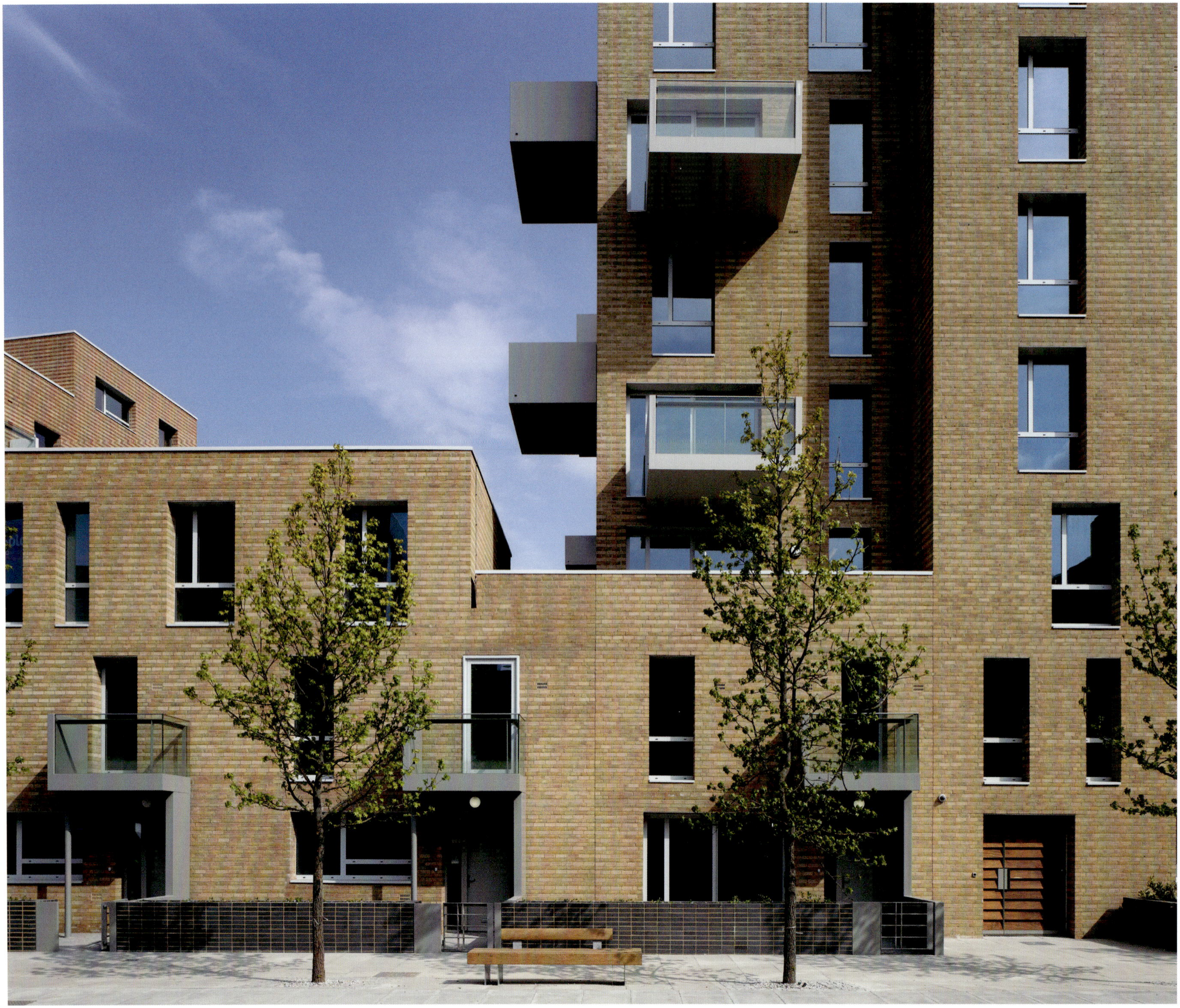

ST ANDREW'S BOW
Bromley-by-Bow, London
2008–11

Because of its extent, and the presence to the east of an elevated section of an inner-city motorway and to the north of a railway cutting, a new development in this rather fragmented east London setting needed to establish a strong, urban structure that would allow the new buildings to be integrated into the surrounding urban fabric and secure continuity of the associated public realm.

Three large residential courtyards, aligned north-south, dominate the plan. Between them, tight streets provide access to residential cores and ground-floor apartments, and combine car parking and play areas in an informal landscape. While the streets are fully public, the courtyards are communal spaces intended exclusively for use by the residents, thereby providing secure areas for smaller children to play, unaccompanied but overlooked.

The heights of the main buildings vary between eight and ten storeys, their stepped profiles allowing the introduction of large private balconies to the top-floor family duplexes. Along the south side, however, the height of the blocks is reduced to allow sun into the gardens

Typical floor of residential court A

1 *residential court A – Allies and Morrison*
2 *health centre – Allies and Morrison*
3 *residential court B – Maccreanor Lavington*
4 *residential court C – Glenn Howells Architects*
5 *residential tower D – Allies and Morrison*
6 *residential tower E – Allies and Morrison*
7 *community centre – Allies and Morrison*

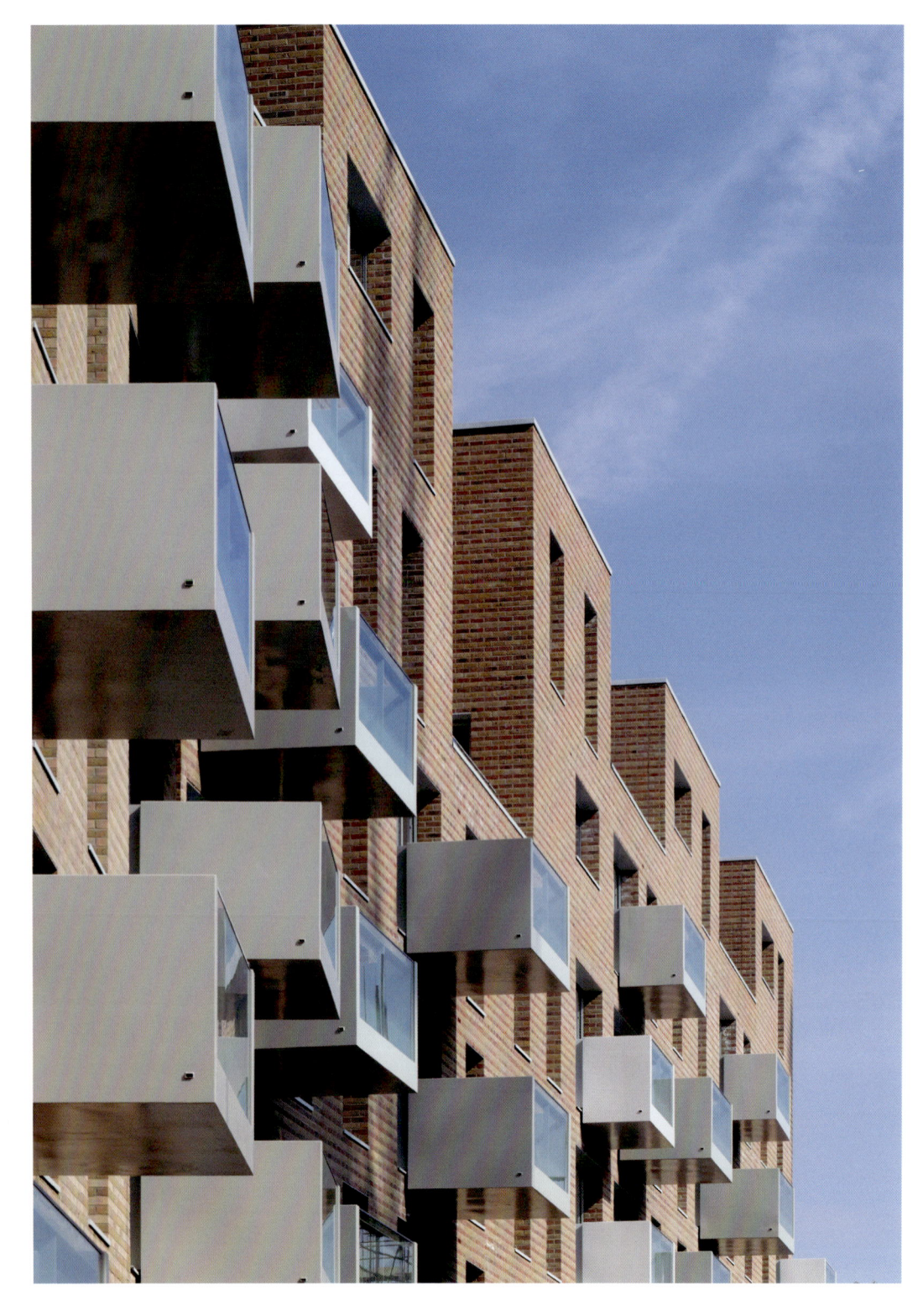

throughout the day. In addition to the three courtyard blocks, the masterplan envisaged two taller towers, in the north-west and north-east corners. The latter occupies a key location next to the motorway and to Bromley-by-Bow underground station, as well as forming the backdrop to a new urban park.

Having prepared the masterplan, Allies and Morrison was commissioned to design the first courtyard, with the other two by Maccreanor Lavington and Glenn Howells Architects. All of the buildings are faced in brick, and in Allies and Morrison's first phase this takes the form of horizontal stripes in two colours, offset by deep window reveals and punctuated by projecting steel and glass balconies.

◀ *Detail of residential balconies*
▶ *Communal space between the blocks*

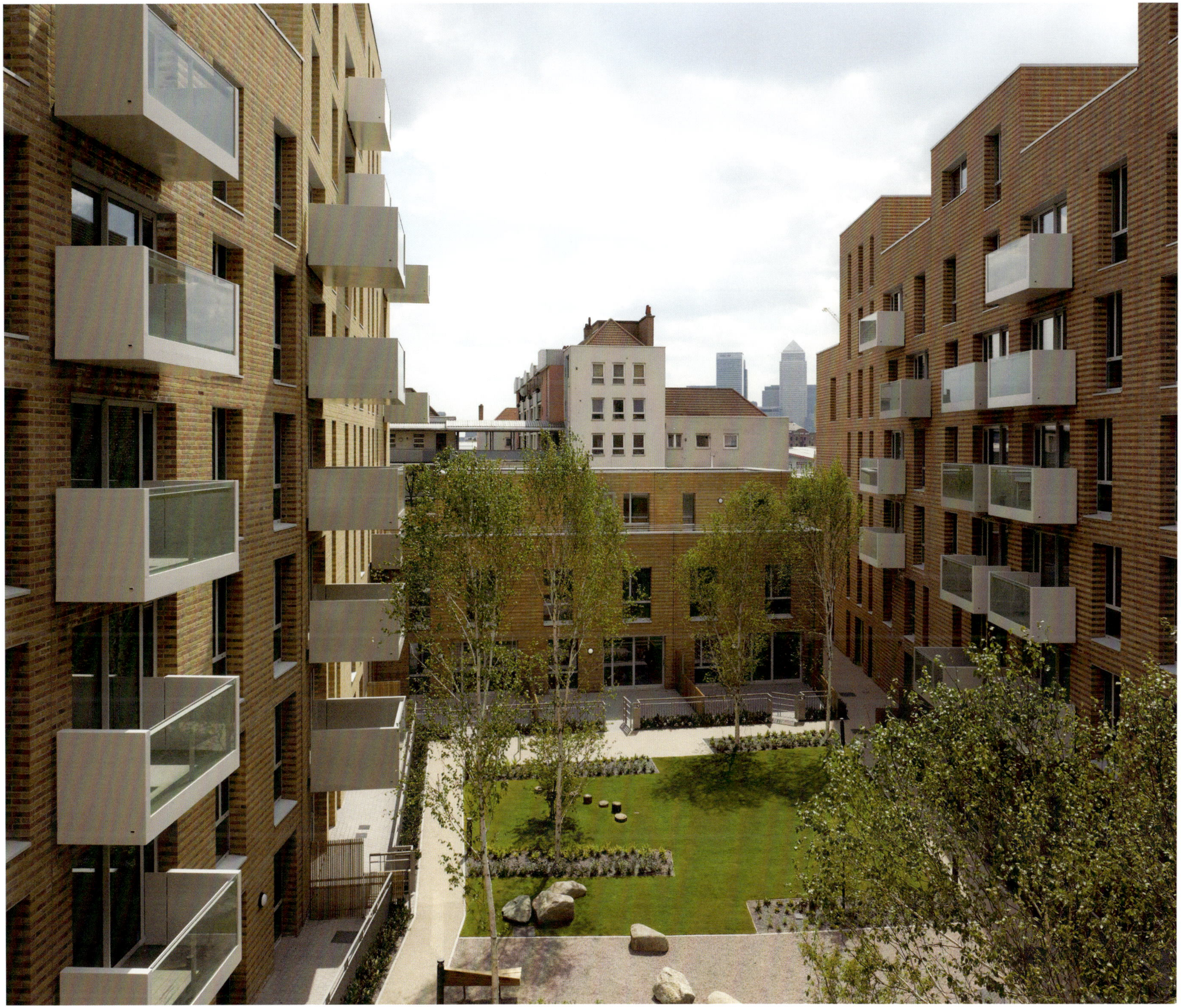

A community centre, forming a barrier between the busy road and the public park, is arranged over two large flexible floors, with potential access to a roof terrace. The ground floor opens up onto the public space, providing space for a community cafe.

Allies and Morrison revisited the first courtyard block, fitting out a new health centre and completing the community facilities. The accommodation is arranged over two floors around a small courtyard, providing natural light and privacy to the consultation rooms, with residential accommodation above.

In the residential tower, the flats are expressed in a range of colours, using different bricks for each vertical element. A central linear core gives access to the flats, freeing the entire external perimeter for ample windows and projecting balconies throughout. The stepped roofscape, which reflects the required mix of units, provides roof terraces at each step, some of which are private to the adjacent units.

The tower and community centre complete the scheme at the eastern end of the site. They face onto the principal public space, a park designed to allow step-free access to the adjacent underground railway station, sheltered from the busy road.

At ground level, a fitness centre, the site-wide concierge office and a convenience store enliven this key entrance to the development. A limited amount of car parking is provided on two levels below the park.

◀ *Community centre brick facade*
◀ *Interior of St Andrew's Health Centre*
▶ *Residential tower D with sculpted landscape*

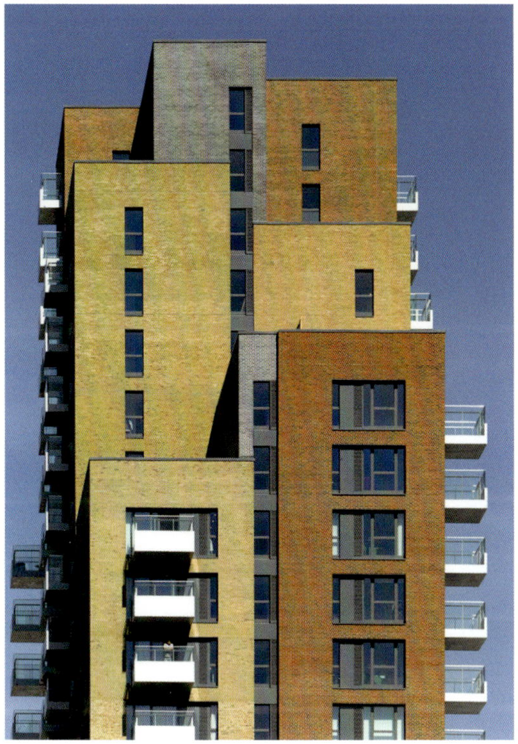

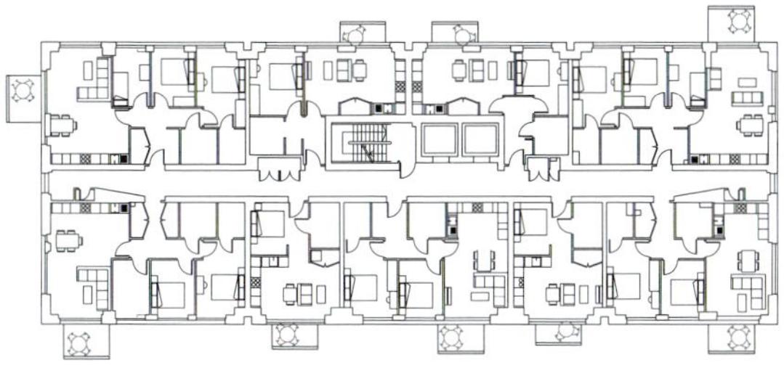

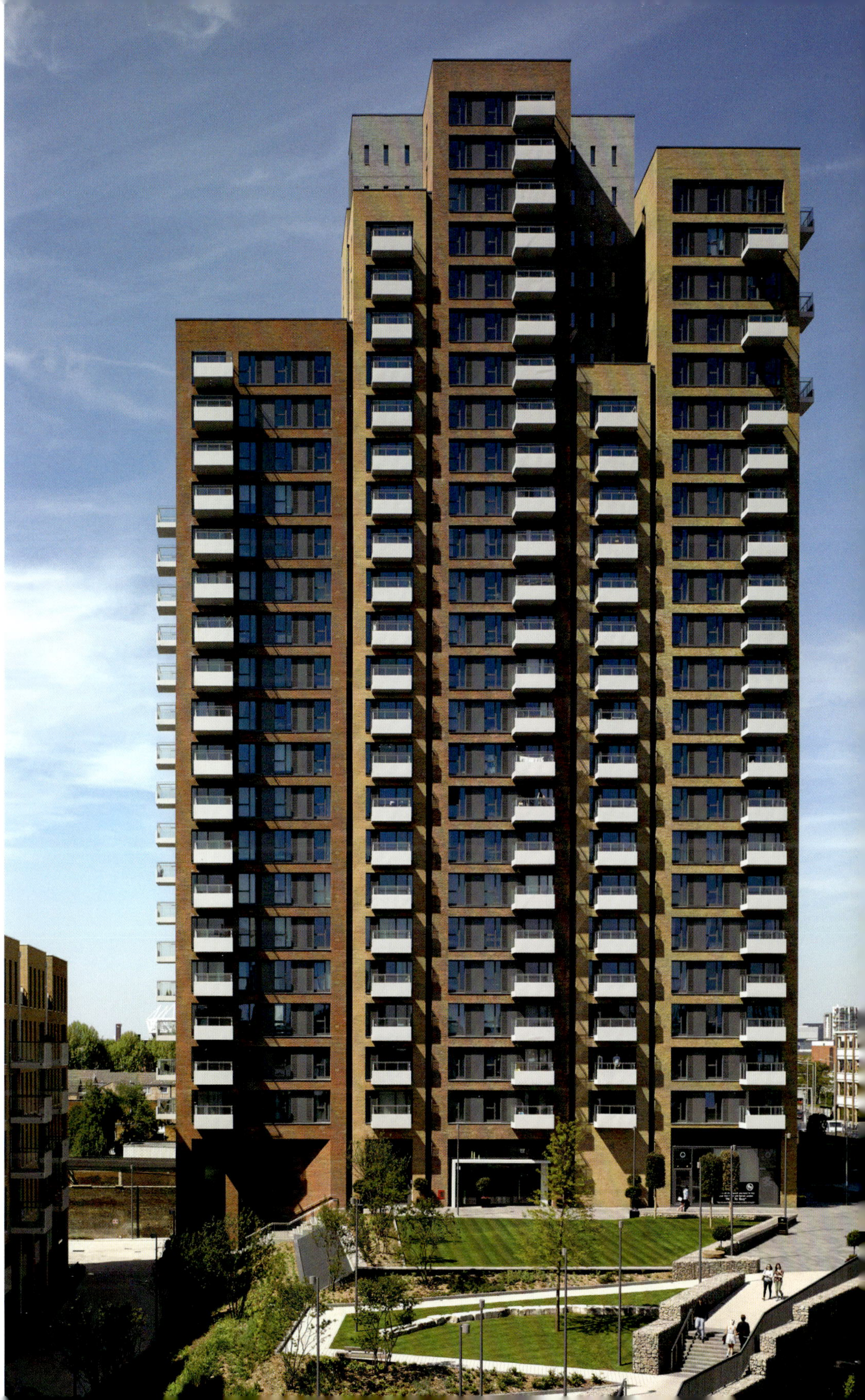

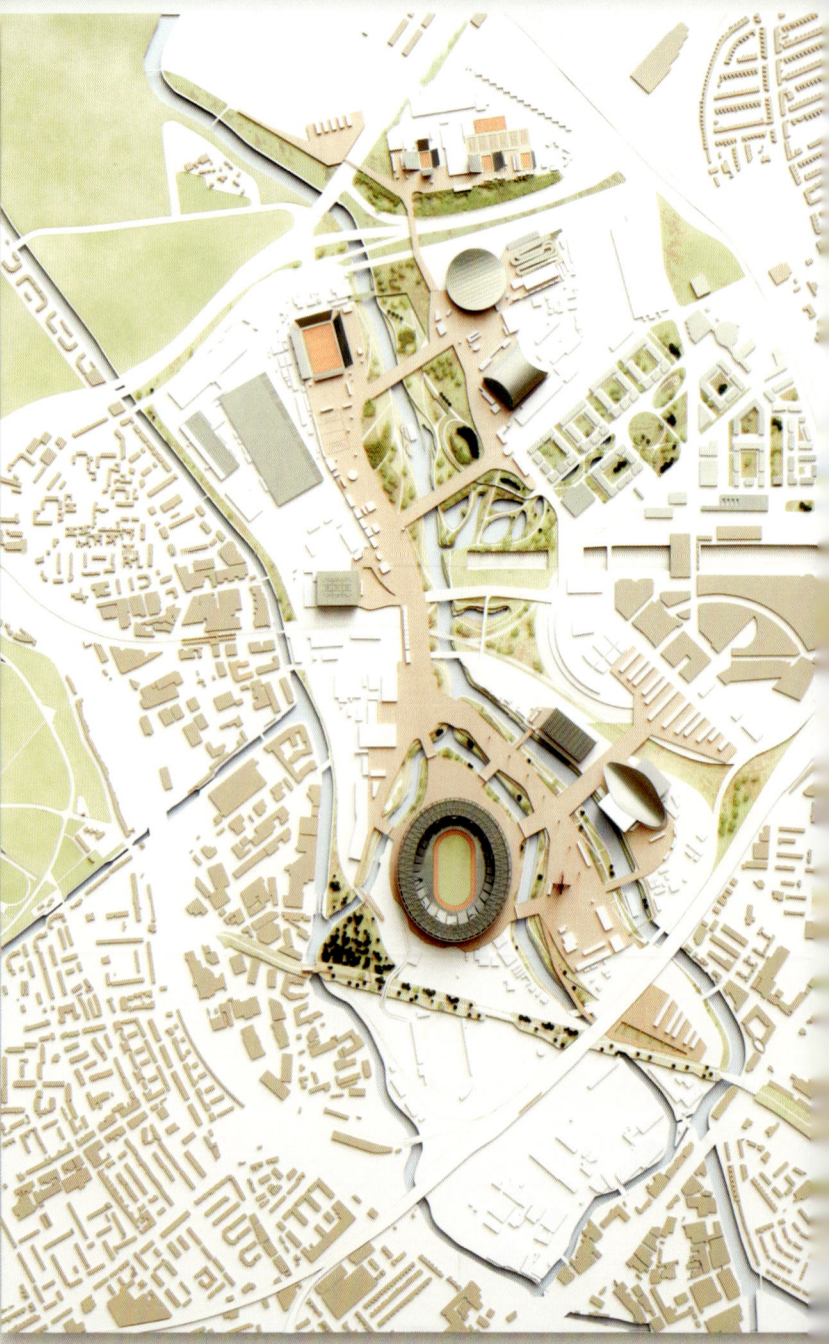

2000

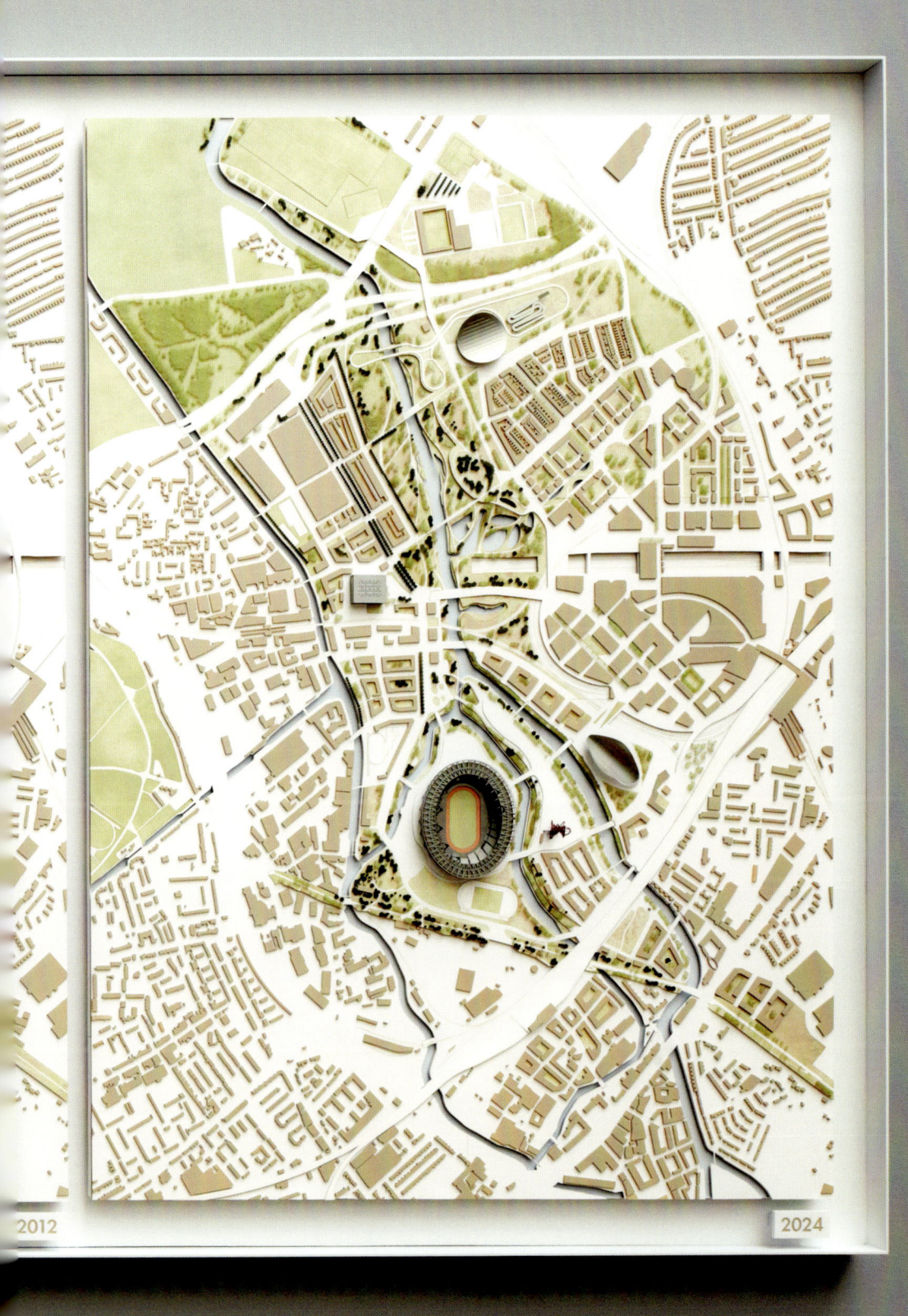

2012 OLYMPIC GAMES AND LEGACY

Stratford, London
2003–12

Allies and Morrison was one of a team of four consultants responsible for preparing the masterplan that underpinned London's successful bid to host the 2012 Olympic and Paralympic Games. The practice was subsequently appointed to develop and implement the masterplan for the 240-hectare site that formed the Olympic Park, to design much of its infrastructure, to prepare its 'legacy' masterplan and, to design many of the temporary structures at other key Olympic venues.

The location for this bid was the Lower Lea Valley at Stratford in East London. Here the River Lea, which flows south into the Thames, had long formed a divide separating the body of the city from its eastern extension. The river's low-lying, marshy and flood-prone valley was difficult to

◀ *Tryptich masterplan model showing site before, during and after the Games in legacy mode as exhibited at the Royal Academy Summer Exhibition in 2012*

bridge or develop, so it had become the location for many of those essential back-of-house functions needed to sustain the growing metropolis. In effect, it acted as London's backyard, with bus depots, stabling for underground trains, sewage treatment works, gasworks, power generation and transmission facilities, railway sidings, warehousing, goods distribution, urban motorways, waste storage and waste treatment, all neighbours to a significant group of eighteenth-century mill buildings lying immediately to the south of the Olympic site.

Ironically, the more its roads and buildings were configured to fulfil this strategic role, the more fragmented its local infrastructure became. The series of trunk roads that cross the site from east to west contrasted, prior to the Games, with only one east-west local road. A key aspect of the Olympic plan was, therefore, to initiate a more complex and comprehensive network of connections across the valley – including a series of new bridges – which in turn provided the framework for the legacy development planned to follow the Games. A similar opening-up was also possible in the north-south direction. With the

▲ Aerial view looking north, with Regent's Canal and the Olympic site in 2012
◄ Fridge 'cemetery' shows the former character of the site (far left) and the site in 2003 (left)
▶ The two drawings were produced to expose the difference between the frequency and variety of existing east-west vehicular and pedestrian routes pre and post Olympic Games.

Pre-Olympic Games

Post-Olympic Games

New local Road
Major Road
Local Road
Minor Road
Rail

185

Legacy park 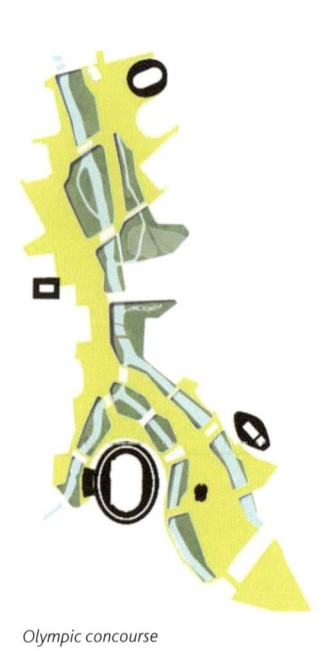   *Olympic concourse*    *Valley landscape*

catalyst of the Games, the River Lea offered the prospect of a continuous footpath and cycle path linking the city with its rural hinterland – the first of its kind in London and perhaps the only one that will ever be feasible.

Though the local infrastructure needed repair, a surprising asset of the site was the quality of its existing public transport provision: three underground lines, two main line railways, and in recent years, an extension of the Docklands Light Railway and the Eurostar station at Stratford International. The high-speed international station and future Crossrail station at Stratford provided the focus for a major new urban development – Stratford City – the construction of which was substantially progressed prior to the Games. During the Games, Stratford City provided the location for the Olympic village, a temporary home for 15,000 athletes designed to revert to permanent residential use after 2012.

Olympic Park

The Olympic Park was planned across two discrete topographical layers: a lower level established by the waterways that meander through the site, and an upper level defined by the platform of the public concourse on which the various venues were constructed. The scale and configuration of the concourse was developed principally in response to the predicted visitor numbers – up to 250,000 people during the busiest days of the Games. After the Olympics the extent of the concourse was substantially reduced, replacing much of the previously paved area with planting. In this way, a landscape designed initially to accommodate huge numbers of people at a global event evolved into a public park, meeting the future needs of a community. Of the principal sporting venues, just four were retained – the Stadium, Aquatics Centre, Handball Arena and Velodrome – and while each of these buildings continued to maintain a relationship with the park, they have also become part of the new urban district.

Legacy Masterplan

A key aspect of the Legacy Masterplan was that each of the new, predominantly residential neighbourhoods surrounding the Olympic Park was designed to look out as well as in, forming explicit connections with adjacent parts of the city. This approach would benefit those living in the new district as much as those who live around it. Indeed, in parallel with the development of the Legacy Masterplan, a series of discrete 'fringe' masterplans were prepared to explore how neighbouring areas might be improved and restructured to ensure that they obtained the maximum long-term benefit. The process of reconnection was not straightforward, however, and when the Games were over, more than a year was required to strip out the temporary structures and return the retained venues to full operation. By the summer of 2013 the public returned to limited parts of the Olympic Park in advance of its full re-opening in 2014.

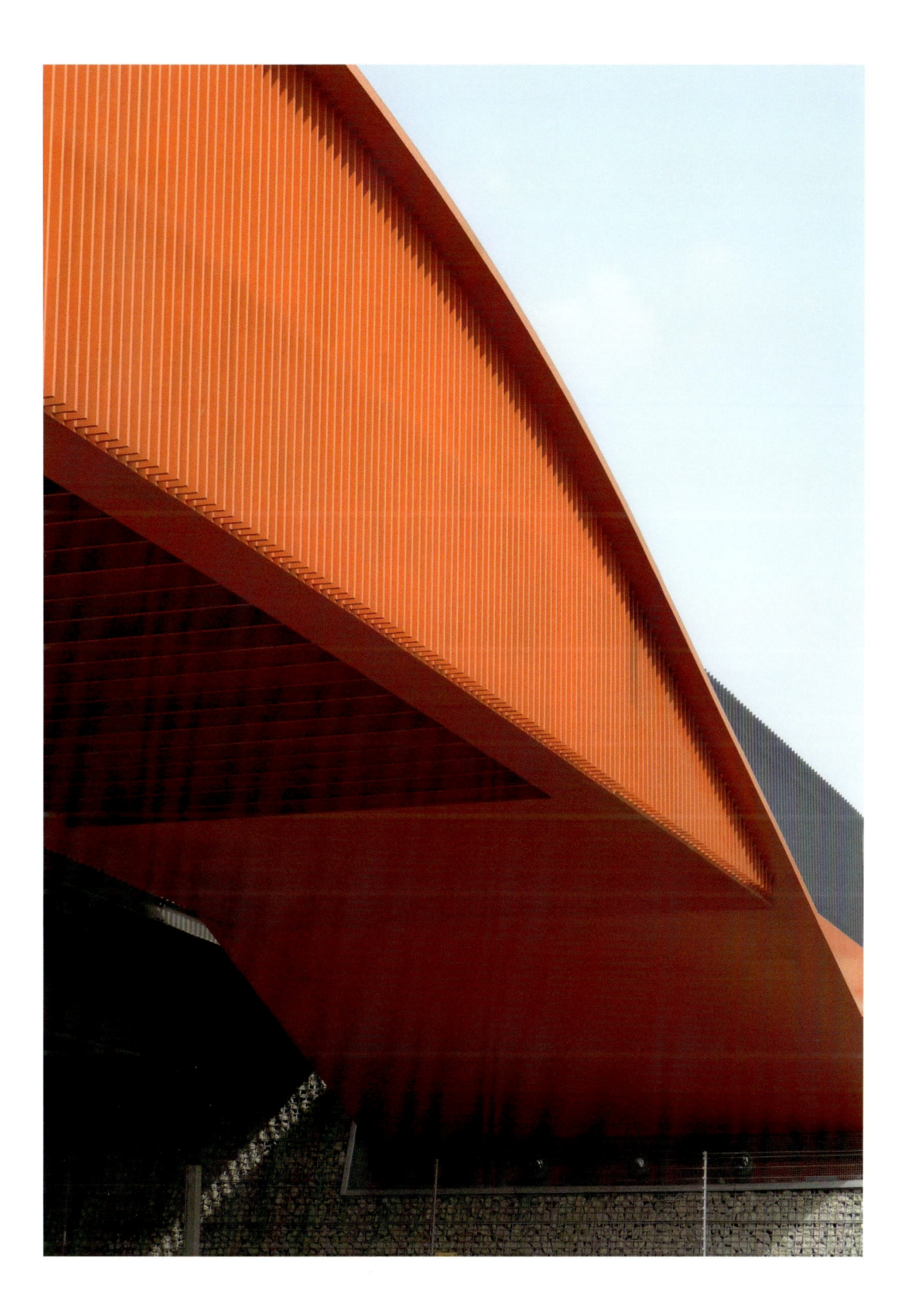

2012 INFRASTRUCTURE
Stratford, London
2003–12

Key to both the Games and Legacy Masterplans was the construction of a significant number of new permanent and temporary bridges. A large number of pedestrian and cycle crossings over water, existing roads and railways were required within the park to connect venues and, in Games mode, route widths of up to 40 metres were required to accommodate the large crowds.

The 13 permanent bridges form a family, with common geometries, details and components. The 15 temporary bridges, however, were designed as 'overlay' elements

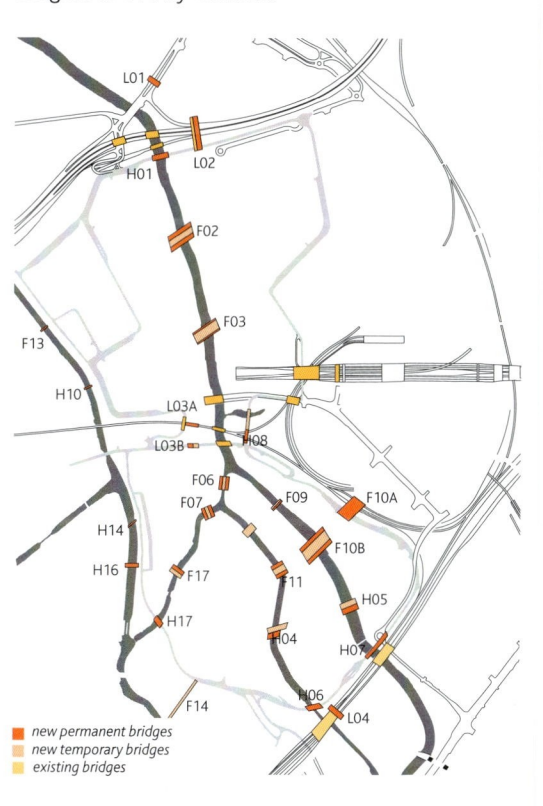

- new permanent bridges
- new temporary bridges
- existing bridges

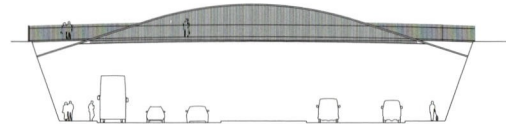

Northern Access Bridge

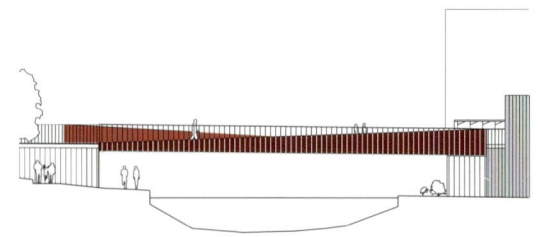

The Lea Navigation bridge

The Lea Navigation bridge

which were removed after the Games to reveal a pre-formed river valley of landscaped terraces. Maximum investment was made in the permanent structures while temporary installations were designed in an economic and sustainable way that would allow ease of removal and re-use wherever possible.

The permanent bridges are embedded within the landscape, and designed simply to extend the concourse across the water. This strategy allows other bridges, particularly those at the park's perimeter, to adopt individual forms responding to their specific locations, and thus constitute an essential component of the public realm.

Among the most significant is the Northern Access Bridge, which connects the Northern Park over the busy Eastway to Eton Manor. A propped steel arch structure helped minimise the height of the bridge deck above the road, thereby reducing the extent of land modelling and the length of the approach ramps. The bold red-orange colour highlights the sculptural quality of the steel bridge elements and distinguishes it from the adjacent, grey parapets of the landscape approach. A number of bridges were constructed to enable pedestrian and cycle crossings over the Lea Navigation, a canal that runs north-south along the western edge of the park.

The Lea Navigation bridges were conceived initially as identical structures although each responds to its context and constraints differently. They are all steel box structures with alternating tapered edge beams forming parapets that gradually fall to deck level over the spans. Sets of steel bars, spaced 110mm apart, emerge out of the reducing edge beam to provide a parapet in a rhythm that echoes the repetitive geometry of the Northern Access Bridge. The ramps and stairs that provide the approaches to the bridges are set into the landscape.

Some of the key bridges crossing the River Lea were designed to be reduced to a more appropriate permanent width after the Games. These bridges are predominantly box girders, which allowed the secure concealment of utility routes (water, power, data etc) and provided surfaces for lighting, wayfinding and colour. The parapets were designed to run off the bridges onto the landscape, blurring the definition between structure and context.

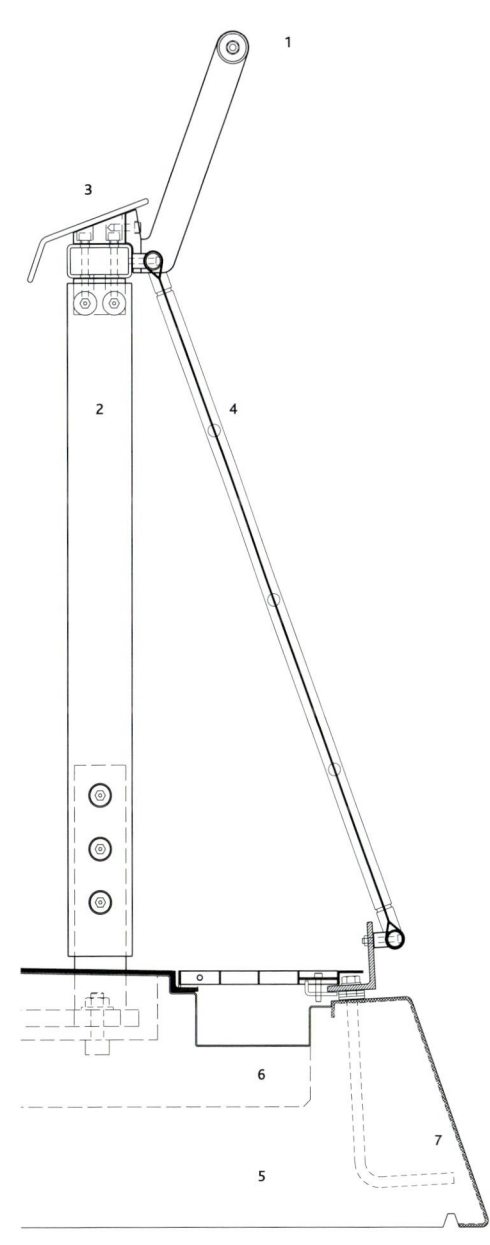

1 extended stainless steel cyclist rail
2 painted steel post assembly
3 stainless steel leaner
4 stainless steel mesh infill
5 precast concrete deck and surfacing
6 drainage channel
7 metal profiled edge

Section of over 6km park-wide balustrade

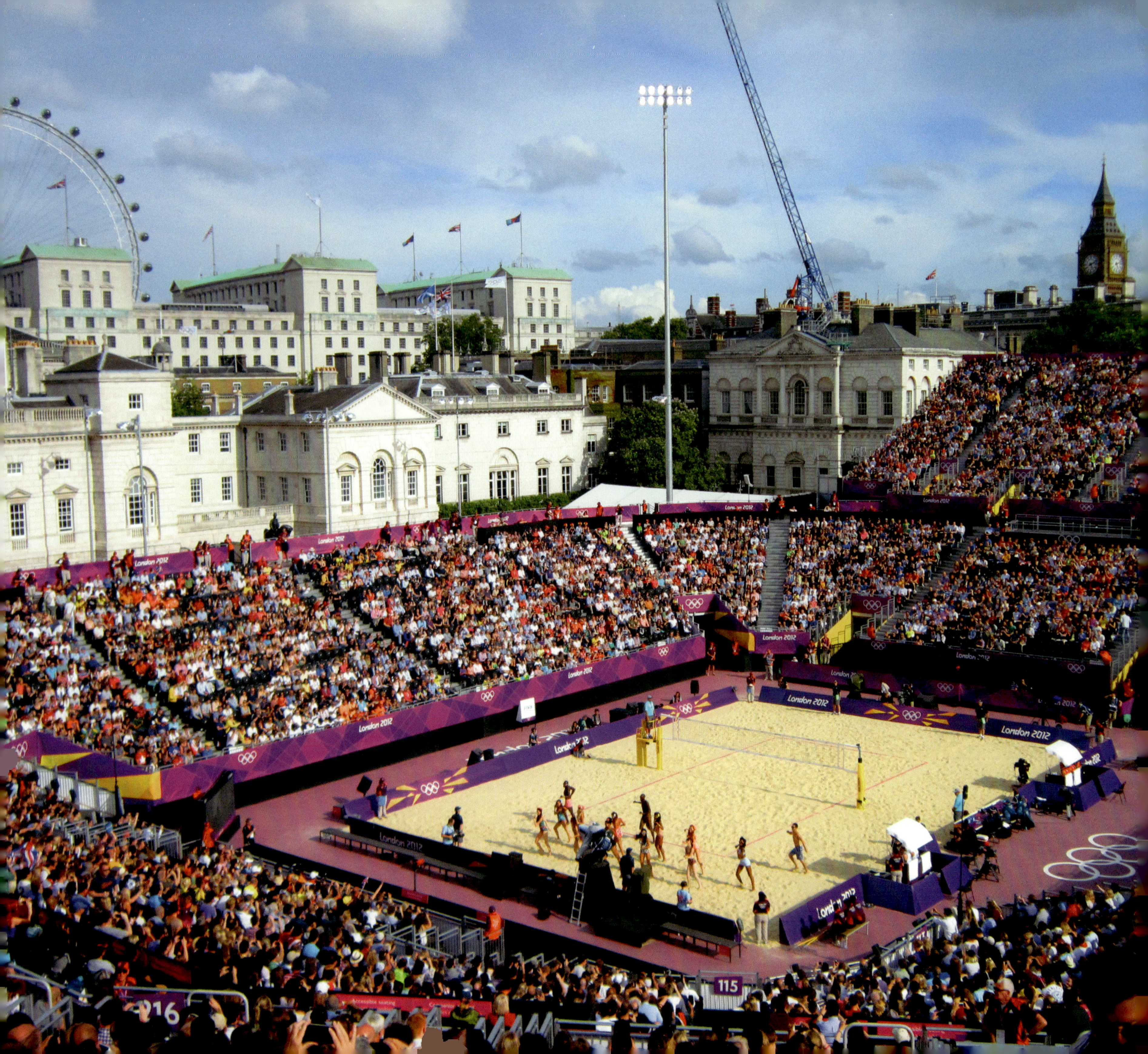
London 2012
115

2012 BEACH VOLLEYBALL
Horse Guard Parade, London
2012

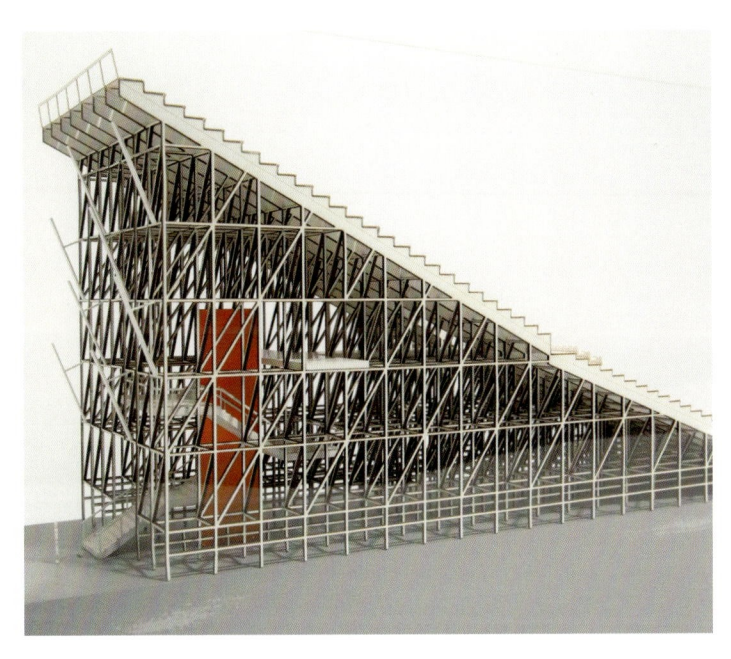

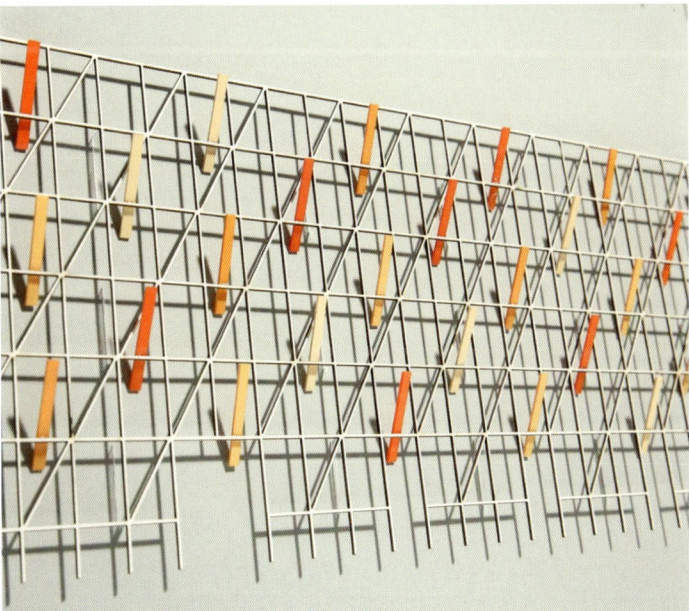

Hosting the Games required the construction of new venues not only across the 90-hectare domain of the Olympic Park but also at historic locations elsewhere around the capital, a commitment that formed an integral part of London's original bid. Allies and Morrison worked with the London Organising Committee of the Olympic and Paralympic Games to design a series of elements, structures and temporary pavilions to accommodate sporting events not only at Stratford, but also at Horse Guards Parade, The Mall, Greenwich Park, the Royal Artillery Barracks in Woolwich and further afield at Eton Dorney.

The Mall, which stretches from Admiralty Arch at its east end to Buckingham Palace at its west end, provided an atmosphere of grandeur as the start and finish for marathon events, cycling and race walks.

Seating for spectators was designed in small stands tucked between the trees on both the north and south sides of The Mall, and entrances, spectator facilities and service areas were incorporated within St James's Park, where they were shared by visitors to Horse Guards Parade and the beach volleyball venue.

Horse Guards Parade provided one of the most memorable backdrops of the entire Games. While a lower bowl of seating wrapping the venue on all four sides served to contain the high-energy atmosphere appropriate for beach volleyball, an upper bowl embraced only three sides, allowing spectator and camera views over the fine Palladian facade of William Kent's Horse Guards to the London skyline beyond.

◀ Beach volleyball event during Games
◀ Scaffold support designs for beach volleyball
▼ Days before the event

2012 EQUESTRIAN STADIUM

Greenwich, London
2012

The Maritime Greenwich World Heritage Site provided the setting for equestrian and modern pentathlon events. A primary field of play, surrounded on three sides by a 23,000-temporary arena, framed views of Christopher Wren's Old Royal Naval College and Inigo Jones' Queen's House. A second field of play, for the equestrian cross-country course, ran for six kilometres around Greenwich Park, exploiting its varying topography and stunning scenery to provide a memorable setting for the 75 competitors and 75,000 spectators.

◀ *The venue during Games*
▶ *Equestrian site at the Greenwich World Heritage Site*

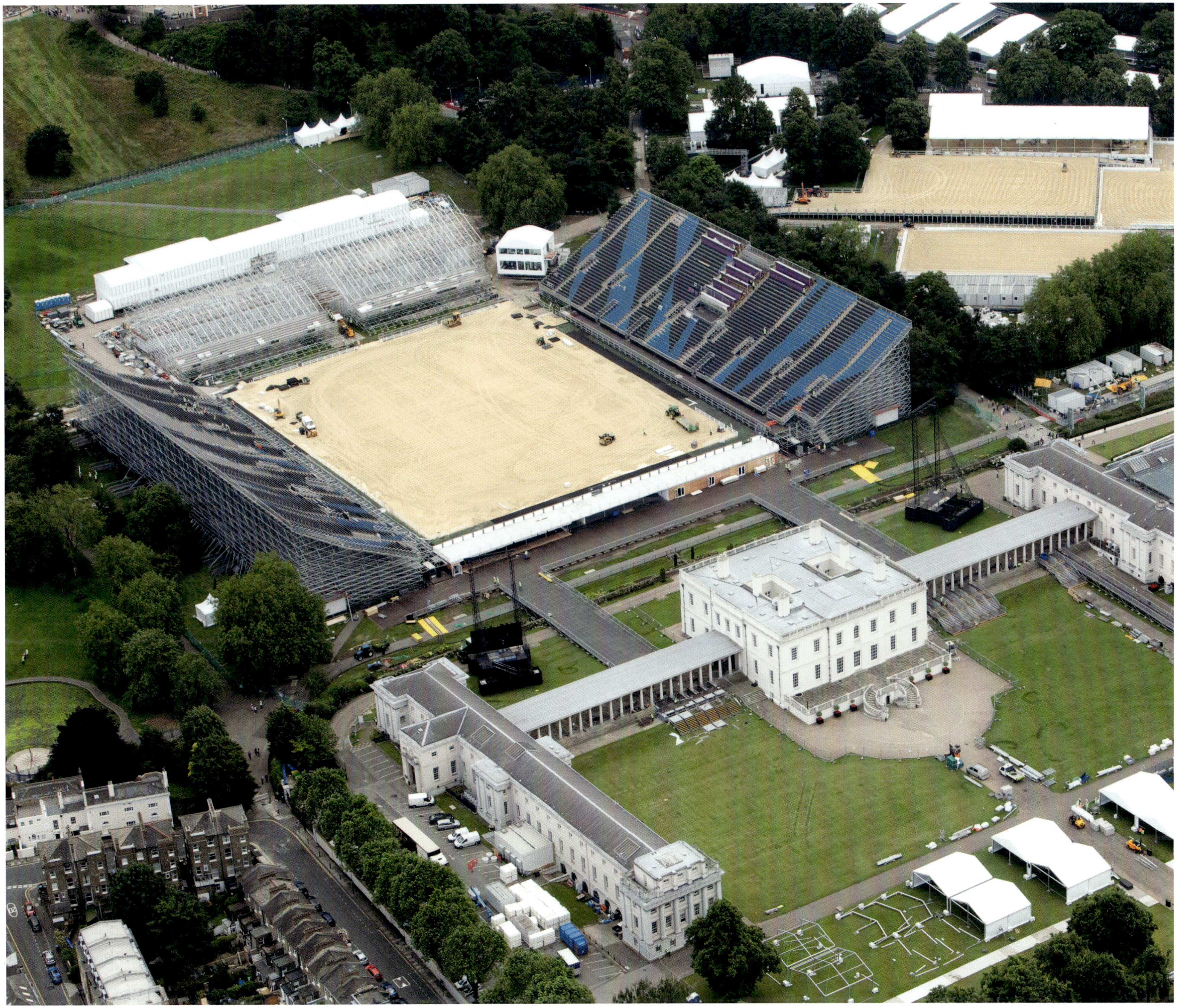

2012 PRESS AND MEDIA CENTRE

Stratford, London
2012

The permanent five-storey Main Press Centre (MPC) and the more temporary International Broadcast Centre (IBC) provided the base for 5,800 journalists. Designed to accommodate the studio and office space for broadcasting organisations during the games, they were planned for post-Games adaptation or sustainable dismantling.

The exacting acoustic performance of the very large spaces of the IBC generated significant cooling loads. The mechanical plant, housed in a distinct four-storey steel gantry, formed the entire elevation of the building facing the Olympic Park. A temporary 700-seat Conference Centre hosting daily press briefings and media events was strategically located between the IBC and MPC and joined the Catering Village, assembled from hired and reusable sectional building systems and sheathed in a perforated timber facade. The buildings, all linked by a 'High Street,' accommodated independent retail and catering outlets, banking facilities, a gym and a faith room.

◀ *Primary facade*
▶ *Interior views towards the City*

195

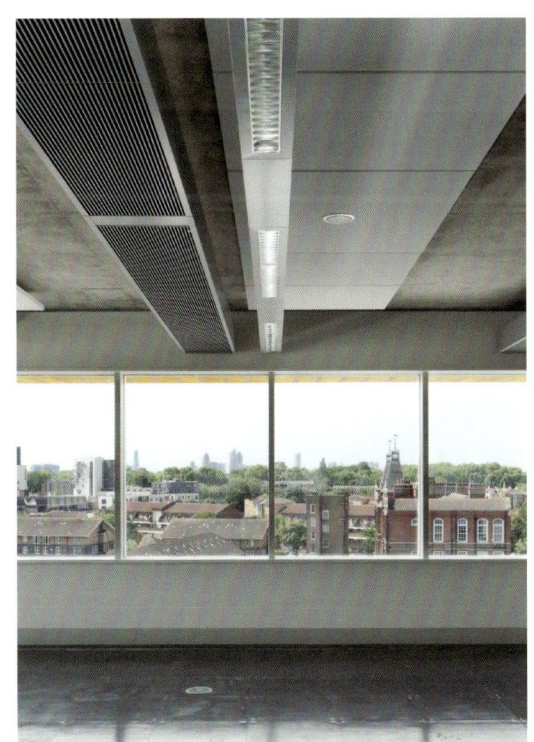

2012 MULTI-STOREY CAR PARK
Stratford, London
2012

Serving the press and media centre, a three-storey car park also accommodated a bus station at ground-floor level. Built using a standard precast concrete construction system, but with purpose-designed, curved ramps on its north facade, the car park was clad in a corrugated skin of perforated aluminium. The cladding provided the necessary enclosure to the car park while maximising daylight within. The corrugated profile allowed the cladding to span directly from floor to floor, obviating the need for any secondary supporting steelwork.

◀ *External cladding*
▶ *Internal spaces*

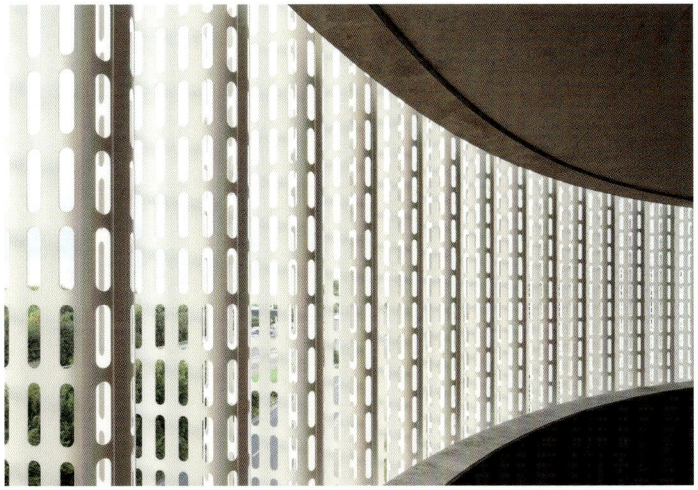
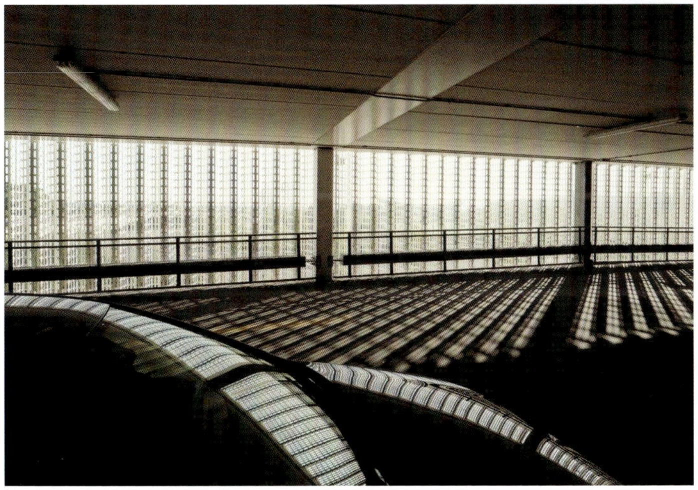
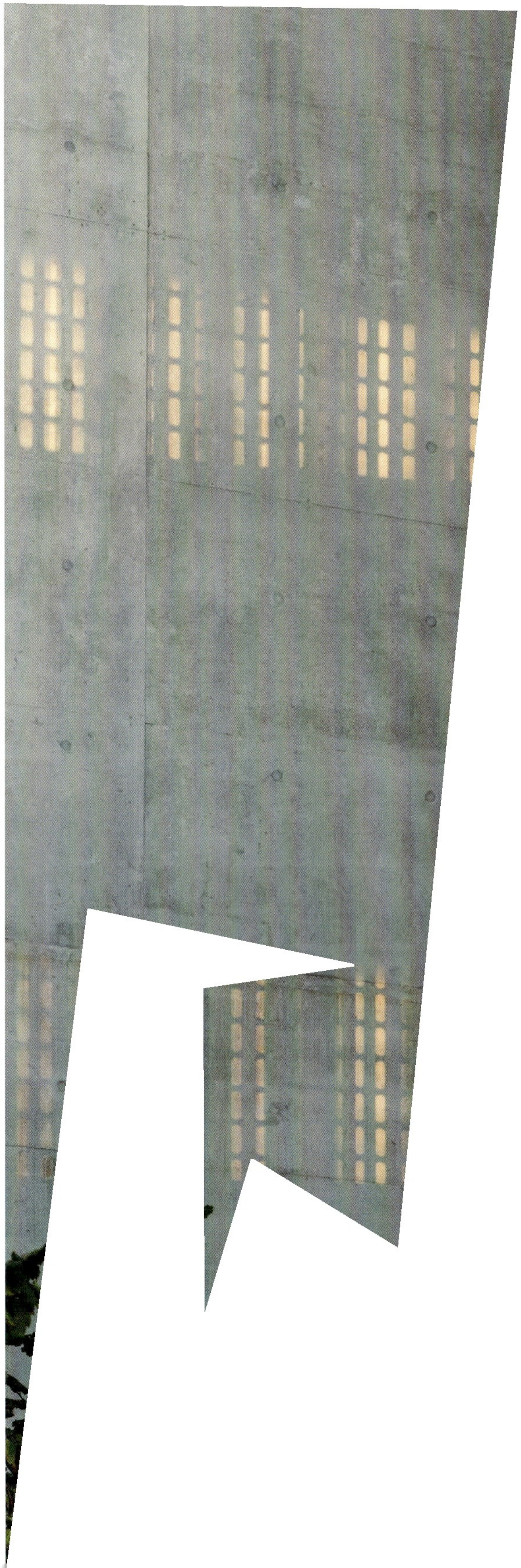
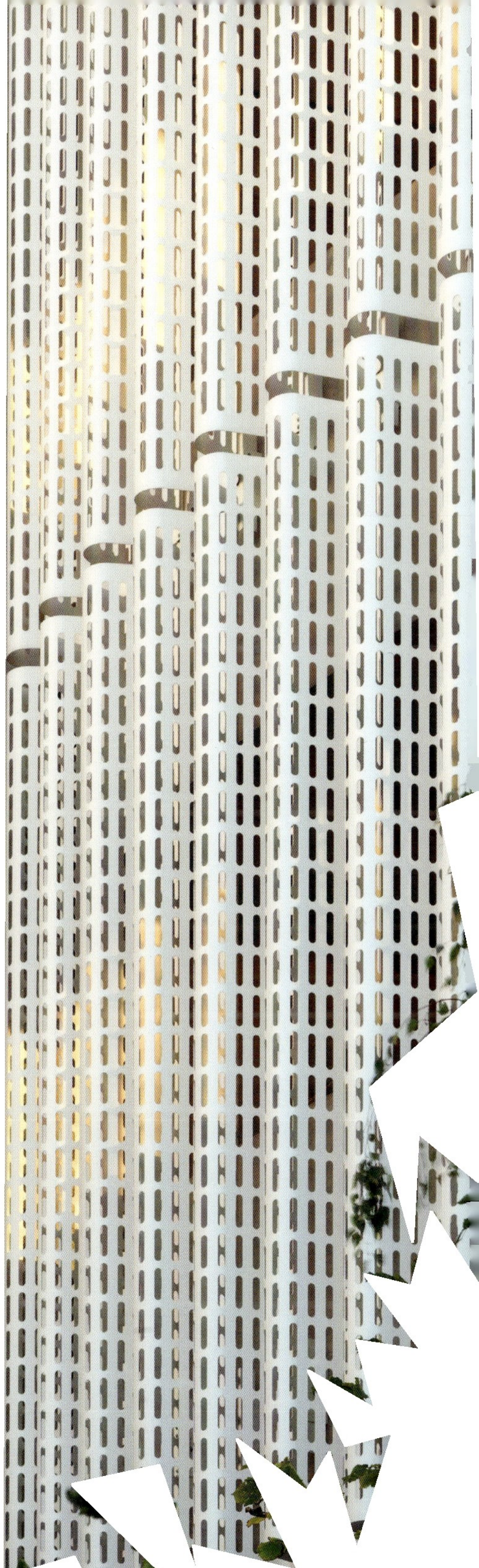

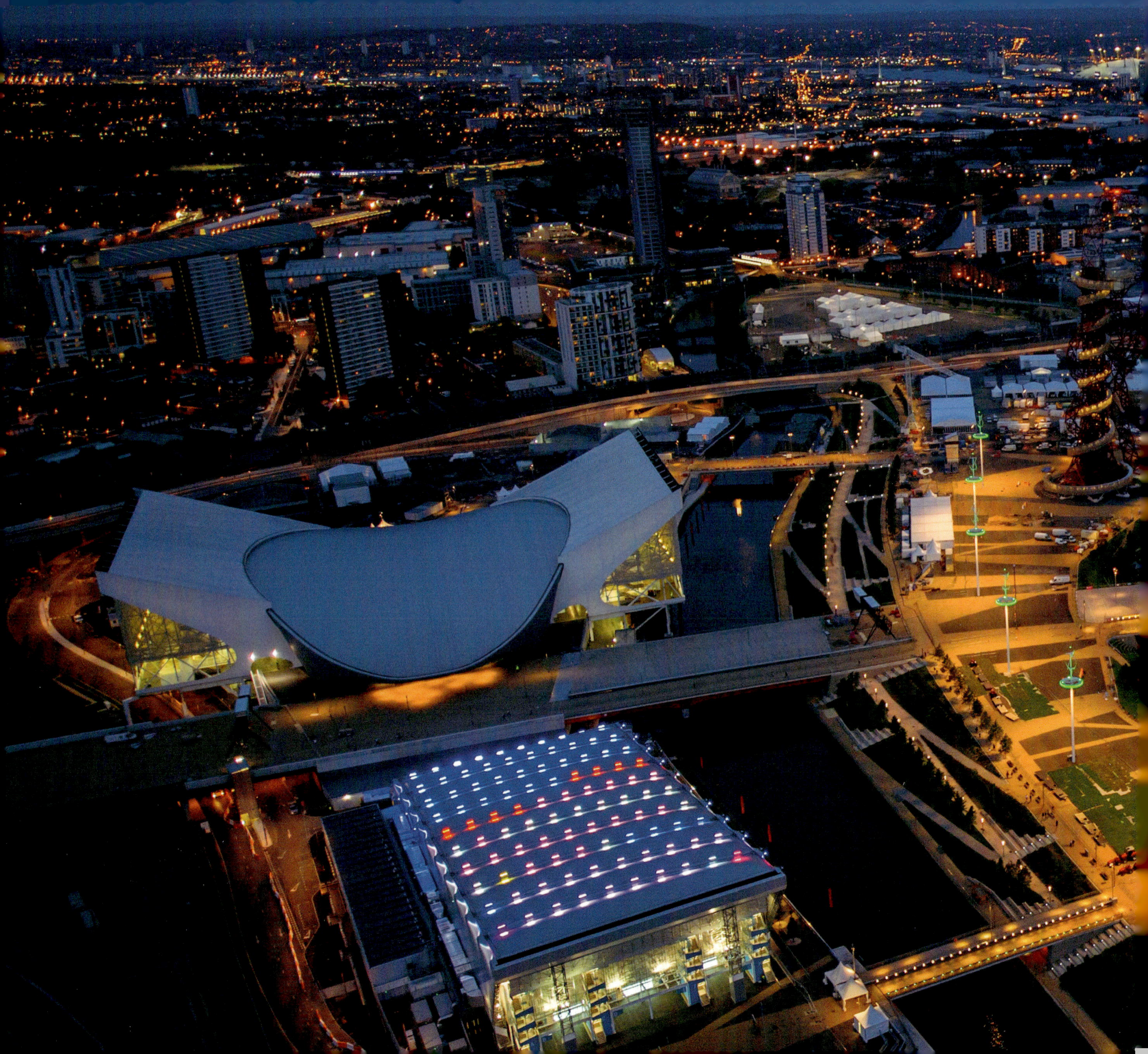

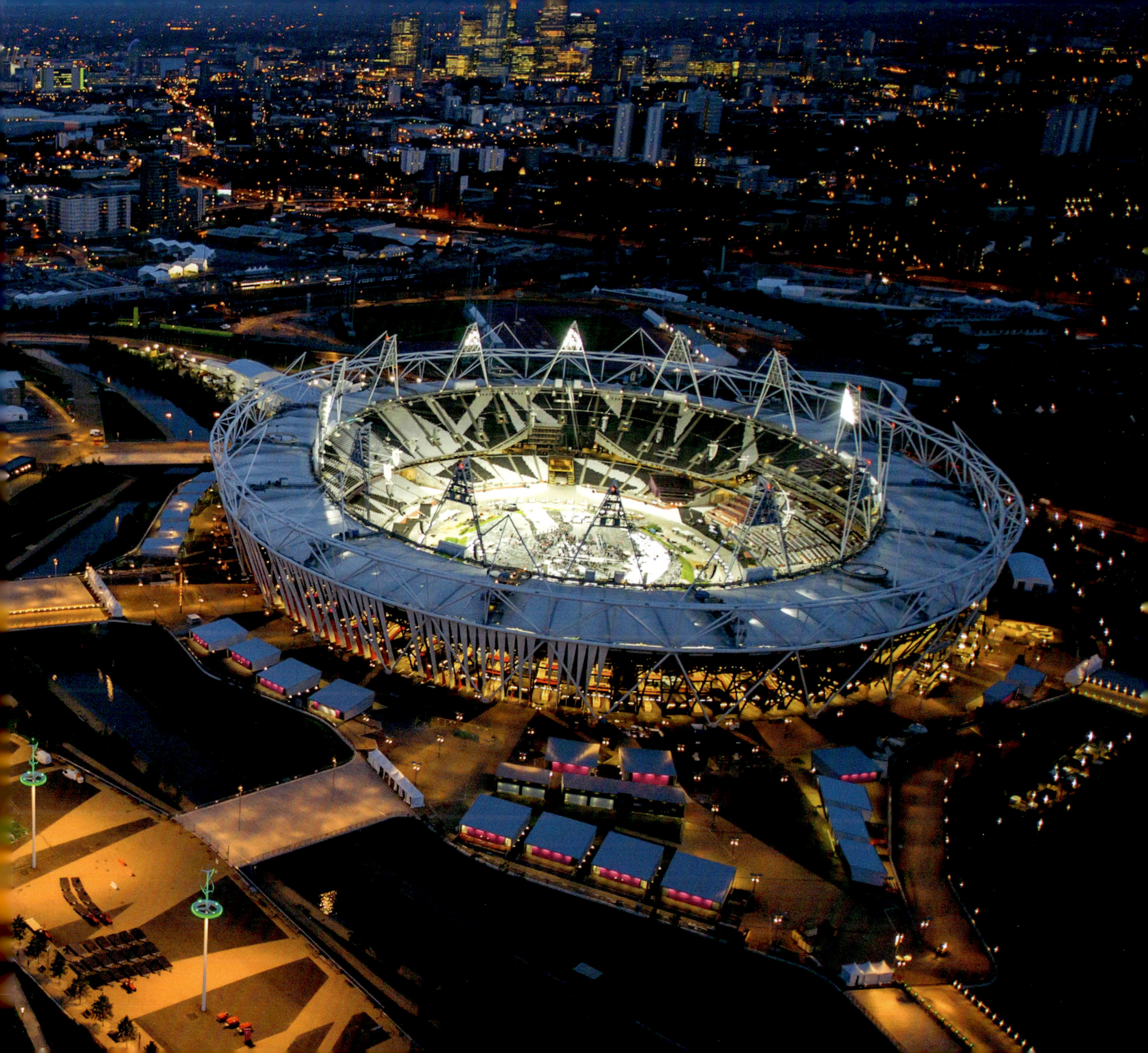

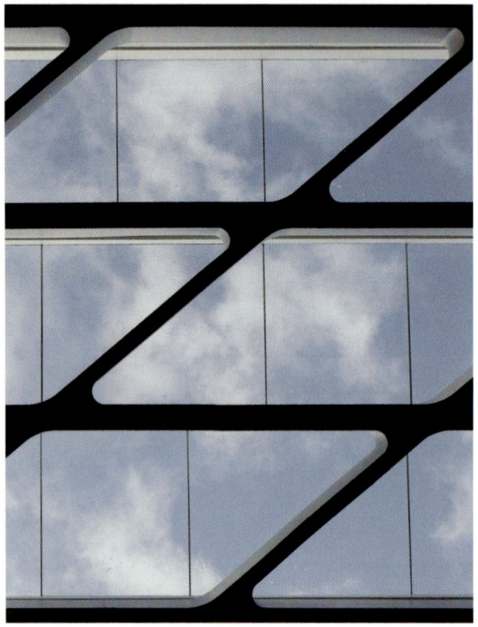

Appendices

Chronology
2003–2012

1999-2003
Allies and Morrison studios, London
Studio and office space
page 18

2001-03
Arnold House School, London
Improvements to entrance, orientation and accommodation

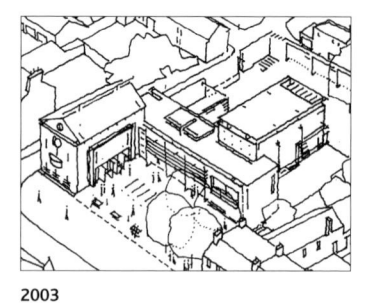

2003
Art Centre, Limavady
1st prize competition for town hall, art centre and museum

2003
Bristol Cathedral
Visitor centre

2003
Cheapside, City of London
Office building

2003
Girton College, University of Cambridge
Conference centre, kitchen and serveries

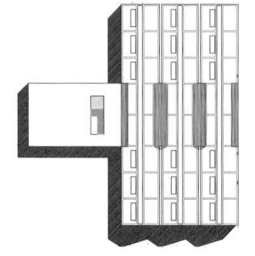

2002-03
Christ's Hospital School, Horsham
Design technology school building

2003
Bligh's Meadow, Sevenoaks
Residential development

2000-04
BBC Media Village, London
Headquarters for the BBC
page 38

2003
Sidgwick Site, University of Cambridge
Arts and Humanities Campus masterplan
page 44

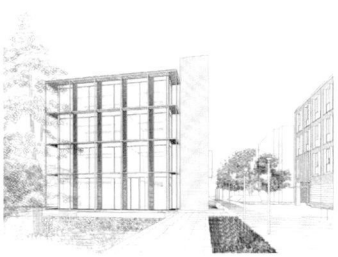

2001-04
Department of Land Economy
University of Cambridge
Faculty building

2001–04
Faculty of English
University of Cambridge
Faculty building
page 45

2001-04
Institute of Criminology
University of Cambridge
Faculty building
page 50

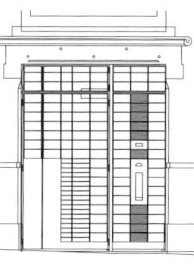

2004
Newton Street, London
Residential development

1999-2004
Fitzwilliam College, University of Cambridge
Student accommodation and auditorium
page 54

2004
History Centre, Kent
Competition for museum and research building at Leeds Castle

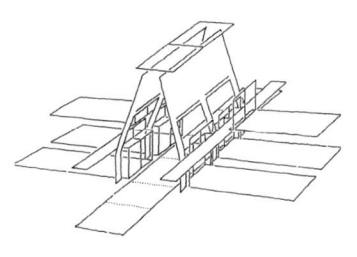

2004
Merchant Village, Glasgow
Retail development

2002-04
Merton College, Oxford University
College administration
page 64

2003-05
Lumina House, London
Office and retail building

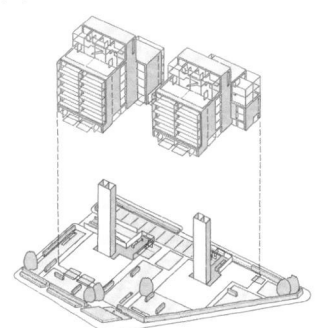

2005
Hamilton Gardens, Felixstowe
Residential development with Edwardian hotel conversion

2005
The Table, London
Fit-out of cafe
page 34

2005
British Council, Lagos, Nigeria
Reception facilities

2002–05
Grosvenor Waterside, London
Residential development
page 68

1998-2005
City Lit, London
Adult education college
page 72

2005
New England Square, Brighton
Hotel and residential tower

2005
University Hall, Bath
Refurbishment of university hall and foyer

2001–05
Chelsea College of Art and Design, London
Art College
page 76

1998-2005
Girton College, University of Cambridge
Archive and library building
page 82

2005
Wolvercote Paper Mill, Oxford
Housing, offices, retail and restaurant buildings

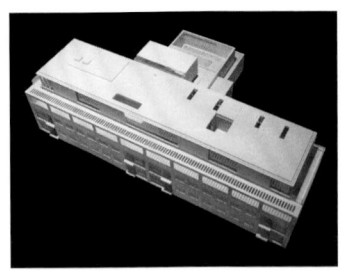

2006
Portland Place, London
Single-storey penthouse

2006
Canons Park, Arnold House School, London
Sports facilities for primary school

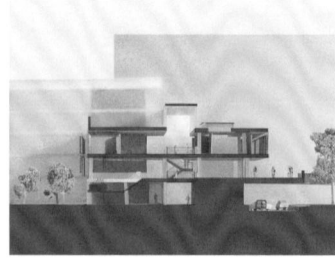

2006
4 West Building, University of Bath
Faculty building

2005
Tottenham Hale, London
Mixed-use masterplan

2005
African Institute of Science and Technology Abuja, Nigeria
Competition for an education masterplan

2005
Elizabeth House, London
Commercial, residential and public realm development

2006
Burnley JCP
Office building

2006
Centre Point Restaurant, London

2005-06
Sandbanks
Private house

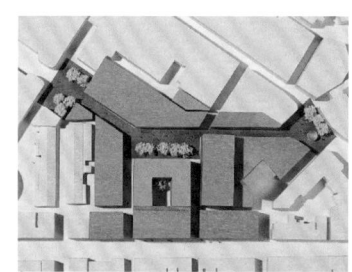

2006
Granville Square, Swindon
Mixed use masterplan

204

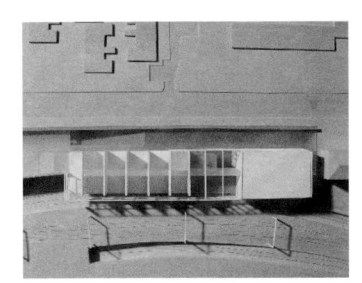

2006
South Hampstead Synagogue, London

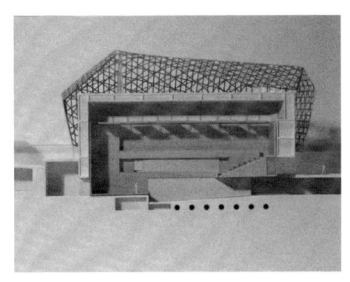

2006
Hemel Hempstead
Town centre masterplan and performing arts centre

2006
Arts and Crafts Exhibition,
Victoria and Albert Museum, London
Exhibition design

2006
Al Falah, Abu Dhabi
Competition for a masterplan

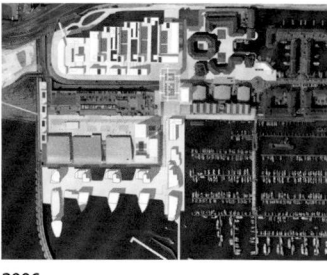

2006
Brighton Marina
Residential and mixed-use development

2006
Goodge Street, London
Mixed-use development

2007
Queen Square, London
Facade for University College London, Neuroscience Institute

1999-2007
Royal Festival Hall, London
Refurbishment of foyers and auditorium, new retail and landscape
page 88

1999-2007
Liner Building, Royal Festival Hall, London
Administration building
page 98

2006-07
Canteen, Royal Festival Hall, London
Restaurant and bar fit-out
page 100

2007
Prakrithi Rose, Bangalore
Hotel, residential and commercial building

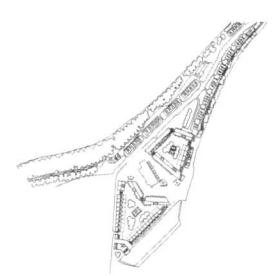

2007
Kirkstall Forge, Leeds
Competition for residential masterplan

2004–07
Welney Visitor Centre
Visitor centre and footbridge for the Wildfowl and Wetlands Trust
page 102

2007
Yeomans, Cowes, Isle of Wight
Residential development

2003-07
IQ Business Park, Farnborough
Office buildings and refurbishment
page 106

205

2004–07
Royal Observatory, Greenwich
Gallery and planetarium
page 112

2007
Belsize Square Synagogue, London

2007
Warwick Road, London
Apartment hotel

2007
Blackburn Road, London
Residential development

2007
UBC Vancouver, Canada
Invited competition for a university hub

2007
Crawley
Mixed-use town centre development

2007
King's Cross, London
Masterplan

2007
Great Northern Hotel, King's Cross, London
Hotel refurbishment

2003–07
Heart of Sheffield
Masterplan, office buildings and multi-storey car park
page 118

2007
Utrecht, Netherlands
Residential and commercial development

2007
Chelsea Barracks, London
Competition for a residential development

2007
Southmead Hospital, Bristol
Hospital masterplan

2008
Forest Hill Pools, London
Public swimming pool, leisure centre and residential development

2005–08
Liverpool One, Liverpool
Retail building
page 126

2008
Eton College
Competition for teaching facilities

2008
Addenbrooke's Hospital, Cambridge
Hospital masterplan

2008
Broadway Chambers, Stratford
Residential towers and mixed-use

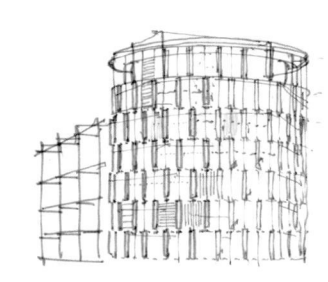

2008
Paddington Central, London
Commercial building

2005-08
Monk Bridge, Leeds
Two office buildings

2008
Somerset House, London
Competition for a hotel and gallery

2008
North End Road, London
Mixed-use masterplan

2008
Bata Fields, East Tilbury
Residential masterplan

2004-08
One Vine Street, London
Retail, commercial and residential development
page 132

2009
Silver Hill, Winchester
Residential and mixed-use town centre development

2009
Hafencity, Hamburg, Germany
Office development

2009
Foreign Office Courtyard, London
Government building

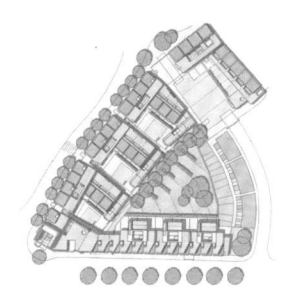

2009
Godalming, Surrey
Residential development

2005–09
Highbury Square, London
Transformation of former football stadium into residential units
page 136

2004–11
Bankside 123, London
Office and retail
page 146

2007–09
Thecentre:mk, Milton Keynes
Shopping centre extension, car park, residential units, retail and infrastructure

207

2008-09
Bofors Tower, Dunkirk, Kent
Restoration of redundant gun tower building
page154

2009
Canteen, Baker Street, London
Restaurant

2006-09
Ericsson, Ansty Park, Coventry
Research and development facilities
page 158

2009
Victoria Street, London
Mixed-use development

2009
Hanover Square, London
Commercial and residential building

2005-09
Olympian Tower Stratford, London
Commercial and residential tower

2005–09
Mint Hotel, Leeds
Waterfront hotel
page 162

2006–10
Great Suffolk Street and Lavington Street, London
Student accommodation and hotel
page 166

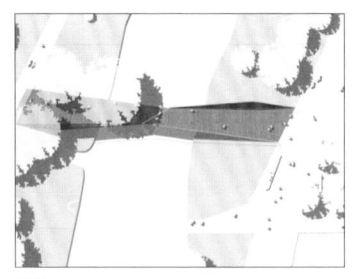

2010
River Soar Footbridge, Leicester
Competition
page 172

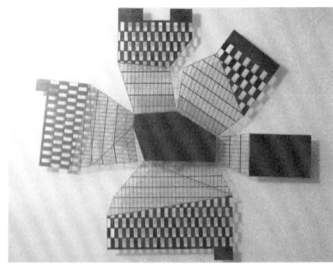

2010
120 Moorgate, London
Office building
page174

2010
Westgate, Oxford
Retail development

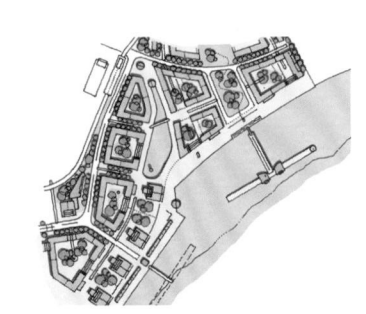

2010
Beckton Gas Works, London
Residential masterplan

2010
King's Cross Underground Station, London

2010
Oak Yard extension, London
Private house extension

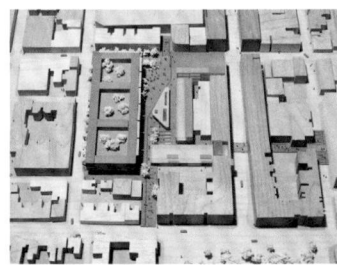

2010
Leamington Spa
Retail, residential and office development

208

2010
Queens Court, Milton Keynes
Retail development

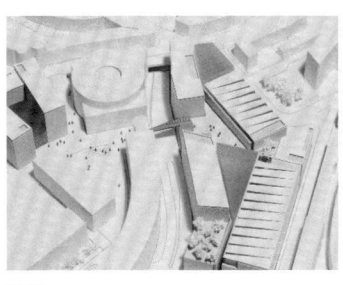

2010
City Inn, Edinburgh
Hotel

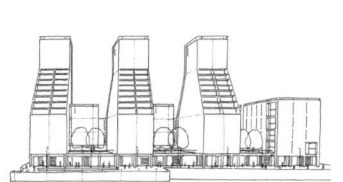

2010
Sugar Quays, London
Mixed-use development

2010
Tetra, Bucharest
Residential development

2010
London City Airport
Feasibility study for airport building

2010
Beethovenhalle, Bonn Germany
Invited competition for concert hall

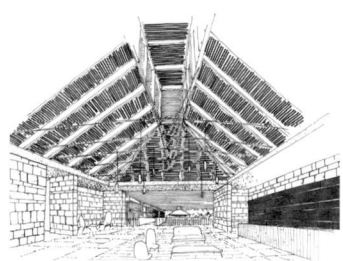

2010
Feroke Hotel, Calicut, India
Hotel and spa

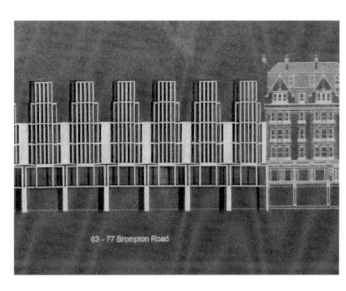

2011
Knightsbridge, London
Commercial development

2008-11
St Andrew's Bow, London
Residential development and masterplan
page 176

2012
Health centre, St Andrew's Bow, London

2009-12
New Court Rothschild Bank, City of London
Office building (with OMA)

2009-12
89 Southwark Street and Farnham Place, London
Studio space for Allies and Morrison
page 26

2012
Contemporary Applied Arts, London
Retail and gallery space
page 35

2012
Farnham Place landscape, London
Landscape and urban design

2003-12
2012 Olympic Games and Legacy
Masterplan
page 182

Bibliography

General Works

Good design is Good Business
Architectural Record, vol 205, no 4, 2017 Apr, p103-131

Learning from… Spaces Between
Graham Morrison
Architecture Today, no 266, 2016 March, p10

Bob the Builder
Mary Miers
Country Life, vol 200, no 1, 2006 Jan 5, p53

Public Buildings
Ed Vaisey et al
Building Design supplement no 13, 2007 Dec 7, p3-38

Building, vol 275, no 8626 (16), 2010 Apr 23, p36-43

Profile: Allies and Morrison
Martin Pearce
Brick Bulletin, 2010 Autumn, p12-17

Still Allies after more than 20 years
Building Design, no 1926, 2010 July 16, p20

Design through Dialogue: a guide for clients and architects
Karen A Franck, T. von Sommaruga Howard
Wiley, 2010

City Architecture: redesigning the City of London, 1991-2011
Richard Saxon et al
Architects' Journal, vol 233, no 2, 2011 Jan 20, p17-123

Allies and Morrison teams up with urban specialist
Building Design, no 1963/1964, 2011 May 6, p3

Working Abroad: Allies and Morrison
Elizabeth Hopkirk
Building Design, no 1949, 2011 Jan 21, p6-7

Allies and Morrison studios

Building a Strong Work Ethic
Allan Haines
Concrete Quarterly, no 223, 2008 Spring, p12-14

Empire Building
Ellis Woodman
Building Design, no 2079, 2013 Oct 4, p10-13

Architects' Offices: Steven Holl and others
A+U, no 1 (424), 2006 Jan, p12-156

BBC Media Village, White City

Place Making
Building, vol 282, no 8928 (24), 2016 June 17, p9

And now from the BBC
Martin Spring
Building, vol 269, no 8322 (9), 2004 Mar 5, p38-42

Allies and Morrison at White City
Adrian Gale
Architecture Today, no 157, 2005 Apr, p64-76

Sidgwick Site: University of Cambridge

Taming the Zoo
Gavin Stamp
Building Design, no 1645, 2004 Oct 8, p12-17

Cambridge Campus Masterplan
Building Design, no 1478, 2001 Mar 16, p7

Gatehouse and Auditorium, Fitzwilliam College

Civic Domesticity: Allies & Morrison at Fitzwilliam College
Patrick Lynch
Architecture Today, no 150, 2004 July, p50-61

Not just a Pretty Face
Kester Rattenbury
Building Design, no 1507, 2001 Oct 26, p14-15

Brick Bulletin
George Demetri et al
Building, vol 270, no 8406 (45), 2005 Nov 11

City Lit

City Literacy
Ellis Woodman
Building Design, no 1678, 2005 June 17, p16-19

Chelsea College of Art and Design

United Front
David Littlefield
Building Design no 1527, 2002 Apr 5, p13

Hit Parade
Amanda Baillieu
RIBA Journal, vol 112, no 9, 2005 Sept, p44-52

Archive and Library, Girton College

Perfectly Pitched
Eleanor Young
RIBA Journal, vol 121, no 1, 2014 Jan, p16-18

How to Beat the Big Heat
Tom De Saulles
Concrete Quarterly, no 254, 2015 Winter, p12-14

Royal Festival Hall

Musical Chairs
Christopher Woodward
Building Design, no 1773, 2007 June 1, p10-15

Reinvigorating 20th Century Masterpieces
Paul Needham et al
A+U, no 3 (474), 2010 Mar, p8-130

Refurbished Royal Festival Hall
Peter Kelly
Blueprint, no 255, 2007 June, p28

Roll over Beethoven
Thomas Lane
Building, vol 272, no 8482 (22), 2007 June 1, p42-49

South Bank Show
RIBA Journal, vol 114, no 6, 2007 June, p28-63

Royal Festival Hall
Dean Hawkes
Architectural Review, vol 222, no 1329, 2007 Nov, p58-67

Tuning up the Royal Festival Hall
Hattie Hartman
Architects' Journal, vol 226, no 9, 2007 Sept 13, p38-40

Slice of Life
RIBA Journal, vol 114, no 6, 2007 June, p8-9

Architecture in Detail II
Graham Bizley
Architectural Press, 2010

Visitor Centre and Footbridge, Welney

Detail in Contemporary Timber Architecture
Virginia McLeod
Laurence King, 2010

Fens and Fowl
Building, vol 271, no 8428 (17), 2006 Apr 28, p12

Strictly for the Birds
Eleanor Young
RIBA Journal, vol 113, no 7, 2006 July, p30-36

Wet Look
Building Design, no 1719, 2006 Apr 28, p5

Cost Model: Visitor Centres
Neal Kalita
Building, vol 272, no 8485 (25), 2007 June 22, p60-66

IQ Business Park, Farnborough

High Flyer
Architecture Today, no 183, 2007 Nov, p76-82

Planetarium, Royal Observatory Greenwich

Space and Time in Architecture
Robert Harbison
Architecture Today, no 179, 2007 June, p38-45

Heavens Above
Museums Journal, vol 107, no 7, 2007 July, p42-43

Heart of the City

Sheffield Master Work

Building Design, no 1789, 2007 Sept 28, p5

Allies and Morrison in Panel Game
Richard Vaughan
Architects' Journal, vol 224, no 14, 2006 Oct 19, p14-15

Paradise Street

Liverpool One
Martin Spring
Building, vol 273, no 8531 (21), 2008 May 30, p38-42

One Vine Street

Alison Turnbull
Andrew Mead
Architect's Journal, vol 228, no 9, 2008 Sept 11, p48

Highbury Square

A Game of Two Halves
Stephen Mullin
Architecture Today, no 205, 2010 Feb, p36-42

Life Beyond Football
David Stanley
Building Services, vol 30, no 5, 2008 May, p25-28

Bankside 123

Have you met the Tate's new neighbours?
Ike Ijeh
Building, vol 275, no 8628 (18), 2010 May 7, p40-44

The Beautiful South Bank
Building, vol 272, no 8499 (39), 2007 Sept 28, p14
Commercial/Offices
Pamela Buxton
Building Design, no 1990, 2011 Nov 18, p11-16

Land Securities: a 21st-Century Client
Peter Rogers et al
Building (Land Securities supplement), vol 271, 2006 Dec, p3-50

A&M reveals £175m Tate Modern neighbour
Zoe Blackler
Architect's Journal, vol 214, no 16, 2001 Nov 1, p16

Bofors Tower

Remake-Remodel
Greg Penoyre
Architecture Today, no 193, 2008 Nov, p22-49

Hotel, Leeds

Leeds Granary Wharf
John Whiles
Architecture Today, no 202, 2009 Oct, p22-32

Coming up Roses in the North
RIBA Journal, vol 117/118, no 12/1, 2010/2011 Dec/Jan, p10

Great Suffolk Street

Innovations in Cladding
Martin Spring et al
Building Design, no 1928, 2010 July 30, pI-XI after p8

120 Moorgate

Practice: IT
Rebecca Haines-Gadd et al
Building Design, no 1792, 2007 Oct 19, p20-21

St Andrews Phase 1

Hidden Houses
Building, vol 276, no 8680 (21), 2011 May 27, p10

Solutions: Brick Structures
Amanda Birch
Building Design, no 1919, 2010 May 28, p14-17

Housing: Bromley by Bow
David Birkbeck
Architecture Today, no 233, 2012 Nov, p36-94

Housing and Regeneration
Joey Gardiner et al
Building, vol 273, no 8557 (47), 2008 Nov 28, p21-22

2012 Olympic Games and Legacy

Gardens of the East
Oliver Wainwright
Building Design, no 2024, 2012 July 27, p14-19

Ready, set, saunter...
Building Design, no 1930, 2010 Aug 27, p5

Let it Snow
Building, vol 276, no 8666 (7), 2011 Feb 18, p9

Double Take: Down to Earth
RIBA Journal, vol 118, no 3, 2011 Mar, p57

London Now
Cathleen McGuigan
Architectural Record, vol 200, no 6, 2012 June, p62-100, 132

It's Here...
Emily Wright
Building, vol 277, no 8709 (1), 2012 Jan 6, p26-34

The Year of the Groundhog
Building, vol 277, no 8709(1), 2012 Jan 6, p36-40

Living in Glass Houses
Building, vol 279, no 8807(1), 2014 Jan 10, p9

Progetti Olimpici
Arca, no 201, 2005 Mar, p92

London Olympisch
Jay Merrick et al
Deutsche Bauzeitung, vol 146, no 8, 2012 Aug, p16-55, 83-88

Eastside story vol 2: Olympic Park
John Armitt
Architects' Journal supplement, vol 236, 2012 Sept, p2-104

Olympic Structures for London 2012
Chris Wise
Structural Engineer, vol 90, no 6, 2012 June, p12-88

Credits

Photographs
Dennis Gilbert: Frontispiece, 11-12, 18-27, 36, 38-45, 47-51, 52-55, 56-65, 66, 69, 74-77, 79-83, 84-89, 90-97, 89, 102-105, 106-111, 113-117, 119-125, 126-131, 133-135, 136-145, 148-153, 158-161, 162-165, 166-171, 176-179
Peter Cook: 38-45, 70-73, 99
Nick Guttridge: 21, 28-35, 48-51
Michael Franke: 36, 100-101
Fisher Hart: 37
Richard Bryant: 93
Paul Riddle: 136-145
IPC Media: 146
Andrew Putler: 147, 153
Charlotte Wood: 154-157
Robin Hayes: 166-171
Edmund Sumner: 180-181
Jack Hobhouse: 182
Jason Hawkes: 185, 198-199
Jim Stephenson: 194-195
Ståle Eriksen: 196-197
Allies and Morrison: all other photography

Models
Kandor: p132, p137, p153
Allies and Morrison: all other models

Every effort has been made to acknowledge the source of photographs and illustrations; we apologise for any errors or omissions.

Exhibitions

2003
Building the BBC: A Return to Form, RIBA, London

2004
Summer Exhibition, Royal Academy of Arts, London

New City Architecture: People Places and Buildings, Broadgate, London

2005
Summer Exhibition, Royal Academy of Arts, London

2007
Royal Festival Hall Revival, V&A RIBA Architecture Gallery, London

Global Cities, Tate Modern, London

2008
Summer Exhibition, Royal Academy of Arts, London

Beyond Measure: Conversations across Art and Science, Kettle's Yard, Cambridge

Housing Design Awards, RIBA, London

2011
City visions 1910/2010: Urban planning – Travelling exhibition in London, Berlin, Paris and Chicago

Projecting London, The British School at Rome, Italy

Southwark Reborn: The Next Chapter, Letchworth

2012
Summer Exhibition, Royal Academy of Arts, London

Re-Made Exhibition, 85 Southwark Street, London

Awards

RIBA Awards

1991
The Clove Building, Butler's Wharf, London

1996
Sarum Hall School, London
Nunnery Square, Sheffield
Newnham College, Cambridge

1997
British Embassy Dublin, Ireland
Abbey Mills Pumping Station, London

1998
Rutherford Information Services Building, Goldsmiths College, London

2000
Private House in Holland Park, London

2003
Blackwell House, Cumbria

2004
Allies and Morrison Studios, London
The Horniman Museum, London
One Piccadilly Gardens, Manchester

2005
BBC Media Village, White City, London
Gatehouse Court and Auditorium, Fitzwilliam College, Cambridge

2006
Girton College Library and Archive, Cambridge

2007
Farnborough Business Park, Hampshire

2008
Royal Observatory, Greenwich, London
Royal Festival Hall, Southbank Centre, London

2009
13b Paradise Street, Liverpool One
Charles Street Car Park, Sheffield
One Vine Street, Regent Street, London
Bofors Tower, Kent

2010
Highbury Square, London
Bankside 123, London

2012
New Court, Rothschild Bank Headquarters, London

2013
The Olympic Park Masterplan, Stratford
Royal Albert Memorial Museum, Exeter

2014
Boarding House, Brighton College, Brighton
Rambert, Southbank, London

2015
Addenbrooke's Multi-story Car Park, Cambridge

2016
Maurice Wohl Clinical Neuroscience Institute, King's College, London

2017
King's College School, Wimbledon, London

Stirling Prize shortlist

2008
Royal Festival Hall, Southbank Centre, London

2012
New Court, Rothschild Bank Headquarters, London

Allies and Morrison
1983 – 2012

Bob Allies
Graham Morrison
Paul Appleton
Joanna Bacon
David Amarasekera
Robert Maxwell
John Pardey
Josephine Saunders
Tim Makower
Robert Wood
Martin Markcrow
Chris Bearman
Robert Payne
Pauline Stockmans
Ian Sutherland
Paul Summerlin
Grainne Crooks
Deborah Bookman
Lucy Britton
Mark Way
Laurie Hallows
Michael Greville
Stephen Archer
Cathy Milligan
Penny Gardiner
Glen Millar
Ioana Sandi
Joe Witchell
Graham Vicary
Liz Parr
Tina Bird
Helena Thomas
Di Haigh
Andrew Green
Jill Annarino
Eddie Taylor
Steve Taylor
Stefanie Eberle Parkyn
Julia Davies
Indu Ramaswamy
Martin Bradley
Suzie Lloyd
Simon Fraser
Cecilia Dubois
Vicky Thornton
David Bonta
Rawden Pettitt
Tommy Chung
Hendrik Heyns
Natalie Black
James Fraser
John Barber
Nina Quesnel
Robin Gray
Gabor Gallov
Lien Lu Sin

Oliver Ralphs
Sarah Beatty
Adrian Leer
Sheila Corbett
Rebecca Huggins
Sarah Simmon
Aaron Fletcher
Lisa Donnell
Pat Seymour
Robin Walker
Toby Birtwistle
Emma Huckett
Helen Logan
Frank Amankwah
Joanne Robinson
Miranda Webster
Iona Foster
John Morgan
Keith Evans
Laura Stephenson
Alex Wraight
Nicholas Champkins
Adam Parkyn
Ashley Munday
James Parkin
Jason Syrett
Jenny Lovell
Robert Nisbet
Andrew Dean
Oli Heywood
Robert Yates
Lynn Taylor
Finbarr Finn
Simon French
Camilla Wilkinson
Miranda Reynolds
Liz Nettleship
Michelle Stott
Robin Williams
Terence Seah
Neil Shaughnessy
Peter Besley
Rupert Fisher
Suzanna Heape
Joanna Rippon
Mark Taylor
Michela Ruffatti
Miles Leigh
Ricardo Gandolfi
Adam Smit
Chris Butler
Mark Reimer
Mammad Tabatabai
Shona Fox
Alistair Twiname
Anne Milbank

Helen Berry
Jan Kuzminski
Liz King
Mark Simpson
Mike West
Ruth Treacher
Chantelle LaRose
Erin Reynolds
Katerina Mathioudaki
Lawrie Robertson
Rob Gregory
Saskia Vandersee
Simon May
Thomas Kopplemann
Hina Farooqi
Jason Cully
Lola Sheppard
Richard Myers
Eric Yeung
Corinna Simon
Donald Matheson
Genna Ryder
Michael Durran
Nick Peri
Robert Park
Susan McLean
Zeya Win
Marco Gelsomini
Bärbel Gamm
Ernest Tsui
Paula Craft
Greg Holme
Eric Martin
Jacqueline Milmo
Jake Noble
Julian Coward
Marianne Voswinkel
Oliver Houchell
Matthew Stares
Neil Dusheiko
Yves Racine
Sue Potter
Miles Wilkinson
Andreia Lima
Graham Simpson
Jonathan Schwinge
Dave Stanley
Debra Penn
Nicola Schroeder
Gail Stott
Andrew Dowding
Julia Chambers
David Stanley
Abel Law
Aoife Keigher
Patrick McLeod

Emma Wiren
Sarah Lyne
Andre Rodrigues
Emma Jones
Victoria Baynes
Billy Choi
Amanda Heagren
Mirei Yoshida
Ben Flatman
Denis Olette
Leyra Villoria
Richard White
Jim Rooney
Anthony Martin
Kirstin Church
Oxana Krause
Lianne Peterkin
Lucia Pflucker
Young-in Oh
Oliver Cooke
Peter Clarson
Ewan Morrison
Daniel Prinz
Jonathon Broughton
Kirsty Yaldron
Matthew Cochrane
Amy Lam
Amy Ewing
Drusilla Powell
Helen Sparks
Charlotte Barrows
Susannah Shaw
Goksen Kolcak
Andrew Dowding
Jonathan Mann
Cathy Milligan
Matthew Stares
Miles Wilkinson
Sue Potter
Yves Racine
Sian Hughes
Margarita Kolokotroni
Christopher Davies
Ana Sutherland
Artur Carulla
Danny Hunter
Kaye Wong
Kazuya Yamazaki
Graham Williams
Erin Klassen
Danny Sze
Jonathan Size
Thomas Horsley
Cristina Monachello
Leonard Sequeira
Juliet Harris

Andrew Fortune
Evi Suominen
James Krikler
Maria Kolokotroni
Rachel Logie
Sasha Sattar-Lothore
Susie Ray
Bettina Willers
Dominic Sharland
Elena Polycarpou
Frank Czudai
Juanita Cheung
Marc Le'Strange
Robert Foy
Sabrina Hill
Stephanie Gladbach
Amy Siu
Frederico Fialho
Giles Omezi
Judith Klingebiel
Philip Veall
Richard Sharam
Rui Baptista
Tina Webb
Vasiles Polydorou
Charlie Dammerell
Deborah Paul
Gudjon Erlendsson
Ian Grant
James Hamilton
Josephine Glyn
Nathan Jones
Silvia Ullmayer
Weibke Rosler
Andrew Simpson
Catherine Phillips
Fiona Ma
Gary Burman
James Bichard
Marija Gucaite
Moyo Otukeko
Barbara P Marina
Ben Clement
Ivana Sehic
Ling Luong
Michelle Murray
Karen Bates
Elena Schymczyk
Owen Aishford
Jeremy Mitchell
Suzanna Wong
Lee Howard
Alfredo Caraballo
Stefan Schoenefuss
Anat Talmor
Vanessa Carswell

Angie Jim Osman
Clare Varrall
Mark Foster
Clare Hamman
Tim Leslie
Lorenzo Viola
Libby Rinaldi
Nina Sahebkar
Oliver Dufner
Damien Mulvhill
Omid Kamvari
Yolandi Hattingh
Peter Von der Osten
Rukeya Khanam
Daniel Hayes
Dominique Chan
Gorana Vucic Shepherd
Kai Ming Wong
Anja Haubold
Diogo Alvim
Isabelle Chatel de Brancion
Julie Simpson
Kayvahn Kavoussi
Richard Beere
Takako Hasegawa
Corrine Armstrong
Francois Guyot
Jade Van Baaren
Sarah Miller Willamson
Clara Martins
Alessandra Beffa-Boggia
Siobhan Thorpe
Rachel MacIntyre
Nicola Zech
Max Kettenacker
Nick Weston
Nicky Malik
Mandy Ng
Sandy Sterzl
Eric Voignier
Simon Gathercole
Mark Dorward
Oliver Wong
Jackie Springford
Karen Cheung
Elke Zinnecker
Paul Eaton
Stephen Griffin
William Lowe
Imogene Potter
Andrew Boateng
Rosie Chang
Stephen Workman
Andrew Lavelle
Kaz Leslie
David Calvert

Jessie Turnbull
Robert May
John Ross
Peter Tindall
Karin Templin
Thomas Windley
Alastair Warburton
Jason Mascurine
Luigi Pecco
Helen Kiritopoulos
Elvin Chatergon
Christian Schwedler
Alejandro Botero Robledo
Laura Guenzi
Martin Birgel
Farid Ghali
Yasmeen Shami
Romy Berlin
Giedre Domzaite
Camilla Carlson
Emily Wandless
Jack Young
Lisa Tobin
Roberto Puchetti
Bartosz Lipnicki
Carla Booth
Jason Williams
Jenni Calzini
Nicola Steele
James Bennett
Ruben Marcos
Fiona Dunn
Ramona Njie
Bodo Schumacher
Lorna Getty
Paula Tinazza
Bobby Open
Tom Clark
Ben Jacobs
Charu Gandhi
Christopher Schulte
Claire McConnell
Natalie Waters
Caroline Andersen
Ines Kramer
Suzy Harris-Brandts
Matthew Smith
Henry Virgin
Niki Gardner
Tom Stemmer
Eleni Stylianidou
Louise Mackie
Simon Platt
Soni Diamond
Stefan Schoebel
Francois Cottier

Ludwik Chelkowski
Kelly Medhurst
Melina Nowak
Yasumasa Kitajima
Pearl Burnet
Joel Davenport
Josef Huber
Amie Lee
Adeline Wee
Cara Jones
Raoul Kunz
Chris Snow
Toby Blackman
Caroline Smithwick
Peter Goulde
Catharine von Eitzen
Ana Hernando
Paul Scott
Iae Won Bang
Vasiles Polydorou
Jonathan Tan
Sabrina Richard
John Carpenter
Nick Tayler
Vimal Mehta
Toby Carr
Kanda Faraj
Paul Morris
Scott Graham
Luke Jackson
Johanna Coste-Buscayret
Andrew McMullan
Sam Hails
Sally Fraser
Andrew Tam
Chris Smith
Desmond Hung
Alex Warnock-Smith
Mine Duzgen
Matthew Cox
Andrea Harnett
David Dunkley
Julian Krueger
Rhys Jones
Elfreda Chan
Tanya Kohli
Aneta Lipnicka
Bahadir Parali
Heidi Shah
Debola Ojo
Jonathan Mopo
Pablo Urango Lillo
Barbara Pfenningstorff
Sandor Ambrus
Jennifer Kwok
Tom Sinden

Alex Bowers
Jennifer Ricketts
Helena Gomes
Clare Loftus
Oliver Fisher
Anthony Earp
Peter Lowe
Evelyne Owen
Fabrice Goacher
Parveen Abdulraman
Alex McAslan
Debra Baker
Jason Amarasekera
Simon Spencer
Ayaka Suzuki
Richard Horton
Andrew Dodd
Erica Elmes
Erin Hunt
Graham Reid
Rachel Catt
Ania Bothe
Michelle Fernandes
Jayden Ali
Max van Wageningen
Roxanne Campbell
Sofia Henriques
Andreas Schoen
Ben Kirkpatrick
Roberta Margnetti
Ang Li
Chin Lye
Desiree Mann
Lap Fat Ngai
Rebecca Steward
Stefan Kogler
Stefan Wentrup
Carolina Thorbert
Natasha Reid
Anna Zannara
Chris Thomas
Dragana Cebzan Antic
Sarah Sperber
Aaron Peters
Benjamin Walton
Hiromasa Shirai
Lucy Dunman
Maria Jose Castrillo
Sascha Rux
Shireen Talhouni
Sara Leon Velasco
Sophie Jie Lian
Asako Nishimura
Carlos Bermudez Alonso
Irina Bardakhanova
Nicola Alger

Poe Matteo George
Sahil Latheef
Andrew Gowing
Antje Saunders
Nikolaus Wabnitz
Gemma Gasson
Lea Faber
Mark Ellison
Alex Bowers
Emad Sleiby
Marielle Goldstein
Samantha Barran
Hannah Parker
Angie Mitchell
Anthony Silverstone
Bruno Marcelino
Enriqueta Llabres Valls
Eun Zung Baik
Florian Gottschalk
Ian Hazard
Kyle Gudsell
Merce de Cabanyes Gay
Rafael Pena
Carl Harding
Fernanda Palmieri
Marco Sanchez-Castro
Tamara Kramer
Ana Povoas
Pablo Cabrera
Maria Bednarek
Juliao Pinto Liete
Oliver Cooper
Deniz Malonn
Mariana Rodrigues
Valentina Gastaldi
Diana Hernando Navarro
Roger Hands
Amy Christie
Anna-Elizabeth Gulzow
Kelly Burgess
Sara Maria Cruz
Isabella Gerster
Janina Vertriest
Sophia Amend
David Marti Cascales
Dennis van Kampen
Pedro Castelo
Daniel Laubrich
Eric Cheung
Kristijan Cebzan
Anna Dziekonska
Isabel Riese
Pedro Sanchez Reche
Takeyuki Suzuki
Daniela Plesser
David Gormley

Iris Hoffmann
Lourenco Andrade
Monika Kaminska
Anja Bradley De Bruin
Arthur Lo
Frances Taylor
Michael Jardine
Giuliano Cosi
Laura Cowell
Mimi Halova
Emiliano Diego-Franceskides
James Saunders
Simon Knight
Tina Jadav
Paulo Sousa
Verity Rowsell
Andrew Morrison
Arianna Ricciotti
Stuart Thomson
Diana Goldswain
Jorn Rabach
Katie Warren
Oliver Bayliss
Aleksandra Rutecka
Frances Sheridan
James Stevens
Twahaa Begum
Jonathan Pick
Vitoria De Albuquerque
Claire Hinton
James Petty
Julian Huang
Kieran Ashton
Payal Patel
Pierre Shum
Andrea Gritters
Katie Sims
Kirsty Leslie
Ozlem Balicadag
Donna Macfadyen
Ross Harniman
Vladimir Berezovskiy
Charlotte Smith
David Saunders
Candy Hoang
Alastair Warburton
Mihir Benodekar
Isaac Voelcker
Jonathan Orlek
Steven Abbey
Alistair Reid
Jane Mulvey
Lara Maeseele
Rachel Hurley
Sharon Osei
Toby Montague

Christopher Knight
Sanjiv Sangha
Tom See-Hoo
Piero Zagami
Louise Yeung
Sarah Richards
Katie Meaney
Nike Himmels
Andrew Rixson
Maria Papaleontiou
Bowornwan Noradee
Raffaele Nannetti
Padraic Ward
Rupert Walshe
Christine Garcia
Maria Chamorro
Paola Marocchi
Miriam-Sylvelin Kotte
Owen Jowett
Emilie Lemons
Emma Reale
Kirsty Leslie
Siu Lon Liu
Alice Chambers
Casey Sole
Gustavo Balague
Marina Polycarpou
Rasa Karuseviciene
Sarah Curran
Peter Bayley
Karman Wan
Robyn Jones
Hannah Calver
Ian Troake
Thanh Nguyen
Helen Goodwin
Noora Ulis
Una Daly
Elizabeth Burnett
Andrea Fabiana Obiol
Anna Vallius
Kate White
Emma McCracken
Peter Ohnrich
Ulla Tervo
William Sherlaw
Natalie Paul
Ross Powell
Kirsteen Owen-Wahl
Hayden French
Diana Zeferino
Shane McCamley
Anthony Bowles
Christine Peters
Oliver Fish
Kenneth Fitzmaurice

Mariia Pashenko
Fabrizio Primavera
Andrew Nevin
Stephen Bonnington
Lindsay Huse
Chris Hughes-Copping
Daniel Rutter
Rebecca Carter
Alex Teoh
Bridget McKid
David Sharpe
Edward Neale
Jane Ashe
Myung Ho Lee
Thomas Richardson
Carla Smyth
Alberto Bergamo
Sean Joyce
Lia Silva
Amy Lin
Lucia Mannocchi
Senimetu Momoh Abu
Michael Callaghan
Amanda Moore
Brian Sheehy
Sophie Nicholaou
Christopher Wenham
Stefan von Strempel
Nick Haill
Laura Sandiford
Harry Molyneux
Ayden De Luca
Michael Slade
Nischal Gore
Amandeep Kalra
Khaled Gamgoum
Thomas Cartledge
Salvatore Contaldo
Peter Froehlich
Viola Maffessanti
Sonia Dasoar
Georgina Bister
Holly Jayne Barker
Oscar Plastow
Rodolfo Rodriguez
Abigail Lee
Yasir Azami
Katie Jones
Anna Joynt
Anna Melville
Mary-Ann Lewis
Louise Mansfield
Antony Rifkin
Helen Hayes
Peter Bishop
Jane Manning

Steve Walker
Keith Binnie
Anthony Benson
Alistair MacDonald
Yasmin Williams
Alice Raggett
Adam Mills
Peter Nicholas Kelly
Ting Li
Philip Bentley
Jack Stephenson
Philip Simon Wright
Richard Green
Lorraine Dixon
David Sharpe
Julia Day
Monica Asha Lal
Elena Padial Galiana
Katie Holt
Kristina Reingoldt
Alberto Bergamo
Adam Roberts
Edith Wunsch
Kristine Cimane
Federico Palazuelos Botella
Tom Pailing
Fabiana Palusnzy
Matt Drury
Ben Hayes
Sofia De Los Rios
Allan Eunson
Ummar Rashid
Shikha Srivastava
Sarah La Touche
Holly Barker
Ignacio Jaso Ferrer
Andrew Rixson

2010
from left to right: Paul Appleton, Bob Allies, Jo Saunders, Robert Maxwell, David Amarasekera, Graham Morrison, Chris Bearman and Joanna Bacon